Party System Change in Legislatures Worldwide

In this book, Carol Mershon and Olga Shvetsova explore one of the central questions in democratic politics: how much autonomy do elected politicians have to shape and reshape the party system on their own, without the direct involvement of voters in elections? Mershon and Shvetsova's theory focuses on the choices of party membership made by legislators while serving in office. It identifies the inducements and impediments to legislators' changes of partisan affiliation and integrates strategic and institutional approaches to the study of parties and party systems. With empirical analyses comparing nine countries that differ in electoral laws, territorial governance, and executive–legislative relations, Mershon and Shvetsova find that strategic incumbents have the capacity to reconfigure the party system as established in elections. Representatives are motivated to bring about change by opportunities arising during the parliamentary term. They are deterred from doing so by the elemental democratic practice of elections.

Carol Mershon is an associate professor of politics at the University of Virginia. She received her Ph.D. in political science, with distinction, from Yale University. She has served as political science program director at the National Science Foundation. Mershon's articles have appeared in journals such as *American Political Science Review*, *American Journal of Political Science*, *Comparative Political Studies*, *Electoral Studies*, and *Journal of Politics*. She has authored *The Costs of Coalition* (2002) and co-edited *Political Parties and Legislative Party Switching* (2009). The recipient of two National Science Foundation awards, Mershon has also held two Fulbright grants and a Social Science Research Council Fellowship.

Olga Shvetsova is an associate professor of political science at Binghamton University. She received her Ph.D. from the California Institute of Technology. Shvetsova works in the fields of constitutional political economy and institutional design. Her work has been published in the *American Journal of Political Science*, *Comparative Political Studies*, *Constitutional Political Economy*, *Electoral Studies*, *Journal of Democracy*, *Journal of Theoretical Politics*, *Legislative Studies Quarterly*, and other peer-reviewed journals. She has authored several chapters in edited volumes and is the co-author of *Designing Federalism* (2004).

Party System Change in Legislatures Worldwide

Moving Outside the Electoral Arena

CAROL MERSHON
University of Virginia

OLGA SHVETSOVA
Binghamton University

CAMBRIDGE
UNIVERSITY PRESS

32 Avenue of the Americas, New York NY 10013-2473, USA

Cambridge University Press is part of the University of Cambridge.

It furthers the University's mission by disseminating knowledge in the pursuit of education, learning and research at the highest international levels of excellence.

www.cambridge.org
Information on this title: www.cambridge.org/9780521765831

© Carol Mershon and Olga Shvetsova 2013

This publication is in copyright. Subject to statutory exception and to the provisions of relevant collective licensing agreements, no reproduction of any part may take place without the written permission of Cambridge University Press.

First published 2013

A catalogue record for this publication is available from the British Library

Library of Congress Cataloguing in Publication data
Mershon, Carol.
  Party System Change in Legislatures Worldwide : Moving Outside the Electoral Arena / Carol Mershon, Olga Shvetsova.
  pages cm
ISBN 978-0-521-76583-1 (hardback)
1. Party affiliation – Cross cultural studies.   2. Political parties – Cross cultural studies.   3. Legislators – Cross cultural studies.   4. Legislative bodies – Cross cultural studies.   I. Shvetsova, Olga (Olga Vitalievna)   II. Title.
JF2071.M47   2013
328.3'69–dc23   2013004059

ISBN 978-0-521-76583-1 Hardback

Cambridge University Press has no responsibility for the persistence or accuracy of URLs for external or third-party internet websites referred to in this publication, and does not guarantee that any content on such websites is, or will remain, accurate or appropriate.

Contents

List of Figures		page ix
List of Tables		xi
Preface		xiii
Acknowledgments		xv

PART ONE   THE PROSPECT OF PARTY SYSTEM CHANGE
            BETWEEN ELECTIONS

1 The Phenomenon of Party and Party System Change 3
   1.1 Approaches to Analyzing Change in Parties and Party Systems 4
      1.1.1 Change in the Number and Position of Parties as
            Emanating from the Electoral Arena 5
      1.1.2 Change in Competition for the Executive 7
      1.1.3 New Attention to Change in Legislative Parties 9
   1.2 The Possibility and Reality of Party System Change between
       Elections 10
   1.3 The Argument in Brief 15
   1.4 The Map of the Book 16

2 How Parliamentary Party System Change Matters for Policy 18
   2.1 Legislative Coalitions and Policy 19
      2.1.1 Legislative Parties as Coalitions of Incumbents 19
      2.1.2 Legislative Majority Coalitions and Executive Coalitions 20
      2.1.3 The Core, Policy Choice, and Changing the Status Quo 21
   2.2 Manipulating the Core: The Power of Interparty Moves 22
   2.3 Tectonic Shifts out of Party Moves: Empirical Illustrations 23
      2.3.1 Two-Party System: U.S. House 23
      2.3.2 Two-Party System: U.S. Senate 24

	2.3.3	Four-Party System: Canadian House	25
	2.3.4	Five Sizable and Many Minor Parties: Italian Chamber	25
2.4	Conclusion		31
3	Why and How Individual Incumbents Change Legislative Party Systems		32
3.1	An Integrated Model of Inducements and Deterrents to Changes of Affiliation among Individual Incumbents		32
	3.1.1	Inducements to Changing Parties in the Utility Function of Incumbent i	33
	3.1.2	The Incumbent's Time-Contingent Choice and the Parliamentary Cycle	35
	3.1.3	The Electoral Value of Stable Party Labels	36
	3.1.4	Voters' Calculus: Agency Risks and Rewards for Partisan Constancy	38
	3.1.5	Unified Analysis of the Calculations of Politicians and Voters	40
3.2	Testable Implications: Inducements, Deterrents, and the Timing of Interparty Moves		43
3.3	Research Design		47
3.4	Conclusion		50

PART TWO   DISCERNING MECHANISMS THROUGH CASE STUDIES

4	Legislators' Pursuit of Benefits and Legislative Party System Change		53
4.1	Revisiting the Parliamentary Cycle		54
	4.1.1	Operationalizing Stages of the Parliamentary Cycle	54
	4.1.2	Elaborating the Hypothesis on Timing Moves to Seize Gains	58
4.2	Inducements at the Granular Level: 1996–2001 Italy and 1993–1995 Russia		59
	4.2.1	Rationale for Selection of Two Primary In-Depth Terms	60
	4.2.2	Variations in Incumbent Changes of Party across Aggregated Stages	61
	4.2.3	MP Interparty Mobility Disaggregated by Substage	64
4.3	Enlarging the View: MP Interparty Mobility by Stage		69
4.4	The Formation of New Parliamentary Parties		75
4.5	Conclusion		78
5	Avoidance of Electoral Costs and Stability in Parliamentary Parties		80
5.1	Revisiting the Logic on Incumbent Avoidance of Electoral Costs		81
5.2	The Closest Scrutiny of Deterrents to Changing Party: 1996–2001 Italy and 1993–1995 Russia		81
	5.2.1	A First Look at the Timing of Interparty Moves Relative to Elections	82

	5.2.2	Timing and Limiting Moves: Comparisons across Groups of MPs	84
	5.2.3	Finding a Balance? Averting Electoral Costs Yet Reaching for Parliamentary Benefits	88
5.3		Expanding the Investigation of Electoral Deterrents	90
	5.3.1	A First Cut at Locating Moves in Time	90
	5.3.2	What Time Tells about MP Efforts to Curb Electoral Costs	93
5.4		Conclusion	95

PART THREE   GENERALIZING IN A BROADER EMPIRICAL SETTING

6 Setting Up the Analysis of One Hundred and Ten Parliaments   101
   6.1 Measuring Incumbents' Changes of Party   102
   6.2 Inducements to MP Mobility among Parties   104
   6.3 Deterrents to MP Mobility   107
   6.4 Alternative Influences and Controls   109
      6.4.1 Party System Properties at the Most Recent Election   109
      6.4.2 Democratic Institutions   111
      6.4.3 Ascriptive Cleavages and Economic Factors   114
      6.4.4 Cultural Factors and Salient Issues   115
   6.5 Conclusion   116

7 Institutional Inducements and Preference-Based Deterrents to Legislative Party System Change   117
   7.1 Introducing the Statistical Models   117
   7.2 Explaining the Absolute Number of Monthly MP Moves   119
      7.2.1 The Basic Model and the SMD–PR Divide   120
      7.2.2 Inducements, Deterrents, and Country Effects   123
      7.2.3 Inducements and Deterrents with Institutional, Economic, and Cultural Conditions   126
      7.2.4 Inducements and Deterrents with Institutions, Economic Conditions, and Party System Properties at the Most Recent Election   129
      7.2.5 Societal Cleavages as Barriers to Change in Parliamentary Party Systems   133
   7.3 Presence or Absence of MP Switching   133
   7.4 Stability, Solo Moves, or Mass Moves   135
   7.5 The Relationship between Interelectoral Party System Change and Electoral Volatility   141
   7.6 Conclusion   145

8 Comparative Statics: Where Our Assumptions May Not Apply   147
   8.1 What Difference Do Assumptions Make?   147
   8.2 Interelectoral Party System Change as a Function of Voter Preferences   148

		8.2.1 Illustrative Cases Meeting Expectations	151
		8.2.2 Anomalies	153
	8.3	Enforcement of Constraints on Switching as a Function of Voter Preferences	154
		8.3.1 Parchment Barriers	155
		8.3.2 Loose Constraints	157
		8.3.3 Constraints with Confounds	157
		8.3.4 Clear Constraints with Questions on Voter Preferences	158
		8.3.5 Windows and Sunsets	159
	8.4	The Case of Spain as a Reference Group against Our Main Findings	161
	8.5	Conclusion	162
9	Conclusions		164
	9.1	Reappraisal: Of Time and Party System Stability	165
	9.2	Illustrative Applications in Further Research	167
	9.3	Broader Theoretical Implications for the Field	169
		9.3.1 Sources of Institutional Change	169
		9.3.2 Control of Government and the Legislative Agenda	170
	9.4	Rebalancing the Concept of Party Systems	172

Bibliography	175
Parliamentary Records	175
Newspapers and Periodicals	177
Other Primary and Secondary Sources	178
Appendixes	203
Appendix A: Chapter Appendixes	203
Appendix B	211
Author Index	213
Subject Index	218

Figures

1.1 Systemic change – within-term dynamics: Italian Chamber of Deputies, 1963–1968 and 1968–1972. *page* 12
1.2 Parliamentary party system dynamics and continuity in voter choices: from individual members of parliament (MPs') choices to systemic change, Italian Chamber of Deputies, 1963–1972. 13
2.1 The Liberals and the heart in Canada: after the June 2004 election and in May 2005. 26
2.2 The empty core in the Italian Chamber after the 1996 election. 27
2.3 Parliamentary groups in the Chamber, April 15, 1998: the search for the core. 28
2.4 Parliamentary groups in the Chamber, April 15, 1999: contending for the core. 30
3.1 Illustration of the theoretical relationship between time and expected incumbent interparty moves. 42
3.2 Variation in posited motivations for incumbents' changes of party across stages of the parliamentary cycle. 46
4.1 Mean weekly changes of party per 100 members of parliament (MPs) (all and single-member districts [SMD]), by sequential substage in term, 1993–1995 Russian Duma. 65
4.2 Mean weekly changes of party per 100 members of parliament (MPs) (all and single-member districts [SMD]), by sequential substage in term, 1996–2001 Italian Chamber. 66
4.3 (A) Percentage of months with specified counts of moves, by stage of parliamentary cycle, thirty-three terms; (B) Percentage of legislative terms with specified totals of moves. 74
5.1 (A) Log of raw number of member of parliament (MP) moves and number of moves per 100 MPs, by week in the legislative term, Italy 1996–2001 (LOWESS smoothing); (B) Log of raw

ix

	number of MP moves and number of moves per 100 MPs, by week in the legislative term, Russia 1993–1995 (LOWESS smoothing).	82
5.2	The timing of interparty moves relative to elections and parliamentary benefits, 1993–1995 Russia.	89
5.3	The timing of interparty moves relative to elections and parliamentary benefits, 1996–2001 Italy.	89
5.4	Percentage of months with specified counts of moves, by quarter of term, thirty-three terms.	96

Tables

1.1	Percent members of parliament (MPs) ever switched party, by term, in twenty-two established and new democracies.	*page* 11
3.1	Case selection: countries and legislative terms.	49
4.1	Operationalizing stages of the parliamentary cycle for primary and secondary in-depth terms.	55
4.2	Mean weekly moves per 100 members of parliament (MPs) by type of stage and by MPs' mode of election, 1996–2001 Italian Chamber and 1993–1995 Russian Duma.	62
4.3	Mean monthly moves per 100 members of parliament (MPs) by type of stage, electoral system, and regime, thirty-three terms.	70
4.4	New parliamentary parties, by type of stage, electoral system, and regime, thirty-five terms.	76
5.1	Percentage of members of parliament (MPs) with specified numbers of interparty moves, Italian and Russian MPs, by mode of election.	85
5.2	Percentage of members of parliament (MPs) with specified numbers of moves, and mean weeks of first and last moves, by set of MPs, Italy 1996–2001 and Russia 1993–1995.	86
5.3	Percentage of members of parliament (MPs) winning reelection, by number of moves and quartiles of first and last moves among MPs running for reelection, Italy 1996–2001.	87
5.4	Mean monthly moves per 100 members of parliament (MPs), by type of stage and by six-month span in the legislative term, select terms and subset of terms based on length.	91
5.5	Mean monthly moves per 100 members of parliament (MPs), by quarter of term, thirty-three legislatures.	94
6.1	Mean monthly moves per year elapsed in term, by electoral system and active vs. dormant stage (United States excluded).	105

6.2	Fact of switching, by electoral system and stage of parliamentary cycle.	107
6.3	Mean monthly moves during term, by raw number of parliamentary parties and effective number of parliamentary parties at outset of term.	110
6.4	Mean monthly moves during term, by mean and median district magnitude in elections.	112
6.5	Mean monthly moves during term, by institutional design.	113
7.1	Explaining the absolute number of switches (cap of fifty) with stages and time in term; zero-inflated Poisson regression.	121
7.2	Absolute number of switches (cap of fifty) with stages, time in term, and fixed effects.	124
7.3	Explaining the absolute number of switches (cap of fifty) with quadratic time in term, stages, and institutional, economic, and cultural conditions; zero-inflated Poisson regression.	127
7.4	Explaining the absolute number of switches (cap of fifty) with quadratic time in term, stages, party system attributes at start of term, economic conditions, and international context; zero-inflated Poisson regression.	131
7.5	Explaining the absolute number of switches (cap of fifty) with quadratic time in term, stages, and societal fractionalization; zero-inflated Poisson regression.	134
7.6	Explaining the fact of switching with stages, quadratic time in term, party system attributes at start of term, and institutional effects; probit.	136
7.7	Explaining the occurrence of solo and mass moves with quadratic time in term, stages, party system attributes at start of term, and institutional effects; ordered probit.	139
7.8	Explaining electoral volatility in election $t + 1$; GLS.	142
7.9	Electoral volatility in election $t + 1$ with stage-specific cumulative switching and change in the number of parliamentary parties; GLS.	144
7.10	Cumulative number of member of parliament (MP) moves during term, by electoral system and change in number of parliamentary parties.	145
8.1	Voter preferences and aggregated measures of member of parliament (MP) interparty mobility.	149
8.2	Voter preferences and the enforcement of curbs on member of parliament (MP) discretion in party affiliation.	155
8.3	Parliamentary terms with cumulative raw counts of switches, by electoral system and change in number of parties during term.	162

Preface

Party systems bring structure out of chaos. They start with the infinite diversity of the concerns, interests, and conflicts inherent in an electorate and then somehow internalize and alleviate that complexity, boiling it down to a manageable number of policy issues and a manageable menu of policy alternatives. This is delicate work. Its outcome hinges on what exactly is happening with parties and the party system – what they look like and how they evolve. Simply put, if a party system "goes wrong," not only might policies start to go awry but the democratic consensus itself might erode and, with it, the social fabric might fray. Precisely because parties do so much to lead us on policy, set the agenda, and define our options, the question of where parties come from and how they change has long been central in politics.

In *Party System Change in Legislatures Worldwide*, we argue that people who make politics their profession and who strive to meet their professional goals – just as anyone with a career would do – have a hand in adjusting what a party system becomes. How free are the hands of professional politicians in altering party systems? Should we worry that incumbents might override voters, or should we be relieved? The latter is a thorny normative question that we leave for others to consider. What we address here are the theoretical and empirical questions: why do we see shifts in parliamentary parties, and what are the forces that rein in this potential for change? We establish as a fact that parliamentary incumbents can and, under certain circumstances, do effect change in parliamentary party systems and that their behavior can be traced and is to an extent predictable. Their impact on policies can be and occasionally is immensely significant.

This is not a new analytical angle. Everyone agrees that politicians broker politics. Call it elite conspiracy or call it political leadership, but political incumbents are not merely deputized to do the work of government in their constituents' stead. They bring value added and are collectively capable of accomplishing what a direct plebiscite would never be able to reach: some measure of consensus on a reasonably broad range of concerns. This is why we value representative democracy even though we at times supplant it with our right to referenda. There might well be many venues in which political incumbents exercise their autonomy. Amending the party system, relative to what voters and election rules generate with each round of parliamentary elections, is but one.

Even though we all know that politicians broker politics, the capacity of officeholders to alter parties and party systems without the direct involvement of the electorate is an understudied phenomenon. Yet it is vitally important to democratic governance. The very fact of such autonomy also sheds light on the enduring question of party system origins. The book explores this capacity as it descends all the way down to individual members of parliament, discovering that their party affiliations are by no means fixed, and following how those affiliations change as incumbents walk the corridors of power. As *Party System Change in Legislatures Worldwide* shows, when representatives shift partisanship, decision making in legislatures and the options for future elections shift as well.

While the choices of voters create a party system in the electoral arena, the choices of strategic legislative incumbents outside that arena, between elections, can reshape the contours of a party system. Sitting legislators introduce change when doing so can benefit them in parliament. The basic democratic rule that citizens have the right to choose their representatives in repeated elections lends a measure of stability to parliamentary party systems between elections. The reality of recurring elections, in which voters might punish representatives who abandon their original electoral party label, places a limit on change in parliamentary party systems.

Acknowledgments

We wish to express our gratitude to the many individuals who have helped make this book possible. For their ongoing, extremely valuable input and support, we are indebted to Mikhail Filippov, Will Heller, Brian Humes, Michael McDonald, and Norman Schofield. A special word of thanks goes to Scott Mainwaring, who graciously shared his data on electoral volatility; he bears no responsibility for the analyses here or our interpretation of them.

Many scholars have generously offered comments on portions of our work at different stages in the research and writing of the book: John Aldrich, Barry Ames, Raj Arunachalam, Scott Barclay, Ken Benoit, Osvaldo Croci, Bonnie Field, Kristin Kanthak, Junko Kato, Richard Katz, George Krause, Michael Laver, Luis Fernando Medina, Tim Nokken, Lucio Renno, Lynn Sanders, Ken Shepsle, and Jonathan Woon. Our thanks go to each and every one of them. Graduate students in Will Heller's seminar at Binghamton University provided helpful remarks on the near-final book manuscript; we thank each student and also, again, Will Heller for assigning the manuscript.

We acknowledge with gratitude the support of our home institutions and departments, which furnished collegial environments in which to write and permitted us to hire talented graduate research assistants with whom to work. Our diligent research assistants have contributed to this project in numerous ways over the years. We thank them all, for all they have done: Sarah Andrews, Nina Barzachka, Scott Boddery, Susan Brewer, Adriana Buliga-Stojan, Lindsay Flynn, Samantha Gassie, Miriam Hurley, Rado Iliev, Elizabeth Kaknes, Drew Kurlowski, Susanna McCarthy, Nikolay Merkulov, Brenton Peterson, and Michael Steen Thomas.

At Cambridge University Press, it was our good fortune to work with Lewis Bateman as editor, who we thank for his support, patience, and encouragement to broaden our book's appeal. We are indebted to the anonymous readers engaged by the Press for their detailed, extremely thoughtful remarks and suggestions on the manuscript, and to the production team at the Press for the close attention and quick turnaround.

All of these individuals and institutions have helped strengthen the book. We are responsible for the product.

PART ONE

THE PROSPECT OF PARTY SYSTEM CHANGE BETWEEN ELECTIONS

Political parties and party systems are essential foundations of democratic politics. Competition among elites for popular support, along with widely shared rights to participate in the selection of representatives, defines a democratic regime (Dahl 1971). Political parties organize the teams and terms of elite competition and thus offer and defend alternative choices to voters. Parties also organize the agenda and work of legislatures and thus translate citizen preferences into policy decisions. Fittingly, one of the most oft-cited judgments in political science is that democracy without parties is "unthinkable" (Schattschneider 1942, 1).

This book aims to restore balance in the discipline's thinking about parties and party systems. For Ostrogorski (1902), parties were creatures of politicians' interactions in parliament. For Key (1964), it was at least equally important to study parties in the legislature as in the electoral arena. And yet political science as a discipline has acquired a bias in favor of an elections-dominant understanding of what parties and party systems are and do. This book corrects this bias by focusing the inquiry squarely on party and party system change in sitting parliaments. To this end, our central question is: why and how much do political parties change, merge, split, and even occasionally form in the intervals between elections – without immediate recourse to the voters' verdict – as legislators meet? Scholars have recently discovered that parties and entire party systems can change between elections in part due to the decisions of individual elected members of parliament (MPs), as those MPs choose to change or retain the party labels under which they won their seats. We use this recent research as the springboard for a novel approach to the enduring question of change and stability in party systems.

Through elections, rich streams of information pass and are dispersed, and voters' consent and representatives' right to govern are established and renewed. Elections are not the end of the story, however. In a democracy, votes determine who wins and who loses. Yet the initial distribution of legislative seats need not last throughout a legislative term. By showing why and how much legislative party systems can and do change in the intervals between elections, *Party System Change in Legislatures Worldwide* invites readers to look at party systems with a new and powerful lens. It thus shifts the focus of research on institutions and parties and illuminates a subject central to democratic political life.

The three chapters making up Part One state the goals of the book and stake out the claim that the book's question, argument, and evidence enrich the understanding of party systems and hence of democratic politics. Chapter 1 introduces the central question of party system change between elections. As a critical step, this chapter illustrates the phenomenon of change in interelectoral party systems, depicting differing degrees of instability in several real-world party systems. To pave the way for pursuing the question of why such change occurs, the chapter juxtaposes the book's theoretical framework and empirical foundation with extant studies of parties and party systems. Chapter 1 also outlines the aims of the study and the answer it offers to the question of party system change.

Chapter 2 demonstrates the significance of interelectoral change in party systems. It shows that legislative incumbents, by changing party affiliation, have the capacity to improve their own bargaining position, alter the overall partisan balance of power, and affect policy outputs in the legislature. Chapter 3 develops an integrated model of change and stability in parliamentary party systems. It presents a general mechanism of what brings legislators to change party and what instead leads them to hold fast to their partisan affiliations. The chapter advances testable hypotheses about the determinants of legislators' decisions on partisanship and of interelectoral party system change. As a whole, Part One provides the analytical grounding for the inquiry conducted throughout the book. We now turn to elaborate the question anchoring and inspiring the book: why and how much do political parties change in the intervals between elections, without direct voter involvement, during the legislative term?

1

The Phenomenon of Party and Party System Change

In a democracy, political parties link the people to the government. Parties enable citizens to choose representatives, aggregate popular preferences, mediate interests and conflicts, and broker compromises. As crucial components of democracy, parties are political institutions operating within a context defined by other institutions.[1] Joining citizens to their representatives and government, parties logically could emerge, evolve, and change either from the bottom up, as the people provoke shifts among those who rule, or from the top down, as the rulers redefine options for the people whose consent they seek. Yet this is not an either/or proposition: change can be driven both by the determinants within and by those outside the electoral arena.

This book offers and evaluates explanations for change in parties and party systems that move beyond the electoral arena. We examine change and stability as products of the strategies of and interactions among representatives serving in the legislature as those representatives pursue the goals of winning votes, gaining office, and influencing public policy. Our premise is that an account of incumbents' strategic choices of partisanship in parliament, in addition to the study of voter dynamics and the electoral arena, can enhance understanding of both the origins of change and stability in parties and party systems and the mechanisms by which change is generated and continuity sustained.

We open this chapter by discussing what it means to explore the prospect of party system change between elections. As part of the discussion, we take stock of the extensive literature on party system change in the electoral arena because the two processes – change occurring in elections and change unfolding outside

---

[1] With Ostrom, we adopt a broad definition of institutions, as "enduring regularities of human action in situations structured by rules, norms, and shared strategies, as well as by the physical world" (Crawford and Ostrom 1995, 583; cf. Munger 2010; Ostrom 1990; Calvert 1995; Greif and Laitin 2004; Hall and Taylor 1996; Knight 1992; North 1990; Riker 1990; Shepsle 1989; Thelen 1990; Weingast 1995).

of elections – are, of necessity, connected through the incentives facing and the strategies pursued by both politicians and the citizens electing them. The second section shows why and how the legislative arena holds such interest for comprehending change and continuity in parties and party systems. In the third section, we outline our main theory of the inducements and constraints that shape the choices made by members of parliament (MPs) on partisan affiliation. The chapter's last section maps the organization of the book.[2]

1.1 APPROACHES TO ANALYZING CHANGE IN PARTIES AND PARTY SYSTEMS

Given the centrality of parties to democracy, it is not surprising that the analysis of parties and party systems has united diverse, rich, and distinguished traditions in political science (e.g., Downs 1957; Franklin, Mackie, and Valen 1992; Key 1964; Laver and Schofield 1990; Lipset and Rokkan 1967; Mainwaring 1999; Mair 1997b; 2006; Powell 2000; Przeworski and Sprague 1986; Sartori 1976; Schofield and Sened 2006; Stokes 1999; Wolinetz 2006). The field has reached basic agreement on its objects of study. In accord with scholarly wisdom, we define a political party as an entity – a team of politicians – that competes or intends to compete for popular support so as to hold elective offices. We also adopt the consensual definition of a party system as a patterned or structured set of interactions among parties.

The consensus breaks down when it comes to the criteria to be used to identify party system change. Scholars fully recognize that the same criteria chosen to distinguish party systems across different units (e.g., countries) at one time can establish change in a party system within the same unit over time. The question is which set of criteria to choose and use. Many political scientists assert or imply that two criteria suffice to indicate the transformation of a party system: change in the number of parties and change in the policy positions of parties. The latter criterion of change in the distance between parties might or might not entail change in the number of dimensions organizing party competition. Mair (1997a; 2006) is prominent among those who insist on other criteria for isolating party system change, maintaining that a party system changes only when change occurs in the structure of interparty competition for control of the executive.

We first flesh out treatments that rely on the two criteria of the number and positions of parties and then turn to analyses adopting other standards. Our

---

[2] Several terms used here and throughout the book deserve definition. We use the words "parliament" and "legislature" interchangeably to refer to the national assembly, regardless of whether the system is presidential or parliamentary. We define the span "between elections" as the time unfolding between one national legislative election and the next and detail the related concept of the parliamentary cycle later in the text (see Section 1.3). The legislative (or parliamentary) arena contrasts with the "electoral arena," in that, in the latter, voters are immediately involved whereas, in the former, they are not.

message throughout is that extant work, even that pointing to party competition for the executive, tends to conceive of change in party systems as a product of the electoral arena. Our aim is not to provide an exhaustive, detailed review of the voluminous body of relevant work, but rather to distill the essence of existing research and to extract guidelines as to how further scientific progress in the field might be achieved.

1.1.1 Change in the Number and Position of Parties as Emanating from the Electoral Arena

Political scientists in the sociological, institutional, and strategic schools have converged on the intuitively appealing notion that a change in the number and positions of parties denotes the passage from one party system to another.[3] For the sociological approach, political parties speak to the historically rooted social conflicts that cleave a national electorate, be they socioeconomic, religious, ethno-linguistic, or urban-rural (e.g., Caramani 2004; Lipset and Rokkan 1967; Rokkan 1970). In this reasoning, when parties first incorporated newly enfranchised lower class and female voters into national electorates (in the early twentieth century, in what are now the developed democracies), they solidified voter loyalties, established organizations, and settled into routines of competition that perpetuated the party system overall. Lipset and Rokkan (1967, 50) famously identified the result: "The party systems of the 1960s reflect, with few but significant exceptions, the cleavage structures of the 1920s." Yet, soon after Lipset and Rokken (1967) pronounced what came to be known as the "freezing thesis," unmistakable evidence of dramatic electoral change appeared. For example, the number of parties winning representation in the Danish legislature doubled in only two years, from five in the 1971 elections to ten in 1973. More broadly, rising values on the index of electoral volatility – a measure of the aggregate shift in electoral outcomes from one election to the next – pointed to an era of flux occurring after roughly 1970 in many developed democracies (Pedersen 1978; 1979; 1983; cf. Katz 1997).[4] Analysts in the sociological and social psychological schools have debated the sources and impact of electoral dealignment (the detachment of voter loyalties to social groups and voter allegiances to political parties) and realignment (the rise of new voter orientations and new attachments to parties). These researchers have thus treated the

---

[3] Counting rules for parties have generated debate (e.g., Ordeshook and Shvetsova 1994; Sartori 1976). Analysts now routinely adopt the measure of the effective number of electoral (or parliamentary) parties, which weights the raw number by parties' electoral (parliamentary) size (Laakso and Taagepera 1979; Taagepera and Shugart 1989; on the related measure of party fractionalization, see Rae 1971).

[4] This index is computed in two steps: first, the analyst tallies the absolute values of changes in all parties' vote shares from one legislative election to the next; then she divides the sum by two, so as not to count gains and losses twice (Pedersen 1978; 1979; on volatility in seat shares between two successive elections, see, e.g., Ferree 2006; Lindberg 2007; Strøm 1985; 1990b).

evolution of voter alignments and electoral outcomes as tantamount to party system change (e.g., Caramani 2006; Clarke and Kornberg 1996; Dalton, Flanagan, and Beck 1984; Dalton, McAllister, and Wattenberg 2000; Dalton and Wattenberg 2000; Franklin, Mackie, and Valen 1992; Inglehart 1971; 1977; 1997).

The institutional approach to party systems sounds the overarching theme that societal cleavages and political institutions (in particular, electoral laws) jointly determine the number and array of parties in policy space (e.g., Bartolini and Mair 1990; Benoit 2002; Chhibber and Kollman 1998; 2004; Cox 1997; 1999; Duverger 1954; Filippov, Ordeshook, and Shvetsova 1999; Ordeshook and Shvetsova 1994). Change in either class of factors, then, could herald fundamental change in a party system. Since politicians in countries around the world enacted electoral reforms during and after the 1990s (in Italy, Japan, Mexico, New Zealand, Poland, Russia, and elsewhere), political scientists in this school have assessed the consequences for party systems (e.g., Benoit 2007; Benoit and Hayden 2004; D'Alimonte 2001; Katz 1995; Shugart and Wattenberg 2003). These studies conclude that voters' choices at election time, as shaped by their identifications with societal groups and translated by new electoral laws, can remold the contours of a party system. Even when federalism joins the set of institutions examined (e.g., Chhibber and Kollman 1998; 2004), and even when the analytical focus encompasses parties as organizations (e.g., Mair, Müller, and Plasser 2004), party systems remain creatures of elections in these accounts.

The strategic approach depicts individual politicians and party teams as engaged in a calculus of costs and benefits, competing against their counterparts for some combination of the goods of office, votes, and policy. Adherents of this school often emphasize how institutions constrain choices of strategy and outcomes of competition (e.g., Aldrich 1995; 2011; Cox and McCubbins 2005; 2007 [1993]; Diermeier 2006; Downs 1957; Hug 2001; Katz 2007 [1980]; Giannetti and Sened 2004; Laver and Schofield 1998 [1990]; Laver and Shepsle 1990; 1996; Sartori 1976; Schofield 1986; 1987; Schofield and Sened 2006). In these analyses, national party systems may shift at the margin when parties adjust location for competitive advantage, or they may become entirely reconfigured when party entrepreneurs introduce a new dimension of competition (McLean 2001; Miller and Schofield 2003). Likewise, new party entrants may bring about systemic change. To return to the Danish example, Laver and Schofield (1998 [1990]) identify two Danish party systems, one before and one since the fateful 1973 elections. In this tradition, save for a class of exceptions considered later, politicians and parties are launched into office by voters' choices at election time, and, on that basis, jockey for influence over the executive and the policy agenda. Contributors to this school thus largely disregard the possibility that the players might be rearranged – that players might strategically rearrange themselves – while serving in office during the interval between elections.

For all schools discussed so far, parties are entities constituted in and through elections and fixed from one election to the next. This holds true as well for analysts who look to criteria other than the number and positions of parties to ascertain change in party systems.[5]

1.1.2 Change in Competition for the Executive

Mair (1989a; 1989b; 1997a; 1997b; 1997c; 2001; 2006) extends the natural idea that configurations of the number and positions of parties matter insofar as they affect which parties enter the national executive. In fact, Mair so strongly emphasizes the structure of competition for control of the executive as a criterion for distinguishing party systems that he elevates this feature to the status of the sole criterion for system change (esp. 1989a, 38; 1997c, 206–207; 2006, 65). Mair thus embraces and reinterprets a central, long-standing concern in the study of democratic politics: the fundamental significance of relationships between government and opposition (e.g., Dahl 1966; 1971).

Mair defines party competition for the executive in terms of three factors. He focuses first on alternation in office, that is, the degree to which parties replace each other in holding the reins of the national executive. The second aspect is the set of governing alternatives, or the degree to which the groups of ruling parties are either novel or repeat familiar formulae from the past. Third, Mair considers access to office, which involves whether some parties are treated in practice as unacceptable governing partners. Combining these related but distinct aspects yields a classification of open or closed structures of competition for the executive.

By concentrating on competition for the executive, Mair advances the claim that even substantial electoral change need not signal party system change. In this logic, electoral results may boost the number of parties and inject new issues into political debate while the pattern of competition for national governing office, and hence the party system overall, exhibit basic continuity. Mair adduces the case of Denmark here and flags the open structure of competition for the executive both before and after 1973 (1997c, 215–216); he seizes the usual suspect, but turns the usual reading of the evidence on its head. For Mair, the entry of new parties into the executive may disrupt – or even end – one party system marked by long-standing rigidity in government composition and thus herald a new party system, even as electoral outcomes remain much the same. As

---

[5] The most prominent such analyst is arguably Mainwaring (1992–1993; 1998; 1999; Mainwaring and Scully 1995; 2008; Mainwaring and Torcal 2006), who adds institutionalization as another property that differentiates party systems. This influential approach is also largely rooted in the electoral arena. Mainwaring defines four dimensions of institutionalization: predictability in patterns of party competition, societal anchoring of parties, popular support for and legitimacy of parties, and organizational solidity of parties.

illustration, Mair cites Ireland since 1989, when Fianna Fáil, for the first time in the country's history, governed in coalition (1997c, 219–220; 2006, 67–68).

In numerous writings, then, Mair implicitly or explicitly criticizes what he sees as the "electoral bias" (esp. 1989a, 271–273; 1997b, 70–73) displayed by much work on party system change. He also underscores the distinction between change (or stability) in parties and change (stability) in the party system overall. Furthermore, Mair argues that what parties do to adjust – to change in a changing environment – preserves continuity at the systemic level. In his words, "party systems freeze into place precisely because the parties themselves refuse to be so pinned down" (Mair 1997a, 16; cf. Bartolini and Mair 1990; Katz and Mair 1994; 1995; Mair, Müller, and Plasser 2004). Hence, where many scholars detect party system change, Mair perceives exaggeration or misunderstanding on the part of the analyst and substantial continuity in the real world.

We echo Mair by recognizing the electoral bias present in most political science research on parties and party systems. Unlike him, however, we note that early social science work did not exhibit this bias. Only for the past fifty years or so has the bulk of political science research on parties and party systems gravitated toward the electoral arena. Ostrogorski (1902) depicted politicians and their tendency to form relatively short-lived alliances and more permanent coalitions within legislatures as the mechanism for the emergence of parties. To Duverger (1954), the importance of the parliamentary arena to party origins and change reflected the historical and institutional circumstances of relatively limited suffrage. In renowned work, V. O. Key (1942; 1958; 1964) insisted that parties should be studied in the electorate, as organizations, and in government. In testimony to Key's influence, political science as a discipline has continued to pay lip service to parties as existing in these three incarnations. Nonetheless, save for contributors to a recent literature, to which we soon turn, since about 1960 analysts have neglected the possibility that parties and even party systems might change between elections.

We also observe that Mair, like most political scientists, assumes that parties operate as entities whose legislative memberships are fixed from one election to the next. We jettison that assumption, as stressed at the outset. Because Mair instead assumes stasis in legislative parties, he portrays change in party systems as a product of the electoral arena. For Mair, parties' capacity to compete for the executive derives from their performance in the electoral arena and from the choices of their leaders as constrained and enabled by electoral performance; parties alternate in the executive, try out new formulae for government composition, and gain access to executive office all on the basis of their electoral success. Mair does not consider that individual legislative incumbents might move from one party to another during the legislative term so as to alter the size, position, and number of parties and thus redefine party competition for the executive. In this sense, perhaps ironically, the elections-dominant approach to party system change extends to Mair.

1.1.3 New Attention to Change in Legislative Parties

In recent years, contributors to a new body of work have relaxed the long unquestioned assumption that parties operate as unitary actors whose legislative memberships are fixed between elections and have sought to explain the phenomenon of legislative party switching.[6] Scholars in this field now concur that multiple factors motivate representatives to jump from one legislative party into another. The theoretical models and empirical findings highlight the benefits of office, policy influence, and electoral advantage as incentives to abandoning the party ship. They reveal that legislative incumbents switch parties as constrained by institutions and in response to their environments (e.g., Aldrich and Bianco 1992; Canon and Sousa 1992; Desposato 2006; Desposato and Scheiner 2008; Heller and Mershon 2005; 2008; 2009d; Kato and Yamamoto 2009; Laver and Benoit 2003; Reed and Scheiner 2003; Schofield 2009; Shabad and Slomczynski 2004; Thames 2007).

This literature demonstrates the consequences of the legislator's switch for the level of the parliamentary party system, yet its analysis of why party systems change remains piecemeal and incomplete. The work documents that, trivial exceptions aside, individuals' moves from one party to another alter the balance of power among legislative parties and shift the profile of preferences within parties (Kato and Yamamoto 2009; Heller and Mershon 2009a; 2009c; 2009e).[7] To date, however, each of these studies has investigated a single country or at most a few legislative terms in several countries over a relatively short time; each on its own has captured relatively limited variation in potential sources of system-level change (but see Mershon and Shvetsova 2008b; 2009). Together, the studies display substantial similarities in the theoretical and empirical analysis of individual-level behavior but do not develop or test a shared, integrated account of change at the level of the party system. Hence, scientific cumulation of theoretical and empirical findings has proceeded at the individual level but has proven quite difficult at the systemic level. In the end, this research sheds light on why individual incumbents switch and how such choices of partisanship leave an imprint on parties and parliamentary party systems but does not explain why party systems change or remain essentially the same.

Nonetheless, precisely because the arguments and findings in the comparative literature on legislative party switching have now gained acceptance, we see a compelling need to examine change in party systems with a new lens. The discovery of change at the individual level invites a fresh inquiry into forces for change and stability at the systemic level. Guided by the literature on party switching, we reconstruct and explain how individual incumbents' choices can, under some conditions, aggregate into change at the level of parliamentary party systems.

---

[6] This field defines a party switch as "any recorded change in party affiliation on the part of a politician holding or competing for elective office" (Heller and Mershon, 2009a, 8).

[7] Seat shares would be unaffected by switching only if each exit from a party were offset by an entrance from another. Likewise, switching would leave intact the distribution of party-member preferences only under very restrictive conditions (Heller and Mershon 2009d, esp. 174–175).

1.2 THE POSSIBILITY AND REALITY OF PARTY SYSTEM CHANGE BETWEEN ELECTIONS

It is logically possible for sitting MPs, through their changes of party affiliation, to redefine the balance of power among – and even the identities of – parliamentary parties without the direct involvement of voters. To what extent does this occur? And, when it does occur, is it tantamount to party system change? To introduce the answers elaborated throughout the book, we first offer evidence on interelectoral change in legislative party membership and then discuss how to identify party system change.

First, consider data on the percentage of legislators who have ever switched party in a given legislative term. Table 1.1 sorts the countries it covers into four groups; it gathers those with the least frequent switching at the top and the most frequent at the bottom. As the table conveys, in some places and times, the proportion of incumbents changing affiliation between elections is negligible or nil, whereas, in others, substantial MP partisan mobility occurs. The variation in the percentage of incumbents jumping party per term is quite pronounced overall; even within the set of established democracies, differences are clear. It is obvious as well that variation over time can appear within a single country, even though the table covers relatively short spans. By the measure used here, some legislatures exhibit what can only be seen as very high levels of MP partisan mobility.

Table 1.1 has both strengths and weaknesses. It dispels the notion of stasis in the membership of legislative parties. Representatives need not stick to the party labels under which they were elected. Yet the table omits any record of whether an individual legislator changed party more than once, and it also omits the impact of those moves. Its aggregate measure masks how the membership of particular parties might fluctuate from month to month during a term. The table thus obscures any change in the number and relative sizes of parties.

To overcome such problems, we modify the conventional index of seat volatility from one election to the next so that it tracks shifts in party seat shares during the course of a legislative term. This new measure of *within-term seat volatility* registers change in legislative parties once the individual politicians winning election have taken their seats.[8] Figure 1.1 plots the within-term seat volatility for the 1963–1968 and 1968–1972 terms of the Italian Chamber of Deputies. The upticks in volatility portrayed in the figure capture the switches of

---

[8] The measure of within-term seat volatility sums absolute values of shifts in party seat shares from month j of a given legislative term to the next month $j + 1$, divides by two, and repeats the measure for every pair of successive months throughout a term (cf. Note 4). This index of aggregate change in the party composition of a sitting parliament avoids a problem found in studying electoral or seat volatility from one election to the next: in systems with more than two parties (i.e., most systems), shifts in party vote (or seat) shares very likely conceal individual-level flows in multiple directions (cf., e.g., Birnir 2007). In contrast, the analyst builds the index of within-term seat volatility as an aggregate of the actions of individual legislators and can preserve the disaggregated data at the individual level.

System	Term 1: % switched	Term 2: % switched	Term 3: % switched	Term 4: % switched
Australia	1975–1977: 3	1977–1980: 0	1980–1983: 0	1983–1984: 0
Denmark*	1966–1968: 3	—	—	1994–1998: 2
Germany	1969–1972: 2	1972–1976: 0.4	1976–1980: 0.2	1980–1983: 1
Switzerland	1999–2003: 0.5	2003–2007: 1	2007–2011: 4	—
United Kingdom	1974–1979: 1	1979–1983: 5	1983–1987: 0	1987–1992: 1
United States	1991–1993: 0.2	1993–1995: 0	1995–1997: 1	1997–1999: 0.5
Canada	1993–1997: 2	1997–2000: 4	2000–2004: 9	2004–2006: 2
France	1997–2002: 4	2002–2007: 10	—	—
Japan	2000–2003: 7	—	—	—
South Africa**	1999–2004: 6	2004–2009: 8	—	—
Spain**	1982–1986: 1	1986–1989: 12	1989–1993: 1	1993–1996: 0.3
EP*	1989–1994: 16	—	—	—
Hungary	1990–1994: 24	1994–1998: 12	1998–2002: 6	—
Israel	1992–1996: 12	1996–1999: 23	1999–2003: 12	2003–2006: 25
New Zealand*	1993–1996: 13	1996–1999: 9	—	—
Romania	1992–1996: 11	1996–2000: 17	2000–2004: 10	—
Turkey	1961–1965: 22	1965–1969: 21	1969–1973: 23	1973–1977: 10
Brazil	1991–1994: 39	1994–1998: 33	1998–2001: 36	—
Guatemala	2000–2003: 35	2004–2007: 52	—	—
Italy	1988–1992: 28	1992–1994: 34	1994–1996: 34	1996–2000: 32
Russia	1993–1995: 33	—	—	—
Ukraine	1998–2002: 56	—	—	—

* Unicameral legislature; other data pertain to lower houses.
** Switching permitted only in two two-week windows in South Africa. In Spain, rules prohibit MPs from joining groups other than the Mixed Group later than five days after the start of the legislature. Chapter 8 discusses such constraints.

This table expands on tables in Heller and Mershon (2008; 2009c, 11). In systems in the top group, percent MPs ever switched is less than 3 %; for second group, 3–10%; for third group, 10–20%; for last, more than 20%.

Sources: Heller and Mershon 2009c, 11, and the two dozen sources therein. In addition: Desposato 2009; Electoral Institute for the Sustainability of Democracy in Africa 2010; Fortin 2008; Israel, Knesset 2010; Italy, Camera dei Deputati 2010; Kopecký and Spirova 2008, 144; Nikoleny and Shenhav 2009, 23; South Africa, Parliament 2008; 2012; Switzerland, Parliament 2010; Vowles 2000, 687; Vowles, Banducci, and Karp 2006, 280.

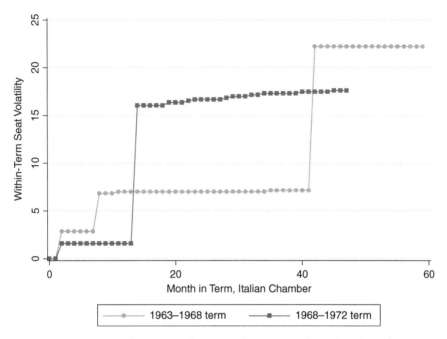

FIGURE 1.1. Systemic change – within-term dynamics: Italian Chamber of Deputies, 1963–1968 and 1968–1972.

one or a few deputies per month and the surges, the (near-) simultaneous moves of many MPs. Specifically, soon after the 1963 election, the Chamber's standing orders forced representatives from tiny parties into the Mixed Group. In early 1964, left-wing Socialists broke away to create the parliamentary group of the Socialist Party of Proletarian Unity. A few deputies executed solo switches between spring 1964 and summer 1966. In late 1966, the Socialists and the Social Democrats merged, forming a single group. Given this record, within-term seat volatility exceeded 22 percent at the end of the term. Now consider the 1968–1972 term. At the outset, parliamentary rules again required that MPs from tiny parties sit in the Mixed Group. The leap in within-term seat volatility reflected the mid-1969 reestablishment of the separate Socialist and Social Democratic parliamentary groups. Several legislators later made solo switches. By the end of the 1968–1972 term, seat volatility surpassed 17 percent.

Analysts typically regard electoral volatility of more than 15 or 20 percent, if observed in an established democracy, as relatively high (e.g., Bartolini and Mair 1990; Mair 1989, 269; Gallagher, Laver and Mair 2006, 294; Mainwaring and Torcal 2006). Figure 1.1 illustrates that party seat shares overall can exhibit this much or even more variation during a legislative term, in the interval between elections, as a result of incumbents' choices – changes – of party affiliation. To be sure, the two particular terms appearing in the figure stand out among all terms

Phenomenon of Party and Party System Change 13

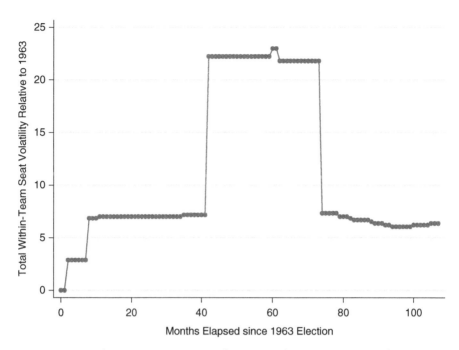

FIGURE 1.2. Parliamentary party system dynamics and continuity in voter choices: From individual MPs' choices to systemic change, Italian Chamber of Deputies, 1963–1972.

we examine. We concentrate on these Italian terms because they are striking: as chronicled by within-term seat volatility, they drive home the message that parliamentary parties can undergo great change without voters casting their votes at legislative elections.

To afford another view of interelectoral change in legislative parties, we anchor the month-to-month seat volatility to a fixed baseline so as to tap total change since the baseline. Figure 1.2 plots the *total within-term seat volatility* relative to the 1963 election.[9] The figure thus charts the evolution of the Chamber's party groups from the start of the first term, in 1963, through the 1968 election, and up to the end of the second term, in 1972. The squiggle at month 61 marks the election of 1968, when the index of total within-term seat volatility relative to 1963 stood at 23 percent. Incumbents' choices then further redefined parties and the party system over the course of the 1968–1972

---

[9] Total within-term seat volatility is computed by comparing the shifts in party seat shares at any pair of months to some baseline, which could be the month of an election accorded special importance (e.g., a democracy's founding election; cf. Mair and Marsh 2004, esp. 242–243 on "system change"). We choose the 1963 election as the baseline in part because it was the first national legislative election after the Christian Democrats and the Socialists had taken concrete steps toward opening the structure of competition for the executive (e.g., Ginsborg 1989, chapter 8). We also use this baseline because it discloses shortcomings of extant approaches.

legislature. As the figure depicts, by the end of that term, incumbents had done much to return the party system to the condition observed at the 1963 election. If we had looked solely at shifts in party vote shares from one election to the next, we would have seen substantial continuity in the party system: electoral volatility stood at roughly 8 percent in 1968 as compared to 1963 (Bartolini and Mair 1990, 342–343; Mainwaring 2011). Yet incumbents, through their actions between elections, can rewrite the menu of voter choice at election time. In this instance, the Italian electorate largely ratified the realignment worked by sitting MPs. If change in voter preferences and choices had driven the evolution of the party system, the (near) return to the 1963 status quo would have been unlikely. The choices of citizens, as expressed in elections, matter, but so do the choices of sitting representatives. Incumbents can exercise their discretion to redefine the contours of a party system between elections. Elite choice can expand and shrink parliamentary parties and inject change into the parliamentary party system overall.

Having demonstrated the reality of change in legislative parties, we define our criteria for identifying change in legislative party systems. Once more, save for work on legislative switching, extant research on party competition conceives of systemic change as a product of the electoral arena. Yet the reigning scholarly assumption of rigidity in legislative party membership falls flat on its face. The notion that voter judgments at election time create a snapshot of political parties, fixing intact until the next election the parties' sizes, platforms, and capacities to contend for the executive, is theoretically misguided and empirically unfounded, as this book claims and shows. The idea of a "photo finish" of the results of party competition at elections, with images surviving untouched until the next election is convened, is political fiction.

Hence, it is possible to observe and analyze, as we do, gradations of change that are grounded in the basic reality that legislative incumbents choose to either switch or retain party affiliation (or independent status) in a given period (e.g., month) of a legislative term. Given our conceptualization and record of individual incumbents' decisions, we adopt a novel criterion for the possibility of system change: at an absolute minimum, for system change to occur, there must be some movement in the membership of parliamentary parties during a term. Along with this, we track as a component of system change a change in the number of parties as brought about by some number of MP switches. In discussing the policy consequences of system change in Chapter 2, we also use the yardstick of a shift, even if small, in the overall configuration of parties' sizes and policies.[10] Equipped in this way, we can discern the extent to which shifts in party seat shares affect the composition of legislative majorities required to set the

---

[10] As detailed later, we draw on extant work measuring party platforms (e.g., Budge and Klingemann 2001; Heller and Mershon 2008; 2009d; Schofield and Sened 2006) or consult primary and secondary sources to estimate roughly the locations of new parliamentary parties founded during a term.

Phenomenon of Party and Party System Change

legislative agenda and approve legislation. We are equipped as well to examine the impact of incumbents' choices on the structure of competition for the executive (cf. Mair 1989a; 1997c; 2006). We can thus arrive at a new understanding of party system change and continuity by following the evolution of parties – and party systems – during legislative terms.

In our theoretical and empirical account, party system change is a matter of degree, of more or less – not of black or white. We aim not to render stark judgments on whether party systems persist or are transformed, but rather to distinguish shades of gray as parties and party systems might evolve in the intervals between elections due to incumbent choices on affiliation. We regard refinement in conceptualization and instrumentation as an advantage, not a disadvantage. Acknowledging that some analysts take a different stance (e.g., Mair 2006), later in the book, we return to the issue of our ability to capture gradations of change – and tectonic shifts – in party systems between elections.

1.3 THE ARGUMENT IN BRIEF

We treat legislative parties as coalitions of strategic individual incumbents. In our account, the party-as-coalition has the potential to shift over the course of the legislative term, depending on what each incumbent decides as she engages in her calculus of party affiliation (cf. Aldrich and Bianco 1992; Aldrich 1995). We assume that legislative incumbents are strategic, ambitious actors who pursue three main goals: policy, office (in all manifestations), and reelection (cf., e.g., Strøm 1990a).[11] Legislators are strategic as they react to and anticipate voter behavior. Legislators are strategic, too, as they respond to institutional constraints and, if they can overcome collective action problems, as they attempt to modify institutions.

We maintain that institutions structure incentives for incumbents and make the pursuit of some goals – and some goods – more salient at some times than at other times. In particular, we use the concept of the "parliamentary cycle" as a device to ascertain how institutions organize legislative activity and impinge on MPs' pursuit of their goals. The parliamentary cycle coincides with the period that many political scientists dub the "electoral cycle" (e.g., among others, Andersen, Tilley, and Heath 2005; Beck 1979; Hellwig and Samuels 2007; Shugart 1995). Even though the spans involved are identical – the time elapsed from one legislative election to the next – the meanings differ profoundly. The notion of the "electoral cycle" highlights that party systems come to life in and through electoral competition; it suggests lulls during the intervals between elections. We stress, on the contrary, that individual politicians, parties, and party systems operate actively outside and between elections, in parliament and

---

[11] As an ambitious politician, an MP acts as if she seeks reelection, even if she does not seek a seat in the upcoming election for the same legislative chamber: voter preferences constrain her behavior since she has career ambition in some form.

in the executive. We interrogate as an open theoretical and empirical issue how much and why party system change outside of elections may occur.

We parse out distinct stages of the parliamentary cycle in order to examine legislative incumbents' pursuit of distinct strategies. We thus endorse and amend the argument that a political actor may calculate that one strategy is advantageous for the stage of electoral competition and another strategy for post-election government formation (cf. Schofield and Sened 2006). Once again, in our approach, the relevant actor is not only the party leader (or the party-as-unitary-team) but also the individual legislative incumbent. Furthermore, the relevant stages to be analyzed extend to distinct moments during the legislative term. Activities on the legislative calendar, as structured and sequenced by institutions, rank priorities for incumbents and make some goals more prominent than others (e.g., policy more salient than office) at some times during the term.

For instance, in some months during a legislature, the party offering the greatest policy benefit to an MP might not be the party to which she currently belongs. For this scenario to hold, the legislature must be in session and acting on policy matters; only if parliamentary parties are engaged in policy debates and decisions can a legislator perceive the heightened salience of policy goods and realize that a new party might be more advantageous than her current party in allowing her to achieve her desired policy aims. As suggested here and as elaborated later, inducements to switch party occur at irregular intervals during the parliamentary cycle, over the course of an entire term.

A map of how the remainder of the book is organized serves to further elucidate the elements of our argument. Moreover, the overview indicates how we marshal and appraise evidence bearing on our claims.

1.4 THE MAP OF THE BOOK

Having presented a novel approach to the enduring question of continuity and change in party systems, we use Chapter 2 to establish the import and impact of interelectoral change in party systems. That chapter illustrates how incumbents who change party affiliation can transform the composition of the legislative coalition controlling decision-making outcomes. We trace the effects of legislators' switches on legislative majorities – and the possibilities for executive formation – across several legislatures varying in the number of parties winning representation. The chapter thus discloses that incumbent legislators who move among parties can bring about tectonic shifts in policy outcomes.

Chapter 3 presents a model of inducements and deterrents to sitting legislators' changes of party affiliation. A chief message of the model, and of the book overall, is that representatives who join a new party – and those who refrain from doing so – take time into account. A politician's strategic calculus on party affiliation involves not only what benefits she stands to gain or lose, but also what times are best or worst to obtain the benefits. At some moments, the MP expects that voter scrutiny is keenest, so that a switch of allegiance will likely cost her electoral support; the incumbent then stays with her original party. At other moments, the legislator calculates that a response to favorable opportunities knocking at the door will likely invite little damage, and so she steps out and moves into another party.

Chapters 4 and 5, which make up Part Two of the book, are devoted to intensive analysis of a relatively small number of legislative terms. The two chapters appraise hypotheses on the timing of MP changes of affiliation within the legislative term, which is shaped by institutions and responds to MPs' expectations of voters. Both chapters proceed on the premise that when a legislator chooses to change party reveals much about why she changes party. Together, the chapters explore the internal validity of the argument that institutions operate as incentives to MPs who effect change in parliamentary parties and party systems, and voters' preferences impart caution to MPs and induce stability in parliamentary parties and party systems.

Part Three examines how well the empirical applicability of our argument generalizes to a broad range of settings. Chapter 6 sets the stage for these tests of external validity by specifying, in a way suitable for large-N statistical analysis, both our hypotheses and alternative hypotheses about the sources of interelectoral change in parties and party systems. Chapter 7 uses our time-series cross-national dataset to probe institutional and preference-based influences on legislative party systems. This empirical analysis yields substantial support for our theoretical argument on institutional inducements and electoral deterrents to change in interelectoral party systems. Chapter 8 reverses that view by weighing institutional forces for stability and by relaxing the assumption that voters punish incumbents who betray their electoral label. Moreover, Chapter 8 expands the empirical analysis to additional countries, encompassing Ecuador, India, and South Africa, among others. Our framework sheds light on change in parliamentary party systems around the world.

Chapter 9, as is customary for conclusions, summarizes our chief findings. We use the argument and evidence as elaborated throughout the book to confirm that MP strategic behavior aggregates into differing degrees of party and party system change outside the electoral arena. Moving beyond convention, we discuss broader implications and sketch how our argument can guide further research in the field. The chapter thus drives home the contributions of the book and the new insights it offers on the workings of political parties and democratic institutions writ large.

2

How Parliamentary Party System Change Matters for Policy

Legislative incumbents can and do change party affiliation during the course of a legislative term, and the incidence of legislators' interparty mobility varies across time and space. In some instances, members of parliament (MPs) substantially redefine the composition of parliamentary parties without legislative elections being held.

Once we grant the possibility of legislative party switching, the pressing question becomes: when incumbents jump party, what happens to policy outcomes? The magnitude of change in policy outcomes that might be wrought by MP interparty mobility is a matter not merely of curiosity but of fundamental theoretical significance. Enacted policy is the product of parliamentary bargaining, as constrained by a bundle of rules and procedures. Enacted policy also reflects the decisive structure of the legislature – the number, weights, and positions of the bargaining partners. In this light, a compelling issue is the maximal effect on policy that might ensue from minimal change – from a single party switch.

This chapter demonstrates the power of legislative incumbents to move policy by changing party affiliation. MPs can enhance their bargaining position by moving across legislative parties, although success in such efforts is not assured: incumbents might face many obstacles to extracting concessions in bargaining, the outcomes of bargaining might be unstable, and an incumbent's capacity to move policy by changing party depends in part on the locations of her original party and her new one. Yet, under some conditions, incumbents who switch party and thus shift those parties' bargaining weights can narrow the range of alternative feasible coalitions and speed the arrival of a compromise they desire. As this chapter shows, a unique viable policy alternative can sometimes be generated when incumbents' changes of affiliation induce the existence of the policy core in parliament.

Legislative incumbents can significantly alter the bargaining environment by executing individual interparty moves to other extant parties and to new parties

How Change Matters

created during the legislative term at some locations in the policy space. By switching party, MPs can induce or move the policy core and thus manipulate policy outcomes in the legislature. Moreover, a single defector can be pivotal to the decisive coalition and legislative decision making overall.

The first section of the chapter sets the stage for our analysis of the policy consequences of legislators' moves among parties. Among other things, we discuss the core as a set of policy outcomes that is invulnerable to defeat. The second part of the chapter argues that MPs who choose to change party can exert an impact on policy. Even when switching is limited in magnitude, mobile MPs can generate a core. The third part of the chapter offers empirical illustrations, drawn from a few of the party systems examined more fully elsewhere in the book.

2.1 LEGISLATIVE COALITIONS AND POLICY

As the foundation for our argument, we depict legislative parties as potentially shifting coalitions of individual incumbents. We then rely on a voluminous body of work to characterize equilibrium outcomes in collective decision making.

2.1.1 Legislative Parties as Coalitions of Incumbents

Here, we expand on the twofold concept of the legislative party as a coalition of incumbents with the capacity to shift. First, in campaigns and elections, a political party operates as a team of politicians (e.g., Downs 1957; Sartori 1976). Then, a party that, once votes are counted, enters into a multiparty legislative coalition or an executive coalition is itself a coalition of incumbents – a collection of individual political officeholders unified for some period of time around shared aims and ideals. In parliament, a party exists as a coalition of legislative incumbents, and the individual incumbents continue to optimize their strategies throughout the legislative term.

Second, we spell out why incumbent legislators might consider a change of party affiliation as an attractive option. We assume that incumbents care about policy, office, and votes, and that their current party membership serves all these goals. Why would a legislator exit her party when she has the option of individual voice on a separate decision (cf. Hirschman 1970)? Several reasons might account for the coupled change of affiliation. A party platform provides an assurance of a commitment to voting in the legislature on a set of linked proposals. This package deal, in contrast to a single proposal considered in isolation, allows for MP calculations on long-term policy coalitions. The party stance on linked proposals implies a commitment to voting on agenda-setting organs and, in parliamentary systems, the implicit or explicit investiture of a government. Participation in those activities requires membership in the party: a legislator who simply shifts her vote does not gain a separate voice in agenda setting, and, as for the party, its role in those activities hinges on the numerical size of its parliamentary group, as enhanced (or diminished) by an MP's move. In the electoral arena, to borrow the memorable metaphor of Pizzorno (1981), parties act as political credit institutions on which voters can bank in the long run.[1] Given these reasons for why moving between parties would yield general policy benefits, those individuals who actually switch may also be able to promote their career when negotiating the move.

This preliminary discussion has introduced the claim that the composition of the legislative party-as-coalition is contingent on the decisions of individual incumbents whose strategic calculations on partisanship can bring them to switch party, either individually or in coordination with others (cf. Aldrich 1995; Aldrich and Bianco 1992). The next step in laying the basis for our theoretical and empirical analysis is to examine party competition for majority control of the legislature and for control of the executive.

2.1.2 Legislative Majority Coalitions and Executive Coalitions

Research on who controls collective decision making stands as one of the most fertile areas in political science. Under the design of parliamentary democracy, theoretical and empirical findings on dominance of legislative decision making identify which actors are in position to command the executive (e.g., Austen-Smith and Banks 1988; 1990; Baron 1991; Baron and Ferejohn 1989; Black 1948; 1958; Diermeier 2006; Franchino and Høyland 2009; Humphreys 2008; Laver 1998; 2006; Laver and Schofield 1990 [1998]; Laver and Shepsle 1990a, b; 1994; 1996; Martin 2004; Martin and Stevenson 2001; Martin and Vanberg 2003; 2005; McKelvey 1976; 1979; McKelvey and Schofield 1987; Riker 1962; Schofield 1986; 1993; 2008; Schofield, Grofman, and Feld 1988; Schofield and Sened 2006; Shepsle 1986; Somer-Topcu and Williams 2008). We draw on this literature to demonstrate that individual incumbents, acting in coalition or occasionally even alone, have the capacity to dislodge the group that has directed decision making so far and hand control to another group.

Like most scholars working in this tradition, we assume that a majority coalition of 50 percent plus 1 is required for approval of any policy decision. In real-world legislatures, this decision rule generally applies, save for constitutional issues and executive veto overrides, which tend to require supermajorities of between three-fifths and two-thirds. We also assume that all deputies of the same party always vote as a bloc. Real-world exceptions to the latter assumption are somewhat more common than are exceptions to simple majority rule. Even so, as political scientists routinely emphasize, the institutions of parliamentary

---

[1] We by no means affirm that such moves are always electorally attractive: negative electoral consequences can ensue, and legislators act as if they expect electoral punishment (Mershon and Shvetsova 2009a; 2011; and below).

democracy reinforce parliamentary party discipline (e.g., Bowler, Farrell, and Katz 1999; Rasch 1999).

We ascribe to the spatial framework, which means that we assume that political parties are located in an issue space defined by N (one or more) relevant policy dimensions.[2] We further assume that it is on the basis of the party's own policy position and the positions of other parties that a party bargains on legislative proposals and enters into a legislative coalition to pass proposals. In particular, a party seeks policy outcomes as near its adopted position as possible, even if it just moved to that position. Each coalition only puts forward policy proposals that its members find to be Pareto-efficient; that is, there exist no alternatives to the proposals endorsed by the coalition that make its members better off, and none that make them worse off. Hence, not all coalitions are feasible for the purpose of reaching a policy decision; the feasible set is defined by the actors' policy positions.

As institutionalists would note, a decisive coalition means different things under different institutional designs. In parliamentary democracies, the formation of majority legislative coalitions is freighted with special importance because the explicit or implicit approval of a majority legislative coalition is required for the executive to come into being and continue in power. The party or parties making up the executive need not command a majority of legislative seats; in fact, minority cabinets rule with some frequency (e.g., Strøm 1990b). In presidential and semi-presidential democracies, the executive has to muster a majority legislative coalition to secure enactment of policy (e.g., Cheibub 2007; Cox 2006; Cox and McCubbins 2005; 2007 [1993]; Haggard and McCubbins 2001). Our treatment in this chapter abstracts away from institutional design because the objective here is to establish in principle the feasibility of substantial policy impact ensuing from MP interparty mobility, rather than estimating degrees of change as dependent on institutional detail. We show that major policy change is indeed feasible. To develop this argument, we take up the concept of the core.

2.1.3 The Core, Policy Choice, and Changing the Status Quo

In the spatial framework, the set of policy proposals that any feasible majority in parliament can advocate is a convex hull of the ideal points of the members of this majority. Although there are a number of theoretical approaches to modeling bargaining outcomes, the concept of the core is by far the strongest and is also the one that links noncooperative and cooperative theory.[3] The concept of

---

[2] The assumption that parties are located in policy space extends to political scientists who do not engage in formal deductive reasoning (e.g., Budge et al. 2001; Sartori 1976).

[3] In noncooperative game theory, and viewing participants' strategies as their decision on which coalition to join, any outcome in the core corresponds to (potentially several) coalition-proof Nash equilibria.

the core is also often used in analyzing legislative coalitions. The core is defined as a set of outcomes that cannot be defeated by any decisive coalition. To see the core's invulnerability, consider that the core, if it exists, is an intersection of the decision sets of all decisive coalitions; it falls within the convex hull of each decisive coalition. Any move away from that policy will be disliked by at least one member of *each* feasible majority; thus, any proposal to amend policy away from an outcome in the core would lose by majority vote. Hence, if the core existed, legislators would recognize its invulnerability; some would propose, and a majority would adopt, policies that lie in that core (e.g., McKelvey and Schofield 1987; Schofield 1986).

The existence or absence of the parliamentary core – and, if the core exists, its size and location in the policy space – are of obvious importance for policy outcomes. When we demonstrate that a very few incumbents' interparty moves can create, destroy, or reposition the parliamentary core, we thus also establish that even small changes of partisanship can transform those policies that the legislature can be expected to adopt.

2.2 MANIPULATING THE CORE: THE POWER OF INTERPARTY MOVES

It is feasible for a parliamentary party (i.e., a coalition of individual legislators) to manipulate the core. Sufficiently large parties in parliaments in which interparty mobility is allowed can unilaterally manipulate the level of predictability in decision making and select final outcomes. Transitional political systems exemplify such extremes in parliamentary fluidity: as affiliation and policy changes destroy one majority coalition and yield another, further changes give rise to still another coalition, and so on. We claim that these observations can be extended to well-established legislatures and offer an account of the empirical realities of party splits, party mergers, and the (rarer) parliamentary walk-outs. If we think of parties as agglomerations of MPs at any given time, then this argument also applies to the mobility of factional subgroups or even individual parliamentary incumbents who might induce the core. A faction within a party can serve as a convenient vehicle for organizing MPs' switches in search of the core. Likewise, a political entrepreneur can maneuver to pull MPs in her wake and lead a collective hunt of the policy core. On rare occasions, the weights and locations of parties can be such that the move of just one incumbent can tip the balance between two or more extant parties, altering their relative weights, triggering new strategic alternatives, and putting into place a new core in collective decision making.

The impact of interparty moves is thus not a linear function of their number. One mobile legislator can endow a party with agenda control that it previously lacked, as Senator Jeffords dramatically illustrated for the United States (cf. Den Hartog and Monroe 2008). To be sure, some real-world legislatures prohibit

How Change Matters

independents from sitting separately and impose a minimum size requirement on parliamentary groups. Still, under some conditions, a single well-placed switch can demolish one decisive structure and create a new one.

Our primary purpose here is to stake this claim: elections set up but do not settle once and for all legislative party systems and decisive structures. Legislative parties, party factional subgroups, and individual incumbents can effect change in the legislative party system and policy outcomes between any two successive elections. Extant theoretical accounts do not portray the potential for change that we identify here (cf. Mershon and Shvetsova 2013). These dynamics can shift feasible policy outcomes from those established by the initial distribution of seats at election time to policies made feasible by incumbents' interparty moves. With few exceptions, the current literature assumes stasis: parties are fixed units, immutable in the interval between one national legislative election and the next. We show why this may not be the case. Even more, mobility between elections can create a new – interelectoral – party system and decisive structure.

The strategic moves made by incumbents can have far-reaching repercussions on policy. This chapter illustrates the plausibility of that claim by focusing on dynamics in several legislative chambers. Our choice of cases affords variation in the number of parties elected to parliament, represented at the outset of the legislative term, which accords with the scholarly consensus that the number of parties stands as a distinguishing trait of party systems. All the chambers that we study here evinced *some* change in the membership of legislative parties. The question is whether the changes in legislative parties prompted shifts in policy outcomes and how much incumbents met with success in remaking the decisive structures.

2.3 TECTONIC SHIFTS OUT OF PARTY MOVES: EMPIRICAL ILLUSTRATIONS

We first examine a legislative party system constituted by two parties immediately after an election and then look at successively larger systems.

2.3.1 Two-Party System: U.S. House

We begin by investigating the U.S. 104th Congress, which served from 1995 to 1997. During this term, the U.S. House of Representatives witnessed five switches, a total not exceeded by any other U.S. term from 1946 to 2002 (our dataset; cf. Nokken and Poole 2004). The 1994 election sent 230 Republicans, 204 Democrats, and one independent to the House. Once the term started, all five members of congress (MCs) who switched became Republican.

This unidirectional flow in itself suggests a search for policy advantage because the 104th marked the Republicans' return to majority status in the

House, with the substantial agenda powers that entailed (e.g., Cox and McCubbins 2005; 2007 [1993]). Moreover, four of the five recruits to the Republicans garnered appointments to key committees: Ways and Means (*CQ Weekly* [*Congressional Quarterly Weekly, CQW*], July 1, 1995, 1894), Appropriations (*CQW*, March 16, 1996, 682), and Commerce. In the Commerce Committee, one switcher retained seniority earned as a Democrat (*CQW*, June 10, 1995, 1612), and another was promised (and received in the 105th) the posts of subcommittee chair and vice chair of the full committee (*CQW*, January 6, 1996, 67). Finally, the roll-call behavior for all five switchers shows dramatic changes at the time of the move, "with pronounced and positive increases in DW-NOMINATE scores expected of a Republican MC" (Nokken 2009, 98). With a floor majority already assured in the House, these mobile MCs did not change the outcomes of bills submitted to a floor vote, after having been brought out of committee. The MCs who enlarged the Republican majority in the interval between elections were, however, in a privileged position to shape committee outcomes, which in turn determined what got to the floor (e.g., Shepsle 1979; Shepsle and Weingast 1987). In this way, the "Republican Revolution" was reinforced by those MCs elected as Democrats who defected to expand the majority and strengthen the Speaker's hand.[4]

2.3.2 Two-Party System: U.S. Senate

The U.S. two-party system also highlights that even a single switch can transform the legislative balance of power. The 2000 election created a Senate exactly evenly divided between Republicans and Democrats. The Republicans constituted a majority only with Vice President Dick Cheney's tie-breaking vote. In May 2001, however, Senator Jim Jeffords left the Republicans, sat as an independent, caucused with the Democrats, and delivered control of the Senate to the Democrats. Before Jeffords' choice, control of a Senate majority had always been established in elections; no interelectoral flips in majority control had ever occurred (Den Hartog and Monroe 2008, 71–72). The literature is unambiguous in judging that the Jeffords switch exerted a substantial impact on policy and financial markets (Covington 2006; Den Hartog and Monroe 2008; Jayachandran 2004; Monroe 2010). Jeffords' votes aligned overall with the Democrats after his switch (Den Hartog and Monroe 2008, 70), enabling that party to possess the policy core. Outside the Senate, the Jeffords move also resonated through the system of separation of powers because it initiated a phase of divided government in the United States (Nicholson 2005).

---

[4] Some observers flag the importance of other outcomes arising from MC moves in this term. In particular, when Nathan Deal switched to the Republicans, he ended cross-cutting House representation for his state. In one observer's view, the move "create[d] a politically and racially polarized Georgia House delegation, consisting of eight white Republicans and three black Democrats" (*CQW* April 15, 1995, 1084).

In the two-party U.S. House during the 104th Congress, switchers enlarged a majority won at election time and served to entrench further the majority's strength on committees that were central to the effort to enact the "Contract with America." In the Senate in 2001, Jeffords deprived the Republicans of a majority, bestowing the policy advantages associated with majority status on the Democrats, a party to which he did not officially belong. Incumbent switching in that case moved the policy core.

2.3.3 Four-Party System: Canadian House

Figure 2.1 follows Schofield (2008) and arrays in a two-dimensional policy space the four parties that won seats in the Canadian House of Commons in June 2004.[5] Shortly after the election, the Liberal premier formed a minority government that, with the informal support of the New Democrats, commanded exactly half of the House. Given the knife-edge balance, the few switches that occurred during the 2004–2006 legislative term had dramatic effect.

Compare the distribution of seats immediately after the election (indicated by boxes on the figure) with the distribution on May 20, 2005 (circles, where change has occurred). By that date, two Liberals had exchanged their electoral label for Independent status, and one Conservative, Belinda Stronach, had defected to the Liberals (data on switching from Canada, House of Commons 2009).[6] On May 20, moreover, the federal budget was put to a floor vote as a matter of confidence. The vote resulted in a tie, with 152 votes on each side, which the Liberal Speaker broke. Along with the Speaker, it was switchers who enabled the government to survive. Stronach was appointed as a minister in the Liberal cabinet on May 17 and naturally toed her new party line a few days later. Another former Conservative who adopted Independent status just before the 2004 election made a "last-minute decision" to vote to express confidence in the Liberal executive (quote from BBC 2005; cf. Desserud 2006; *Economist* 2005a,b; Fox 2005; Gussow 2006; Morton 2006). The policy upshot was approval of an essential omnibus bill – the annual budget – with the simultaneous renewal and enlargement of the authoritative team of policy-makers, the cabinet.

2.3.4 Five Sizable and Many Minor Parties: Italian Chamber

The 1996 Italian parliamentary election awarded seats in the Chamber of Deputies to more than a dozen parties. The center-left Olive Tree electoral cartel formed the basis for the governing coalition allying the Party of the Democratic Left (PDS), Popular Party (PPI), Greens, Italian Renewal (RI), Italian Socialists, and two tiny local parties (South Tyrol and Sardinian Action) with external

---

[5] We adopt the spatial metrics and policy locations of electoral parties for our cases from extant work focused on the countries in question.

[6] Two more MPs changed party affiliation before the end of the term.

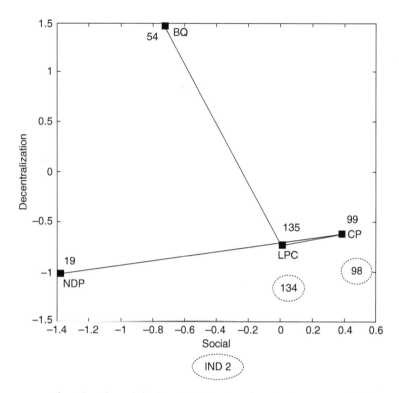

FIGURE 2.1 The Liberals and the heart in Canada: after the June 2004 election and in May 2005.

Numbers next to the circles show seats as of May 20, 2005. For 2004 Canada, Schofield (2008, 120) used mass survey data to place parties in policy space. Schofield often uses Manifesto data to locate parties (e.g., 2008 on Israel; Schofield, Grofman, and Feld 1988; Schofield and Sened 2006; on this major research program, see, e.g., Budge et al. 2001). We make no assumptions about the locations of the two independents (ex-Liberals).
Source: Schofield 2008, 121, fig. 4.11, on June 2004 election result, with information on seat strength at election time added to the Schofield figure. BQ, Bloc Québecois; CP, Conservatives; IND, Independent; LPC, Liberal Party; NDP, New Democratic Party

support from Communist Refounding (RC). As Figure 2.2 illustrates, the 1996 election created an empty core in the Chamber, given the array of electoral actors in the two-dimensional policy space and the seats each won (cf. Giannetti and Sened 2004; Schofield and Sened 2006). The median lines identify alternative majority coalitions, one coalition on and to one side of the line, and the other on and to the other side of the line. A core party, if it exists, sits at the intersection of all median lines; the core does not appear in Figure 2.2.

The ten fairly sizable electoral actors depicted in Figure 2.2 do not correspond precisely to the parliamentary groups as constituted at the outset of the legislative term, in part because rules on the minimum size of groups forced MPs from the smallest parties to enter the Mixed Group. Only nine parliamentary groups,

How Change Matters 27

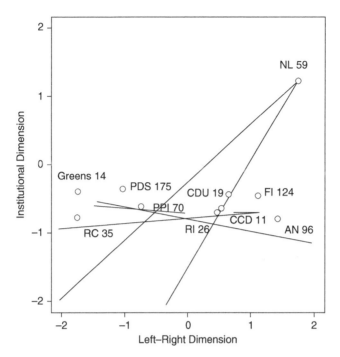

FIGURE 2.2 The empty core in the Italian Chamber after the 1996 election.
Giannetti and Sened use mass surveys and expert judgments to locate party positions for 1996.
Source: Replication of Giannetti and Sened (2004, 504, figure 3). AN, National Alliance; CCD, Christian Democratic Center; CDU, Christian Democratic Union; FI, Forza Italia (Go Italy); NL, Northern League; PDS, Democratic Party of the Left; PPI, Italian Popular Party (Popular Democrats, PD, as parliamentary group); RC, Communist Refoundation; RI, Italian Renewal

among them the Mixed and the combined Christian Democratic Union-Christian Democratic Center (CCD-CDU), thus existed at the start of the term. Furthermore, throughout the 1996–2001 term, one-quarter of deputies changed affiliation at least once (cf. Heller and Mershon 2005; 2008; Mershon and Shvetsova 2008a; 2009b). We analyze this strategic behavior in detail later. To convey the import of change in the legislative party system for bargaining over policy and competition for the executive, it suffices for now to focus on two snapshots of the Chamber, one taken in mid-April 1998 and the other in mid-April 1999 (data on switching from Italy, Camera dei Deputati 2010).

First, in March 1998, life Senator and former President Francesco Cossiga founded a new party, the Union of Democrats for the Republic (UDR), to contest the May 1998 subnational elections. The UDR pulled MPs from the CDU and CCD, the most centrist elements of the center-right electoral cartel (the Freedom Pole, dominated by Forza Italia [FI] and the National Alliance [AN]); in the

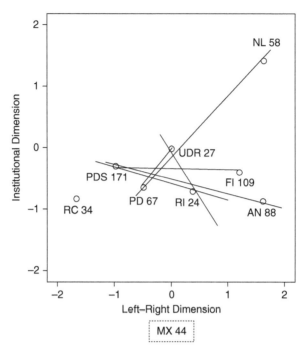

FIGURE 2.3 Parliamentary groups in the Chamber, April 15, 1998: the search for the core.
See Note 7 on our estimates of the location of parliamentary groups founded during the term. We make no attempt to locate the motley Mixed Group (MX) and do not count it in computations of the median and the core (see Note 8). Without the MX, the majority threshold is 294.
Source: Updating of Giannetti and Sened (2004, 503), using data on switching from Camera (2010).

Chamber, both the CDU and CCD shrank so much that their remaining adherents were obliged to enter the Mixed Group. The UDR also attracted a few incumbents with center-left origins. As the campaign unfolded, Cossiga announced the UDR's stance in pressing budgetary and constitutional debates and pursued tightly linked electoral and policy aims. Cossiga declared on launching the UDR that his party would be "outside the Pole, distinct and distant from the right, and, for now, an alternative to the left" (as quoted in Istituto Cattaneo 2010a; cf. *Corriere della Sera* [*CdS*], March 14, 1998; March 15, 1998; March 26, 1998; April 10, 1998; April 29, 1998; May 1, 1998; May 27, 1998; Donovan and Newell 2008; Pasquino 1998, esp. 127–128). Taking him at his word, we assign a centrist position to the UDR in Figure 2.3.[7]

---

[7] We use party leader pronouncements to estimate party locations immediately after their creation during the term. Specifically, we scour the online archives of the Italian newspaper of record for leader declarations near the time of the party's founding and draw on other sources based on

With the parliamentary groups' locations and seats in mid-April 1998 as portrayed in Figure 2.3, it looks like Cossiga was hunting the core. If the policy space in the Chamber had been defined only by the left-right spectrum, the UDR would have qualified as the median party. (Note that we assume that the motley Mixed Group does not count in computations of the median and the core, and we make no attempt to locate it in policy space.[8]) When both dimensions are considered in Figure 2.3, the various median lines that demarcate alternative majorities do not intersect at the UDR where we place it. Yet we cannot reject – and see reason to accept – the possibility that Cossiga's intention was to control policy outcomes from the center. The contrast between the empty core immediately after the 1996 election and the UDR's location in April 1998 is stark: the area bounded by the median lines, which defines a "heart" as opposed to a core (e.g., Schofield 1993), has contracted, if compared to that just after the 1996 election. The UDR now shows on the boundary of the new small "heart." Recall that a player inhabiting the core is the decisive – essential – member of any majority coalition. Cossiga succeeded in landing a sweet spot: he brought into being a new party and brought MPs behind him.

This example suggests that incumbents, by changing party, can alter the bargaining weights of multiple actors and can possibly endow one of them with the ability to participate in every decisive coalition. Can another political entrepreneur "steal" the core – create a new group and attract enough followers so as to enable it to similarly gain dominance in decision making? The second snapshot of the Italian legislative party system appears in Figure 2.4 and captures the legislative party system in mid-April 1999. Preparing for the June 1999 subnational and European Parliament elections, MP and former Premier Romano Prodi, in February 1999, announced the formation of a new party, the Democrats-Olive Tree (Dem-U). By mid-April, sufficient switching had occurred among center-left MPs that the Dem-U came to satisfy the minimum size requirement (20 deputies) for a separate parliamentary group in the Chamber. Prodi emphasized his center-left stances by, for instance, comparing his party to such successful "reformist forces" as those led by Tony Blair and Lionel Jospin (quote from Prodi op-ed, *CdS*, March 13, 1999; cf. *CdS*, February 5, 1999; February 6, 1999; February 14, 1999; February 27, 1999; May 26, 1999; June 22, 1999; Daniels 2001; Di Mascio 2007; Prodi press interview February 9, 1999, excerpted in Prodi and Marinelli 2006, 17). In light of

---

contemporary media accounts. Although our estimates should be treated with caution, we regard them as the most appropriate option; the Manifesto data (as used in some of Schofield's work, e.g., Schofield and Sened [2006]; Schofield [2008] on Israel) and expert judgments and mass surveys (Giannetti and Sened 2004) are unavailable upon the parties' creation, and measures based on MP voting behavior (as used in Heller and Mershon 2008) would not capture the party leaders' efforts to communicate to voters.

[8] The Mixed Group was quite diverse internally, with multiple organized components (minimum size, three deputies) and with no expectations on its members' voting behavior (personal communication, On. Mauro Paissan, December 3, 2000, then President of the Mixed Group).

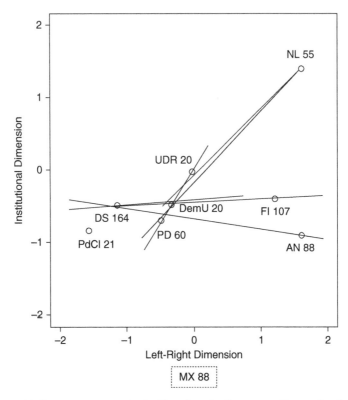

FIGURE 2.4 Parliamentary groups in the Chamber, April 15, 1999: Contending for the core.
Without the Mixed Group (MX), the majority threshold is 272; the majority threshold is 279 if the Communist Refoundation (RC)-organized component is regarded as uniquely disciplined on socioeconomic issues within the Mixed Group.
Source: Updating of Giannetti and Sened (2004, 503), using data on switching from Camera (2010).

Prodi's statements at the founding of the Dem-U and during the 1999 electoral campaign, we locate his party toward the center of the policy space, but to the left of the UDR.

Figure 2.4 registers several other important changes in the legislative party system that occurred between April 1998 and April 1999. In October 1998, the RC suffered a split, with its hardliner chunk traveling to the Mixed Group and retaining the RC moniker; the more moderate majority renamed itself the Communist Party of Italy (PdCI), and we regard it as slightly more centrist than the once-unified RC. What occasioned the party split in October 1998 was internal divergence on a confidence vote in the government, then headed by Prodi. Given the split, for the first time in the Italian Republic, a government fell due to defeat on a motion of confidence. For its part, the UDR denied support to Prodi on the fateful October vote, then scored ministerial appointments in the new government launched by Massimo D'Alema (e.g., Giannetti and Laver 2001; Ieraci 2008, 92; Istituto Cattaneo 2010). Cossiga successfully exploited the bargaining power available to him in October 1998.

By mid-April 1999, as Figure 2.4 shows, defections had reduced the UDR membership in the Chamber to 20. A string of MP departures had moreover extinguished RI as a separate parliamentary group. With these changes and others indicated in the figure, the UDR still sat at the median on the left-right spectrum. If we were to assume, however, that the RC-organized component within the Mixed Group voted with unique discipline on socioeconomic issues (as could well be reasonable for hardline communists), then the Dem-U qualified as the median party on the left-right spectrum. For a two-dimensional policy space, Figure 2.4 displays the median lines that identify a contest for power between the Dem-U and UDR.

Tellingly, both the Dem-U and the successor party to the UDR, Cossiga's Union of Democrats for Europe (UDEur), received ministerial positions in D'Alema's second cabinet, inaugurated in December 1999 (Istituto Cattaneo 2010). Both parties also served in the last executive of the 1996–2001 legislature.

2.4 CONCLUSION

Incumbents' moves matter for policy. Their strategic decisions to change affiliation and move in policy space redefine party systems between elections. Decisive structures are not set at election time.

The distinguished research traditions on parties, party systems, and party system change, despite their signal achievements, do not account for or even attend to legislative incumbents' capacity to change decisive coalitions between one legislative election and the next. To be sure, a new body of research has emerged to demonstrate the importance and ubiquity (at varying levels) of the phenomenon of legislative party switching. These scholars have sought to identify explanations for why individuals would switch and why some places and/or times evince higher switching rates than others. Few contributions to date come to grips systematically with the system-altering implications of switching (but see Giannetti and Benoit 2009; Giannetti and Laver 2001; Heller and Mershon 2009a,b,c; Laver 2008; Laver and Benoit 2003; Laver and Kato 2001; Laver and Shepsle 1999, 36–47; 2006, 257–258; Schofield 2009). Here, we showed the feasibility of system-level change between elections due to MP interparty mobility – change occurring in the party system and in the set of decisive coalitions. Legislators who move among parties can disrupt and realign policy outcomes.

3

Why and How Individual Incumbents Change Legislative Party Systems

Now that we know that incumbents can transform party systems and parliamentary policy agendas between elections, the next task is to explore why and how incumbents bring about such change. Taking up the task, this chapter develops an integrated model of change and stability in interelectoral legislative parties and party systems. In the mechanism presented here, an individual incumbent's choice of party affiliation is a recurring strategic decision. The sitting legislator's strategy is moreover contingent on time: her calculus on partisanship involves not only what she stands to gain or lose, but also when the potential gains or losses likely occur.

The first section of this chapter lays out a formal model of the inducements and impediments to changes of affiliation among individual legislators. The second part draws out the testable implications of the model. The third section outlines the two-pronged research design used to assess hypotheses.

3.1 AN INTEGRATED MODEL OF INDUCEMENTS AND DETERRENTS TO CHANGES OF AFFILIATION AMONG INDIVIDUAL INCUMBENTS

Our model of parliamentary parties as endogenous coalitions of incumbents is premised on the notion that the incumbent's choice of party should maximize her utility in any given period (e.g., month).[1] The assumption that actors maximize utility is routine; the novelty here is that we use this assumption as the basis for an integrated theory of incentives and deterrents to incumbents' changes of party affiliation.

---

[1] As elaborated later, the month serves as the standard time interval in this study's theoretical and empirical analysis.

3.1.1 Inducements to Changing Parties in the Utility Function of Incumbent *i*

The anchor of our model of parties as endogenous coalitions is a statement of the goals that elected members of parliament (MPs) want to attain. We identify three fundamental types of rewards for political actors: policy, office (and its perks), and election (e.g., Desposato 2006b; Heller and Mershon 2009d; Reed and Scheiner 2003 on individual legislators; Müller and Strøm 1999; Strøm 1990a on parties). We express the utility function of incumbent *i* as:

$$u_i(\lambda, \theta, \tau),$$

where

λ is the parameter (or weight) indicating the importance to an MP of policy gains,
θ is the parameter attached to the benefits of office, and
τ is the parameter attached to the incumbent's prospects for reelection.

We assume that an elected representative sees at least some value in each of the three sets of rewards. That is, $\theta, \lambda, \tau > 0$. Granted, some political scientists assert that the goals of individual politicians and parties reduce to the imperative of winning the next election (e.g., Downs 1957; Mayhew 1974; 2001; cf. Aldrich 2001). Like many scholars, however, we assume that an elected representative completely bereft of policy aims is a rare creature. Parliaments approve pieces of legislation that embody decisions on public policy, citizens consider this as they cast their votes, and legislative candidates are recruited, winnowed – and win – in part on the basis of the policy positions they espouse. In consequence, "it is hard to imagine that voters would be willing for long to entrust anyone devoid of policy preferences with policy-making responsibilities.... Few politicians assign a weight ... of zero to policy" (Heller and Mershon 2008, 915).

It is straightforward to assume that candidates who compete for legislative office wish to hold the seat and value the benefits tied to occupying that office. In the MP's utility function as we define it, then, office refers not only to retention of the legislative seat via reelection but also to internal legislative office and related perks (e.g., committee membership and access to staff). In parliamentary systems, a subset of legislators earns promotion to executive office, so that hopes for a cabinet position can enter into a candidate's office objectives as well.

The candidate's pursuit of votes advances both policy and office aims. When a candidate meets electoral success and lands a legislative seat, she is newly equipped to pursue her policy and office goals. Immediately after capturing a seat, the partisan strategy of an elected representative is free from the original drive to win enough votes to be launched into the legislature, although reelection at future electoral rounds naturally remains a concern.

The incumbent almost always takes her seat with status-quo partisanship. That is, in most democratic legislatures, few legislators enter as independents.

The MP's strategy is thus not so much a choice to affiliate as a choice to change party. Even an MP who holds fast to her initial party affiliation over time is making a recurring, strategic, utility-maximizing choice. For the loyal incumbent, too, the utility derived from party membership is a function of the benefits of policy, office, and reelection prospects.

Having identified the aims that a sitting legislator pursues, we now express her prospects for reelection as the summation across all voters of the probabilities that an individual voter in the electorate of size n will vote for incumbent i in the next election:

$$u_i(\lambda, \theta, \tau) = f(\lambda, \theta) + \tau \sum_{k=1}^{n} p_k^i \qquad (3.1)$$

Hence, for a given month j in the life of a legislature, the utility to incumbent i from moving out of her original party, o, and throwing in her lot with a new party π, can be expressed as

$$u_i^j(\cdot, \pi) = \lambda a_\pi^j + \theta b_\pi^j + \tau \sum_{k=1}^{n} p_k^{i\pi} \qquad (3.2)$$

where a_π^j denotes the one-time amount of policy rewards that the incumbent could secure in that month as a member of party π, whereas b_π^j stands for the one-time amount of office- and perks-related benefits available in that month from that party. We assume without loss of generality that $a_\pi^j \geq 0, \forall j \in C, \pi$, whereas $a_\pi^j = 0, \forall j \notin C, \pi$, where C is the set of months during which the legislature addresses an active policy agenda. Similarly, $b_\pi^j \geq 0, \forall j \in B, \pi$, and $b_\pi^j = 0, \forall j \notin B, \pi$, where B is the set of months during which recorded allocations of internal legislative offices (and, in parliamentary systems, executive portfolios) unfold.[2]

The incumbent's expected vote in the next election, the final term in equations (3.1) and (3.2), can be represented as a function of whether or not the incumbent has changed parties during the current term. We discuss this below. For now, we stress the assumption that voting probabilities are affected in two distinct ways. The first depends on the policy distance entailed in a given party change by legislator i; any distance from the original position implies a negative effect; that is, a loss in aggregate vote share, because, by assumption, the original choice of party maximizes constituent support.[3] A second negative and varying effect, and

---

[2] Later, we expand on how we conceive of the B (benefits) and C (policy control) sets of months, or stages, of the parliamentary term.

[3] To underscore, we assume that the MP's policy platform, given other candidates' platforms, already maximizes her vote: after all, she has won election. Because we focus on the MP's strategic choice of affiliation and her perceived policy variance, we do not address change in policy platform as a strategic choice. For theoretical tractability, that is, we opt to address the moving part of loyalty while keeping policy constant.

Why and How Incumbents Change Systems 35

one of central importance in our argument, flows from the simple fact that such change or changes have taken place.

Proposition 1: Strategic incumbents will change parties only during active parliamentary stages.

Proof: The Appendix to this chapter provides the brief proof of Proposition 1 (see 3A.1 in Appendix A at the end of book).

Proposition 1 leads directly to a corollary that lays the basis for our first hypothesis.

Corollary 1: Change at the level of legislative parties and the legislative party system should occur only when the legislature is engaged in those active stages of the parliamentary cycle in which legislators compete for control of policy and office goods. Very little or no change should occur when the legislature is dormant.

Observe that the politician's utility-maximization problem is a period-specific statement. Whereas later we treat voters as sensitive to the temporal distance between their vote decisions and events that inform their beliefs about politicians (specifically, occurrences of MP switching), we make no analogous assumption about legislators. The incumbent's choice of party, however, hinges on time. To this we now turn.

3.1.2 The Incumbent's Time-Contingent Choice and the Parliamentary Cycle

In our approach, each calculation the incumbent makes on party affiliation entails recognition of the benefits and costs available at one moment, and yet each stands independent of the other in time. The incumbent's strategy on partisanship over the course of a legislative term thus amounts to a sequence of separate occurrences; the incumbent makes each of her period-specific (e.g., monthly) calculations afresh. We assume that this "snapshot" model suffices to capture the key intuition that when a legislator perceives benefits at hand, she will reach out and switch party to reap those benefits. In contrast, when she expects that a change of allegiance will cost her voter support, she will stay loyal to her status-quo party.

The snapshot view of the incumbent's sequence of separate calculations, month by month, complements the concept of the parliamentary cycle. This concept reflects the reality of legislatures as complex institutions, with rules and procedures that bundle, schedule, and sequence the activities of legislators on the legislative calendar (e.g., Cox 1987; 2006; Cox and McCubbins 2005; 2007 [1993]; Döring 2001; Martin 2004). As defined in Chapter 1, the parliamentary cycle is the interval between two successive legislative elections – the span from the election initiating a given legislative term to the election ending that term. The length of this interval varies across countries and can also vary across terms for most parliamentary democracies. Such variation notwithstanding, the work of legislatures during the span between two successive elections has a property that generates a *cycle*: during that span, distinct phases of activity appear periodically and, also periodically, highlight different types of gains for the incumbent, who engages in a recurring strategic calculus of party affiliation.

All activities on the legislative calendar do not bear equally on the rewards of policy and office that incumbents can pursue through switching party. Early in a legislative session, committee posts are awarded to MPs. At such times, given the legislative agenda's focus on office allocation, it should be the desire for office benefits that induces an incumbent to consider a change of party. In some months, the legislature actively deliberates on policy. In those months, the prospect of increased policy influence in a new party should come forward as the most salient motive that might bring an MP to switch. To be sure, in some parts of the span between elections, a legislature is largely inactive – most obviously, when it is on recess. In such phases of dormancy, the strategic incumbent should see no benefit in a change of allegiance and should stick with her original party.

Our analysis locates the timing of not only inducements but also impediments to the elected representative's change of party affiliation. Voter preferences for partisan loyalty deter individual legislators from switching party and underpin stability at the level of the party system as well. We now develop this point in two steps: the candidate's need for a stable party label and the voter's evaluation of candidates.

3.1.3 The Electoral Value of Stable Party Labels

What counteracts pressures for change in legislative party systems between elections? In our approach, the legislator's openness to changing parties while serving in parliament is checked by her need for the party label. On one hand, the rewards held out to legislators in active stages of the parliamentary cycle operate as incentives for change, whereas, on the other, switching is deterred by the requirement that the candidate in an election have a relatively clear and lasting association with a party label. The electoral connection (Mayhew 1974) entails electoral costs attached to party switching.

We contend that the key force that works to hold the party system together between elections is the importance to voters of the incumbent's partisan identity and reputation. Consider that a party label serves as an information shortcut for voters in two ways. Party affiliation makes a candidate electorally recognizable in a race by associating her with a well-known political program. A candidate's membership in a party, in addition, can enhance voters' perceptions of her quality because she has the trust of a larger political network. In both of these uses, the party label is important in reducing information costs to a voter – but it is not irreplaceable. In the reasoning so far, moreover, affiliation with one party is as good as with any other; there is nothing wrong with a candidate swapping one label for a second and then a third and even a fourth.

Hence, we place extra weight on still another, distinct contribution of a *stable* party label to the electoral attractiveness of a candidate. This contribution stems from overcoming the individual candidate's inherent deficiency as an agent of voters when compared to the party as an agent. Because of the natural time limitation on an individual's political career and her many alternative opportunities even within her lifetime, a representative-as-person is less beholden – less accountable – to voters than is a representative-as-party. Diermeier (1995), for example, argues that a party, by combining the incentives for many short but overlapping careers of individual politicians, establishes itself as a reliable representative of the principal, a representative feasibly committed to a long-term planning horizon and feasibly fully preoccupied as an entity with its reputation in office (cf., e.g., Aldrich 1995; 2011; Cox and McCubbins 2005; 2007 [1993]; Heller and Mershon 2009b). Similarly, we contend that it is important for voters that their MP is a known and reliable party member who stands for more than her own qualities and record and who embodies in her partisan candidacy and service in office greater longevity and reputational resource than that offered by any individual or any single personal political career.

The need for a party label is only one of the factors tying an incumbent to her party. Other factors provide tangible contributions to a politician's hold on office: campaign resources, appointments to legislative committees, chances for positions in the executive, the party's backing of her favored policies, and so forth. Yet we believe that these influences need not counter the impetus for an incumbent to change party and may even motivate a decision to switch. All factors other than the party label constitute potentially negotiated benefits – elements of a "package" that leaders can offer an incumbent in an effort to entice her to switch into the leaders' party from her current party. Reasonably enforceable contracts on party benefits can be established between a party's leadership and switching recruits to that party (cf. Heller and Mershon 2008; 2009b,c). The benefits that a party as a coalition of politicians furnishes to one of its own thus exert an influence on an MP's loyalty that is, in the end, indeterminate. The benefits are negotiable: party elites can withhold these benefits from (some of) the new arrivals but can also extend benefits to attract promising politicians from other parties.

What cannot be negotiated when incumbents plan and carry out individual or collective moves between parties is how voters will respond at the next election. We argue that it is the voters – the supporters of the MP's (prospective) new home party and those of the MP's original party – who can constrain an incumbent's decision to change partisan affiliation. The reactions that the MP anticipates from voters in the next election have the capacity to put a brake on the MP's impulse to defect from her party.

The model of the electoral costs of changing parties in parliament must then rely on assumptions about voters' preferences for incumbents' party loyalty. We assume that voters identify with the party of the candidate for whom they cast their vote. We also accept as a premise that voters prefer representatives who exhibit consistency (low variance) in behavior. We assume, in particular, that voters value loyalty – steadfastness – in a representative's attachment to a party. We ground this assumption about voters in the argument that a party's accountability and level of competence, again, exceed those of any individual representative (Diermeier 1995). We assume, moreover, that the consistency of an MP's partisan attachment is especially valuable where it matters the most – where electoral laws allow voters to decide on individual candidates instead of a party list (e.g., Carey and Shugart 1995).[4] Because we treat voters as the key actors whose behavior affects the welfare of legislators, we now specify the voter's utility function and show how the legislator's utility-maximizing behavior hinges on voter response.

3.1.4 Voters' Calculus: Agency Risks and Rewards for Partisan Constancy

Voters balance two tasks when evaluating their prospective representatives on the eve of an election: they assess the policy position that a particular candidate promises, and they judge the policy risk associated with that candidate. The second task arises from the possibility that the policy the representative will actually pursue once in office might diverge from what the candidate promises to voters at election time. Voters might also consider characteristics of candidates that do not pertain to policy, such as the candidates' personal qualifications for office and demographic traits. We assume that these variables enter the utility function of a voter directly and do not change with a politician's change in partisanship.[5]

The policy variance associated with the candidate is quite another matter. It reflects both the limits on the voter's information about the candidate's true policy position and the risk of the candidate's deviation from the platform on which she was elected. The partisan history of the candidate influences both components of policy variance.

Thus, we specify the utility function of voter k as reflecting the importance of policy and variance associated with candidate i. We write this function as

$$u_k^i = u_k(x_i) - \sigma_i^2(I_i, L_i(\alpha)), \qquad (3.3)$$

where x_i is candidate i's policy position and the policy variance of candidate i is $\sigma_i^2(I_i, L_i(\alpha))$. In turn, I_i is an indicator function taking the value of 1 if a candidate belongs to a political party and 0 otherwise. We assume that the fact of partisanship gives a partisan candidate a lower perceived policy variance than the perceived policy variance of an independent competitor. L_i is a loyalty

---

[4] Hence, we work with the premise that candidate-centered voting and party-centered voting are not mutually exclusive. Instead, pure candidate-centered and pure party-centered voting are but extremes of a continuum.

[5] To be sure, no real-world electorate likely fully meets our set of assumptions (e.g., Converse 1964; Lupia and McCubbins 1998).

Why and How Incumbents Change Systems 39

variable indicating the dependability of the candidate's current party membership in the voter's eyes; it is a personal attribute of an incumbent that depends on her partisan behavior during the term; that is, on her history of moving in and out of parties. The degree to which partisanship remains constant – loyalty – also serves to reduce variance and hence to increase the incumbent's electoral appeal; changing parties instead reduces L_i, and so increases $\sigma_i^2(I_i, L_i(\alpha))$. The variable α stands for the degree to which the electoral system induces voters to focus on individual candidates.

To appreciate the impact of an incumbent's history of switching on the voter's calculus, first denote the utility to a voter from unquestionably loyal incumbents (those who have not switched in a given term) as $L_o > 0$. Now, consider a voter at the moment immediately after an incumbent's switch in month j of the term. The voter experiences a utility loss due to the erosion of her perception of the incumbent's loyalty and thus due to an increase in the variance associated with this incumbent. The utility loss comes from two sources: the MP has betrayed her status-quo or electoral party, which demonstrates the opportunistic nature of the incumbent's affiliation in the first place; and the novelty of the MP's new party affiliation means that it has unproven strength.

The voter's appraisal of a switch depends on the move's timing relative to both the election starting a given legislative term and the election ending the term. The voter perceives maximal utility loss due to an MP's switch at election time; this utility loss fades over time, weakening with each month into the term. Denote the (maximal) utility loss due to a switch immediately after the election initiating a term as $\Delta L(\alpha)$, and the (maximal) utility loss arising from a switch immediately before the election closing the term as $\Delta l(\alpha)$, where $\Delta L(\alpha) \leq 0, \Delta l(\alpha) < 0$. Because we assume that the maximal reputational damage occurs at the minimal distance from an election, we can specify the decay rate of the damage. For the initiating election, the damage decreases by a factor of $0 < \phi < 1$ with each month of the term, so that a switch executed in month j will signify betrayal of the incumbent's status-quo party with the factor of ϕ^j. Intuitively, ϕ^j shows the degree to which voters feel the switcher's disloyalty to the original party label, given that the switch occurs j months from the moment voters elected the legislature. Similarly, for the election closing a term lasting m months, the reputational damage decreases by a factor of $0 < \delta < 1$ with each month of distance to the term's end, lessened by the factor of δ^{m-j} if a switch occurs in month j. Thus, $0 < \phi < 1$ and $0 < \delta < 1$ capture the degrees to which the voter's disutility due to an MP's switch wanes over time.[6]

Because a history of switching increases the negative term in (3.3), it reduces the utility to voters from supporting candidate i if her policy position, x_i, is

---

[6] Whereas we allow for the possibility that the initial utility loss, $\Delta L(\alpha)$, can be zero in some systems, as discussed later, we assume that the decay factors are the same for all voters everywhere and the utility loss at the ending election, $\Delta l(\alpha)$, is non-zero.

fixed.[7] This dynamic holds regardless of the value of α. The magnitude of the effect and the constraining force of the bracketing elections may vary with α, however. The more voters focus on candidates rather than parties when making their vote choice, the higher α is. Conversely, when voters must choose a party list, as under proportional representation (PR) rules, α is relatively low. Where voters cast votes for a party, not an individual candidate, they are relatively insensitive to the switcher's defection from her electoral label. Yet voters who choose party lists are sensitive to whether lists present teams dedicated to the label and platform when the next election is held.

3.1.5 Unified Analysis of the Calculations of Politicians and Voters

Having delineated the voter's perception of both the unquestionably loyal candidate and candidate i who has switched, we are now equipped to assess the voter's probability of voting for i and so to unify the analysis of voters and incumbents.

Denote as $H_i = \{h_i^1, ..h_i^m\}$ the history of interparty moves by incumbent i, measured by the temporal distance between the move and the month of the election, m, that ends the given term. Define a generic component of H_i as $h_i^j = 1$ if a switch took place in month j of the term and 0 otherwise. The loyalty parameter with which incumbent i approaches the next election is thus functionally linked to the history of that incumbent's interparty moves during the term as follows:

$$L_i(h_i^1, ..h_i^m) = L_0 + \sum_{j=1}^{m} h_i^j (\delta^{m-j} \Delta l + \phi^j \Delta L). \quad (3.4)$$

In this expression, terms $\phi^1, ...\phi^m \in (0,1)$ are, again, the weights on the loss of loyalty arising from switching, respectively, in months 1 to m of the term. An MP who jumps party in the same month as the election inaugurating the term, t, will suffer the maximal reputation loss.

Such loss diminishes, month by month, as time elapses after the initiating election. Terms $\delta^{m-1}, ...\delta^{m-m} \in (0,1)$ are the weights on the loyalty-loss parameter that reflect the length of time the switcher has been enrolled in her new party and thus the extent to which she has been able to compile a history of attachment with it so as to compensate for the disloyalty to her old party. Maximal loyalty loss due to the unproven loyalty to the new party is inflicted if the switch takes place in month m of the term.

---

[7] This discussion suggests that the loyalty variable has two dimensions: (a) stability of party affiliation, the focus here; and (b) propensity to vote with the party of record. That is, if x_i is stable, then changing parties implies either that the (old and new) parties occupy the same observed positions in voting terms (always vote together) or that the switcher must necessarily regularly buck the party line in voting in at least one of the parties in which her membership defines L_i. Investigation of (b) lies outside the scope of this study.

Why and How Incumbents Change Systems

The voter's perception of a candidate's loyalty thus declines with the number of interparty moves and with the moves' temporal proximity to either the election closing a given term or the election opening the term. The voter's utility of voting for the candidate also declines with an increase in the number of moves and the temporal proximity of the move(s) to the two elections bracketing a term.

We now express the probability of voter k voting for a candidate i, $p_k^i(\bullet)$, as a function of k's utility from that candidate, $u_k^i(x_i, I_i, L_i)$, which in turn depends on the candidate's policy, partisan status, and past history of consistent partisanship. Assuming that higher utility increases the probability of voting for the candidate, we observe that $p_k^i(x_i, I_i, H_i)$ declines in $\sum_{j=1}^{m} h_i^j(\delta^{m-j}\Delta l + \phi^j \Delta L)$. That is, the more times the candidate switched in the past, and the closer the move(s) occurred to either of the elections bracketing the parliamentary term (either the election initiating or that ending a term), the less likely, all else equal, the voter is to vote for that candidate. What does this result mean for the calculations and behavior of strategic incumbents?

An incumbent who contemplates a move from one party to another compares her actual state with others not yet observed. In our framework, she compares the net benefits available to her from membership in her current party o and the estimated net benefits to be had from belonging to an alternative party π. As held in Proposition 1, a necessary condition for an incumbent's change of party is that the benefits of office and policy promised by party π strictly exceed those offered by her status quo party o. If the MP's reelection prospects were unaffected by a switch, she would move whenever $f(\lambda_\pi, \theta_\pi) > f(\lambda_o, \theta_o)$ (recall expression 3.1).

Yet that "if" does not apply, and this inequality is woefully incomplete. Once more, voters are less likely to vote for switchers than for loyalists, with the probability of voting depending on the timing and number of moves. The strategic incumbent will thus expect that, if she moves among parties during the term, the impact of the move(s) on her probability of re-election will hinge on how close to election time she switches. This argument leads to the conclusion that legislative incumbents' utility loss from switching parties is minimized and their benefits are maximized, all else equal, if moves are timed near the middle of a legislative term.

Proposition 2: Conditional on the availability of partisan gains, strategic incumbents will time changes of party near the middle of a legislative term.

Proof: The Appendix to this chapter furnishes the proof of Proposition 2 (see 3A.2 in Appendix A at the end of book). The proof shows that, subject to the availability of partisan benefits, the electoral cost to the incumbent from executing a switch is minimized near the middle of the legislative term.

The strategic incumbent's recurring choice on party affiliation is thus a matter of strategic timing. On the one hand, as in Proposition 1, the incumbent seeks to time changes of party so as to reap the gains offered by a new party and available

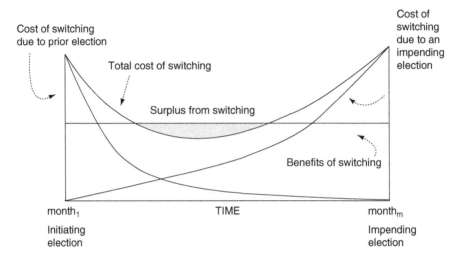

FIGURE 3.1 Illustration of the theoretical relationship between time and expected incumbent interparty moves.

when the legislature actively allocates offices or deliberates on policy. On the other hand, as in Proposition 2, the incumbent knows when voter scrutiny is relatively sharp, so that a switch will invite greater electoral damage. At such times, the incumbent will stick with the status-quo party.[8]

Figure 3.1 portrays the theorized relationship. The horizontal axis shows the timeline of the legislative term from one election to the next. The vertical axis displays the electoral costs and the parliamentary benefits of switching. The cost of switching due to the election initiating the term declines as the term progresses, and the cost due to the election closing the term rises with the approach of the upcoming election. Supposing, for simplicity's sake, that the benefits to incumbents from switching are evenly distributed throughout the legislative term (as expressed via the horizontal line), the net office and policy benefits of switching appear below the benefits line.[9] The shaded area in the figure indicates the phase during the term when switching is probable – when net benefits tempt MPs to

---

[8] In almost all parliamentary democracies, the duration of the parliamentary term is flexible, up to a constitutionally mandated length. We assume that sitting legislators, as they carry out their responsibilities, gather information sufficient to enable them to foresee an early election. We assume as well that incumbents, as a matter of political survival, must act as if voters understand the approach of an early election, which means, in turn, that their moves should be checked by voter preferences for party label loyalty even if a snap election is held.

[9] The depiction in the figure of benefits evenly distributed over the term is convenient for this illustration. Nothing in our concept of the parliamentary cycle requires such regularity. Indeed, we contend that the incentives to change party occur irregularly. We return to this point later.

move among parties. With the groundwork in place, we can extract testable hypotheses.

3.2 TESTABLE IMPLICATIONS: INDUCEMENTS, DETERRENTS, AND THE TIMING OF INTERPARTY MOVES

In our theory, then, sitting legislators make recurring decisions on party membership by consistently striving to maximize parliamentary gains and minimize electoral costs. Whereas incumbents unswervingly aim to exploit benefits and avert costs, the appearance of benefits and costs varies over the course of the legislative term. Hence, at different moments during the parliamentary cycle, MPs' calculations issue different "marching orders" to them, telling them to stay in place at some times and to step out to a new party at other times. By looking at the behavior of elected representatives through the prism of time, we can infer how incumbents respond to incentives as they decide whether to change or retain their coalitional affiliation – their membership in political parties. Our reasoning allows us to reconstruct the linkage between prospective benefits and politicians' moves in a natural and direct way, via time. By observing when incumbents make their moves, we can identify what explains their moves.

Timing matters not only for incumbents but also for voters. Our model reveals that voters should penalize incumbent MPs' moves between parties when the disloyal incumbents come up for reelection. The depth of betrayal of the label that voters punish is a function of the time that a legislator spends with her party. It is voters and their ability to inflict electoral costs that can put brakes on any inclination on the part of incumbents to pursue new gains by reassessing their partisanship while in office. MPs seek to time any move they make so as to minimize the electoral price they pay.

The general logic of the model points to five specific testable hypotheses, each of which comes under examination in subsequent chapters. The first three hypotheses focus on the ways that MPs should time changes of party in attempts to maximize parliamentary benefits and minimize electoral costs.

First, we expect that if MPs make any moves among parties, they should act during those phases when such changes could produce concrete advantage. The advantages that the incumbent may attain by transferring from one party to another must materialize after her initial choice of party. The model shows that when one type of benefit becomes highly salient during the term, it should entice the legislator to consider a move. In particular, incumbents should be tempted to change party in those phases when legislative policy decisions are weighed and legislative internal offices (or executive offices) are assigned. The model implies that incumbents should see incentives to switch, too, when they affiliate in a parliamentary caucus at the start of the legislative term. After all, as emphasized, one core assumption is that legislators recognize the value of political parties, and a caucus constitutes the legislative expression of the political party writ large. On the whole, therefore, if incumbents jump party, they should do so in response to specific inducements during the term, incentives defined by the incumbents' institutional context and their activities within that context. In a nutshell, incumbents should time moves to seize benefits. This first testable hypothesis flows from Proposition 1 and Corollary 1 in the formal model.[10]

- *H1, Time Moves to Seize Gains*: MPs should change parties during active stages of the parliamentary cycle; thus, system-level change should be relatively high during active stages as well.

Second, the deterrent to MP switching imposed by voter preferences for loyalty should be strongest when elections loom. Given voters' fundamental preference for partisan loyalty, voters should look with favor at a legislator who has built her record in a new party for almost an entire legislative term, and they should distrust MPs who change parties immediately before an election in attempts to tack to the prevailing electoral winds. Hence, MPs should grow more reluctant to move between parties as their term in office progresses and the next election approaches. If an MP wants to move to a party different from the one under whose banner she was elected, she should jump as early as possible in the term.

- *H2, Stay Put When Elections Loom*: The electoral cost of acquiring a new party affiliation should rise as the next election nears. Other things equal, the frequency of switching should decline during the term.

The next hypothesis, unlike the second, is contingent on institutional context. Under relatively candidate-centered rules, voters should perceive an abrupt break from an MP's electoral party, timed early in the term, as a signal that this particular MP has a propensity to be disloyal. The MP thus communicates that she affiliates weakly and opportunistically with an electoral organization. She cannot afford to hop parties too soon in the term – unless the inducement is very strong, such as a cabinet post. To the extent that voters decide on individual candidates, incumbent concern about displeasing voters should deter defection immediately after an election.

- *H3, Wait to Jump Ship*: The more candidate-centered the system, the more reluctant MPs should be to switch soon after an election. In relatively candidate-centered systems, the electoral cost of switching should fall as the last election recedes in time and, other things equal, the frequency of switching should increase.

---

[10] Whereas the prose label for the first hypothesis (like Proposition 1) refers to the individual incumbent, the hypothesis itself extends to the system level. This feature forms an integral part of our effort to uncover the microfoundations of systemic change.

Why and How Incumbents Change Systems

In candidate-focused systems, then, two tendencies should operate. As in H_2, the MP needs to establish a legislative record in her new party that she can defend at the next election; the electoral cost of switching should climb as the term unfolds. As in H_3, the incumbent must avoid being seen as irresponsible, so that the electoral cost of switching should wane as time passes since the last election. Weighing these concerns, MPs should be most likely to change party near the middle of the span between the last national legislative election and the next, at the moment that minimizes the electoral cost of switching. This posited minimum in costs and maximum in switching constitutes the *conditional midterm effect*. The expectation of the conditional midterm effect corresponds to Proposition 2 in the formal model.

Whereas H_2 foresees a smoothly decreasing frequency of switching as the term unfolds and H_3 a smoothly increasing frequency over the term, the posited conditional midterm effect envisions the ascent of H_3 until some point near the midterm when that ascent should be overtaken by the descent of H_2. It is roughly at midterm that MPs should begin to respond to the freedom they perceive from the electoral constraint binding them to voters and vote choices from the last election. Near the midterm, too, MPs should discern relative freedom from the prospect of punishment for switching to be meted out at the next election. The net benefits of changing party should be most abundant roughly at midterm, as in Figure 3.1.

Consider the implications of the discussion so far. The benefits from switching should materialize unevenly over time within a given legislative term, whereas the constraints on switching should evince smooth, gradual change, as a function of the temporal distance from the election launching the term and the distance to the election ending the term. Changes of party should thus occur irregularly over the term, which contradicts the notion that incentives to switch are distributed evenly over a term, as depicted in Figure 3.1.

Figure 3.2 illustrates the irregularly occurring incentives to changing party, incentives grouped by stage of the parliamentary cycle. In stage A (for Affiliation), at the opening of the first legislative session, MPs have the option of discarding the party label they wore when campaigning and of announcing a new party group membership for serving in the legislature. In stage B (for Benefits), legislative offices (and in parliamentary systems, executive portfolios) are up for assignment. In stage C (for Control of policy), the legislative agenda addresses the most important policy domains. H_1 holds that, if any MP hops party in stage A, she should be motivated above all by the office perks tied to membership in the new party, just as, if she moves in stage B, the chief incentive should be office benefits: these are the salient goods at the time. Given legislators' heightened focus on policy during stage C, any choice to change party should aim at influencing policy and controlling the agenda. Incumbents should not be induced to switch during any inactive stage, stage D (Dormant), excluded from the figure.

Figure 3.2 simplifies the parliamentary cycle during the span between two legislative elections, presenting the active stages as always consecutive, never

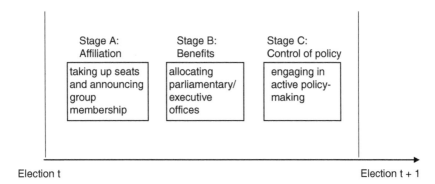

FIGURE 3.2 Variation in posited motivations for incumbents' changes of party across stages of the parliamentary cycle.
Key to posited motivations in stages: A: obtain legislative perks associated with legislative party AFFILIATION; B: aim for office BENEFITS, such as legislative committees and posts, government portfolios; C: secure advantage in CONTROL over policy agenda.
Source: Adapted from Mershon and Shvetsova 2008a.

overlapping, and non-recurring. The lack of realism of this stylization is more than offset by its ability to spotlight the central notion that distinct motivations for changing party affiliation come to the fore depending on the type of activity dominating the legislative agenda. The figure thus illustrates the idea that distinct phases of the parliamentary cycle offer distinct inducements to incumbents to switch; and, given the possibility of individual-level mobility, it is also possible for parliamentary parties and party systems to shift and evolve between two successive elections.[11]

The role of electoral institutions, flagged in H3, deserves further attention. We contend that candidate-focused electoral rules magnify voters' attention to individual candidates' behavior and that, under such rules, voters attend to candidates' policy positions and use permanence of the party label as a tool to assess candidates' policy variance. In such voting systems, the perception of high variance in the politician's type should be compounded when a switcher breaks the contract with a partisan coalition in her well-defined home constituency. Party-based voting should instead shield incumbents from voters' perceptions of disloyalty: voters cast votes for a party. Given this protection, legislative party systems elected under party-list rules should evince greater overall change than do those elected under candidate-centered rules.[12]

---

[11] Figure 3.2 omits the role of elections. Because we posit that that the approach of elections should dampen the propensity to switch, we are well poised to appraise the counterargument: that the drive for reelection motivates switching. We return to this as an empirical question later.

[12] Candidate-centered systems allow independents to enter the legislature more than do party-list systems. We address the behavior of non-partisan MPs later.

- **H4, *Move to the Law*:** The electoral cost of changing party should vary across electoral systems. In particular, switching should be less frequent in candidate-centered systems than in party-list ones.

The fifth implication of the model, like the fourth, concerns the number of switches. Whereas the fourth hypothesis regards overall frequency, the fifth focuses on individual-level behavior and can thus be evaluated only in the intensive case-study component of the empirical analysis. Every time a sitting MP changes party, the voter becomes less likely to cast her vote for the MP at the next election. Recognizing this tendency on the part of voters, the individual MP should refrain from executing multiple moves – she should minimize the number of switches made.

- **H5, *Limit Moves*:** MPs should minimize changes of party. In particular, among switchers, the modal number of moves should be one.

Just as important as specifying the testable hypotheses stemming from our theoretical argument is the task of making explicit what phenomena would appear if our argument failed to hold. If we were wrong, then neither inducements to switching nor voter propensity to punish disloyal representatives would vary over the course of the legislative term. The null hypothesis would thus be that incumbents' changes of party affiliation should not exhibit significant variation across time during the legislative term. No variation should appear across systems with different electoral laws. And, according to the null, a single move among switchers should show no tendency to emerge as the mode.

- **H0, *Null*:** No variation in the frequency of changes of party affiliation should appear across time within terms or across different electoral systems. No effort to minimize the number of moves should be manifested among switchers, whatever the electoral system.

Note that the extant literature on party system institutionalization (cf. Mainwaring 1999; Mainwaring and Torcal 2006) suggests that, in weakly institutionalized systems, the relative malleability of voters' beliefs, orientations, and preferences may loosen or lift constraints on representatives, even those elected under candidate-based rules. The implication would be that Hypotheses 2 through 5 should apply feebly, if at all. This implication is, then, a variant on the null hypothesis.

3.3 RESEARCH DESIGN

Here, we sketch the broad contours of our research design and defer operationalization of our hypotheses, along with specification of controls and rival hypotheses, until we proceed to the empirical analysis. We adopt a two-pronged research design. In the first component, we conduct in-depth case studies of select country-terms. In the second, we estimate large-N statistical models of interelectoral party system change. Each part of the empirical analysis brings distinctive strengths. We exploit the case study evidence, both qualitative and quantitative, in order to search for the mechanisms underlying flux and continuity in interelectoral party systems. The intensive case studies permit us to gauge the internal validity of our argument. We probe whether our hypotheses hold for the "right reasons" – whether the posited causal mechanisms operate as expected to produce the outcomes observed. The extensive comparisons in the statistical models speak to external validity. We aim to establish the generalizability of our theory by analyzing a dataset with comprehensive cross-national and longitudinal coverage. The large-N estimations allow us to discern whether our hypotheses find support even while controlling for variations in, for example, economic conditions and social cleavage structures. The two parts of the investigation complement each other and, in so doing, buttress confidence in the inferences drawn from the empirical analysis overall.

The second chief aspect of research design is case selection. Table 3.1 identifies all country-terms included in the two-pronged investigation. As notes *a* and *b* to Table 3.1 suggest, we choose the subset of country-terms for intensive analysis to ensure substantial variation in the institutions demarcating the boundaries of the parliamentary cycle stages, which is central to evaluating the first hypothesis. The in-depth cases also exhibit different electoral rules, which play a key part in our logic. Moreover, these cases vary in the institutionalization of the party system, which, as discussed, may affect voters' propensity to punish incumbents' party defection. For the entire set of country-terms included in the large-N analysis, where we seek to demonstrate the generalizability of our argument, we deliberately maximize institutional variation across country-terms. In particular, the country-terms examined differ as to electoral system, territorial governance, and regime type (i.e., presidential or parliamentary design).[13] Overall, as Table 3.1 conveys, the large-N estimations span a total of 110 legislative terms in eight countries, for more than 4,000 monthly observations.

Third, Table 3.1 conveys the third feature of the research design, the choice of time frame to be studied. As data availability permits, the main dataset initiates its monthly observations on legislator behavior for each country with the first democratic legislative election after World War II.[14] This starting point aligns with a foundational assumption of our argument, that voters prefer partisan loyalty on the part of elected representatives. To rephrase, an assumption essential to our theoretical and empirical work is unlikely to have held before the advent of

---

[13] As elucidated in Chapters 6 and 7, the vital advantage of institutional variation is offset by the disadvantage that multiple institutional variables easily become de facto country effects, given the relatively small number of countries here. For descriptive statistics on all terms and on the in-depth terms, see Tables 3A.4 and 3A.5, respectively, in Appendix A at the end of the book.

[14] We omit 1949–1955 Australia, given gaps in the monthly data, and we omit 1946–1948 Italy, given the uncertain institutional context at the moment of the founding elections and during the Constituent Assembly (e.g., Mershon 1994). We omit 1994–1996 Italy in light of severe difficulties both in theorizing about voter and MP behavior and in operationalizing incumbent switching when the hybrid electoral rules were first used in 1994. For discussion, see Appendix 3A.3, in Appendix A at the end of the book.

Why and How Incumbents Change Systems

TABLE 3.1 *Case selection: countries and legislative terms.*

	Regime Type	
Electoral Laws	*Parliamentary*	*(Semi-)Presidential*
SMD plurality/majority		
FPTP	CA 1949–2006 (18)	US 1946–2000 (27)[a]
	UK 1945–2005 (16)[a]	
2-round		FR 1997–2007 (2)
AV	AZ 1955–2004 (19)	
List PR		
Closed	SP 1979–2000 (6)[c]	RO 1996–2004 (2)[a]
Open	IT 1948–1976, 1976–1994 (11)[a]	
Hybrid		
	GE 1949–2005 (15)	
	IT 1996–2001 (1)[b]	RU 1993–1995 (1)[b]

Federal and highly regionalized systems are italicized. For each country, numbers in parentheses show terms studied.

[a] Includes secondary in-depth terms: IT 1963–1994; RO 1996–2004; UK 1970- 2001; US 1970–2000.

[b] Primary in-depth terms do not enter into the large-N analysis, as discussed in Appendix 3A.3 Case Selection, in Appendix A at the end of the book.

[c] In Chapter 8, the analysis expands to include Spain. As discussed in Chapter 8, Spanish parliamentary rules since 1982 limit the applicability of the key assumption that MPs are free to change parties.

Key to country acronyms: AZ, Australia; CA, Canada; FR, France; GE, Germany; IT, Italy; RO, Romania; RU, Russia; SP, Spain; UK, United Kingdom; US, United States.

Key to electoral acronyms: AV, Alternative Vote; FPTP, First-Past-the-Post; PR, proportional representation; SMD, single-member districts.

Data sources: Australia, Parliament (2011); *Ballot Access News* (2001a,b); Butler and Butler (2000; 2006, 112–114); Canada, House of Commons (2009); France, Assemblee Nationale (2009a,b; 2010a,b,c,d); France, Ministere de L'Interieur (2010); Germany, Bundestag (2009a,b); Italy, Camera dei Deputati (2009); Nokken and Poole (2004); Timothy Nokken (personal communications, June 2006 and July 2008); Romania, Parlamentul Romaniei (2009); Schindler (1984; 1988); Szarka (1997, 196); Tomás Mallen (2002); U.S. Congressional Biographical Directory (2008).

universal male suffrage (roughly occurring at the end of World War I in a number of systems), when, distinguished political scientists contend, voters had relatively weak attachments to party labels (e.g., Caramani 2004; Lipset and Rokkan 1967; Mair 1997a). Although the interwar years are less often studied (but see, e.g., Luebbert 1987; 1991), it is questionable whether our key assumption would have held for this time as well. Thus, we restrict the bulk of our tests to the temporal context when our key assumption about voter orientations is likely to have applied. That said, in Chapter 9, we briefly look at pre-World War II evidence.

Last, although we defer discussion of details of measurement until we proceed to the empirical analyses, we note that these details differ to some degree from the intensive case studies to the extensive cross-national longitudinal comparisons. Some differences in measurement are understandable, given the different aims and possibilities of each prong of the analysis. At the same time, we underscore what we stated at the outset of the study. At minimum, for legislative party system change to occur, legislators must act so as to bring about movement in the membership of parliamentary parties during a term. We thus devise multiple measures of incumbents' changes of affiliation. We also track change in the raw number of parties. Throughout, we emphasize the analytical advantages offered by our ability to detect gradations of change – and tectonic shifts – in party systems between elections.

3.4 CONCLUSION

Part One of the book has laid the foundation for our empirical investigation. Chapter 2 has shown that incumbents' strategic choices to change party affiliation can shift the legislative balance of power, dislodging the party once capable of dominating policy outcomes. In short, switchers can successfully hunt the core. Incumbents' moves matter. This chapter has advanced a formal model that identifies the factors that induce MPs to change party and that deter them from doing so. We have made explicit the testable hypotheses implied in the formal model and have outlined a two-pronged research design for evaluating hypotheses.

The hypotheses build on the general notion that a legislator who weighs whether to stay in her original party or switch to another party considers not only what goods she will receive or relinquish, but also what times are best or worst to get the goods. MPs should switch in active stages of the parliamentary cycle, moving in time to seize the rewards at hand in the stage they face. Seeking to avert electoral costs, incumbents should refrain from switching immediately before an election. The more electoral institutions invite voter scrutiny of individual candidates, the more MPs should stay loyal to their labels right after an election. Thus, under relatively candidate-centered rules, any change in parliamentary party systems should occur near the midterm, the time at the greatest remove from elections and the time when accountability is weakest. Overall, however, parliaments elected under candidate-centered rules as opposed to party list rules should evince relative stability: voter attention to individual candidates at elections should induce sitting representatives to hold fast to their status-quo affiliations between elections. The same force that underlies our expectations about the timing of interparty moves relative to elections – incumbents' awareness of electoral penalties for disloyalty to the party label – should lead them to limit the number of switches they make.

We combine intensive case studies and extensive cross-national comparisons to appraise hypotheses. The next two chapters, which comprise Part Two of the book, address the first component of that research design. Chapters 4 and 5 are devoted to the task of isolating the causal mechanisms generating overall patterns of interelectoral change and continuity in parliamentary party systems. Both chapters subject to detailed scrutiny the argument that comprehending when parties and party systems change holds a key to comprehending why they change.

PART TWO

DISCERNING MECHANISMS THROUGH CASE STUDIES

Time is of the essence in the argument we advance. Legislative incumbents should schedule any moves they make among parties to maximize gains and avert losses. The timing of incumbents' moves should reveal what propels change and what underpins stability in legislative party systems. Support for our theory about incumbents' redefinition of legislative party systems hinges on two factors: the stage of the parliamentary cycle and the distance from one national legislative election to the next.

If our argument holds, then the two forces exerting opposing effects should act roughly concurrently over the legislative term. Hence, it is especially challenging to disentangle the impact of incentives and deterrents to legislative party system change. This difficulty makes it especially important to track the workings of posited causal mechanisms. The two chapters that constitute Part Two exploit case study evidence to drill down for the mechanisms underlying flux and continuity in interelectoral party systems.

Chapter 4 explores the inducements to incumbents' mobility between parties. The chapter looks at the correspondence between the moments when new rewards become available to incumbents and when those incumbents manifest a response to the new rewards – when they become so compelled by desired gains that they exit their electoral parties and enter others. To anticipate the chief finding, elected representatives time any moves they make among parties during the active stages of the parliamentary cycle. The available evidence supports the first hypothesis and its several corollaries.

Chapter 5 directs attention to the deterrents to party switching. Legislators largely refrain from moving among parties when the upcoming election draws near. We discover that incumbents in candidate-oriented systems, relative to their counterparts in party-list systems, wait until after an election to defect from their electoral party. The second and third hypotheses are corroborated. We also find some evidence of a peak in interparty mobility near the middle of the term.

In multiple ways, then, the temporal distribution of switches within the legislative term tells a tale of incumbent accountability to voters' preferences as registered on election day. What is more, as the fourth hypothesis holds, incumbents elected under candidate-focused rules are less likely to move than are those elected under party-list rules.

The empirical analysis in Part Two demands detailed qualitative and quantitative data. Chapters 4 and 5 thus restrict their focus to a subset of terms, those earlier identified as the in-depth terms in Italy, Romania, Russia, the United Kingdom, and the United States. For two terms within that subset, deliberately selected to limit variation on electoral rules, we compile and inspect especially fine-grained evidence on the behavior of individual legislators that brings change or reinforces stability in legislative party systems. Scrutiny of diverse sets of granular data permits us to probe the internal validity of our argument – to ascertain whether the causal mechanisms we posit work as expected to yield the outcomes observed.

4

Legislators' Pursuit of Benefits and Legislative Party System Change

We seek to gain leverage on the question of why legislators switch party affiliation by establishing when they make their moves. Because we contend that change in legislative party systems is rooted in incumbents' pursuit of benefits, we look for evidence that legislators change parties to obtain rewards. We look for evidence that legislators change parties *in time* to obtain rewards.

To illustrate, if we observed that an incumbent has switched party when committee positions have come up for allocation, then we could infer a relationship between the two events. In this example, we could infer that the availability of office goods has triggered the choice to change party. To increase our confidence about the mechanism behind the inference, we could adduce more evidence on the individual legislator making the leap to another party, showing, for instance, that she received a new committee post in the new party. We could also multiply observations, for many legislators, many months, many legislative terms, and even a fair number of countries. We follow both strategies in this chapter, then further expand the set of countries in Part Three of the book. By linking changes of party affiliation with the time periods when such benefits as office or policy goods are most prominent and available, we bring evidence to bear on the key claim that politicians' search for advantage drives their decisions to switch parties – or to stay in their original party homes.

The first section of this chapter revisits the parliamentary cycle, the construct we use to partition time within the legislative term. In operationalizing the stages of the parliamentary cycle, we also elaborate for case study analysis the first hypothesis on *timing moves to seize gains*. The second part of the chapter assesses the first hypothesis and its corollaries against data from the two terms that we examine in greatest detail, the 1996–2001 Italian Chamber of Deputies and the 1993–1995 Russian Duma. The third section analyzes incumbents' interparty mobility across the set of thirty-three secondary in-depth terms in Italy, Romania, the United Kingdom, and the United States.

We conclude the chapter by using our findings on the determinants of legislative party system change to begin evaluating the determinants of stability, the subject of Chapter 5. Indeed, discovering what motivates incumbents to jump party also suggests what leads legislators to retain membership in their original party. The basic message of this chapter, like that of Chapter 5, is that timing matters both for incumbents' moves among parties and for the forces constraining those moves.

4.1 REVISITING THE PARLIAMENTARY CYCLE

We defined the parliamentary cycle as stretching from one legislative election to the next and as containing distinct stages. Chapter 3 illustrated in stylized fashion three active stages of the parliamentary cycle: A (for Affiliation), B (Benefits), and C (Control of Policy). In each, distinct goods valued by legislators come to the fore. We argue that legislators, recognizing the availability and salience of such goods, might be moved to switch in active stages. In the inactive stage D (Dormant), in contrast, no change in legislative party systems should appear. This expectation is enshrined in the first hypothesis: if not for the label-related constraints, members of parliament (MPs) should be open to switching parties as they pursue goals specific to the stage in the parliamentary cycle.

4.1.1 Operationalizing Stages of the Parliamentary Cycle

The institutions, rules, and procedures structuring legislative activity, along with the content of legislative decision making, define the temporal boundaries of stages of the parliamentary cycle. Table 4.1 indicates that the degree of detail in operationalizing stages varies from the two primary in-depth terms to the secondary in-depth cases. For the most intensively studied 1996–2001 Italian Chamber and the 1993–1995 Russian Duma, we are able to compile abundant information on rules and decision making; fine detail enters into our application of criteria for coding stages.[1] When our purview expands to encompass the additional terms constituting the set of secondary in-depth cases, we must resort to simpler, sparser criteria for identifying stages to maintain consistency across legislatures whose records offer varying degrees of information in varying formats. Our identification of stages must be simplified still further when we analyze the full dataset in Part Three.

The wealth of evidence gathered on the two most intensively studied terms allows us to track most closely the trail of incumbents' efforts to switch party at

---

[1] See Appendix A, Tables 4A.1 and 4A.2. Note that, for 1996–2001 Italy and 1993–1995 Russia, given our ability to tap the wealth of the legislative records in hand, we treat the week as the unit of observation. For the secondary in-depth terms, where weekly information on MP switching and legislative activity is not uniformly available, the unit of observation is the month; all the same, there as well, consultation of legislative records generates the coding of stages.

TABLE 4.1 *Operationalizing stages of the parliamentary cycle for primary and secondary in-depth terms*

Stage and Concept	Factors Shaping Operationalization	Primary in-depth terms — Italy 1996–2001	Primary in-depth terms — Russia 1993–1995	Secondary in-depth terms
A: *Affiliation* MPs take seats and announce group affiliation	Electoral laws affecting independents; legislative rules on groups and on start of session	Election day to last week MPs must state group membership	Election day to day of group selection for SMD MPs; for PR, five weeks after rules specified on group selection	First two months, starting election day
B: *Benefits* Legislative and executive offices are allocated	Rules and practices affecting relative strength of president vs. premier; number of cabinets per legislative term	B recurs with >1 cabinets; week groups announced to the date legislative and first cabinet payoffs completed; week Nth cabinet falls to the week N+1 cabinet named	Given strong presidency, no governing coalition formed; period of allocation of legislative committee posts, as shown in legislative records	For committees, month(s) in which posts allocated, as shown in legislative records; for cabinet(s) in parliamentary and semi-presidential systems, any month in which cabinet negotiated
C: *Control of policy* Policy making dominates agenda	Rules on introducing, considering, and approving bills, including committee role	Legislative record, from week executive sends budget to house to the date bill passed; date constitutional bill presented to the date committee dissolved	Legislative record, from first vote on finance until finance moves off agenda; on war: as indicated by key events that open and close policy episode	Any month that legislature is officially in session, as shown in legislative records
D: *Dormant* All other than A, B, and C	Definition of other stages (residual stage)	As indicated by other stages	As indicated by other stages	As indicated by other stages

All stages save D can overlap or coincide. See text for discussion of operationalization of electoral stages associated with nonlegislative contests, performed only for 1996–2001 Italy.

particular times to obtain particular types of goods. When we enlarge the scope of the inquiry to the secondary in-depth terms, we must sacrifice a degree of specificity in the data to probe the general applicability of our claims. We maintain enough granularity in the evidence on the secondary in-depth terms that we retain the capacity to tap the workings of our posited causal mechanisms. This design enhances our confidence that, if the large-N statistical analysis in Part Three yields findings that fit with outcomes predicted by our theory, those findings are produced due to the operation of the causal mechanisms we posit.

As shown on the top row of Table 4.1, the parliamentary cycle opens with stage A (Affiliation), which runs from the popular vote to the taking up of legislative seats in the first session. In stage A, MPs have the opportunity to alter the label under which they won election when they announce (party) group affiliation for the legislative session. In standard legislative practice, MPs need to belong officially to some legislative group in order to participate in legislative deliberations, whether on the floor or in committee. In most systems, MPs are permitted, as or soon after they take their seats, to declare affiliation with a label different from their electoral label. At this time, too, independents might choose to join a legislative party group.[2] For the primary in-depth terms in Russia and Italy, we code stage A as lasting from election day to the week in which MPs are required to declare legislative group membership, as shown in legislative records. For the secondary in-depth cases, we regard stage A as the first two months of the legislative term, starting with election day.[3]

Stage B (Benefits) is when party leaders negotiate and settle the distribution of committee seats, committee chairs, and other legislative posts – and, in parliamentary systems, executive portfolios. For both primary in-depth terms, we operationalize stage B as including the legislative division of offices. For 1996–2001 Italy and 1993–1995 Russia, stage B follows stage A and ends on the date legislative offices are assigned, as coded from parliamentary records. In a parliamentary system such as Italy's, multiple cabinets can rule within one legislative term. In these cases, we operationalize stage B as including the allotment of not only legislative but also executive office. This executive stage B for Italy covers any period of bargaining over a new government; the first executive stage B runs from the end of stage A to the announcement of the first government in the term; subsequent executive stage Bs extend from the fall of one government to the naming of another.

For the secondary in-depth cases, our approach is similar, although simpler. To capture the allocation of legislative offices in the U.S. presidential system, we code the first month after the election and the first month of the legislative session as constituting stage B (*CQ Weekly* [*Congressional Quarterly Weekly, CQW*]

---

[2] Some legislatures allow an Independent group as well. Note that many scholars have omitted what we call stage A from analytical scrutiny because research has traditionally focused either on the election or on the legislature after it has convened for its first session.

[3] When an election occurs on the last day or two of a month, we mark stage A as starting in the subsequent month.

Legislators' Pursuit of Benefits 57

various dates, e.g., December 8, 1984, 3051; December 3, 1994, 3427; January 16, 1999, 156–157; U.S. House of Representatives, Office of the Clerk 2009). In semi-presidential and parliamentary systems, we also denote stage B as the first month of the legislative session and add as well any month(s) during a legislative term in which a new cabinet is negotiated and formed.[4]

In stage C (Policy Control), the legislative agenda focuses on policy domains relevant to a broad range of issues. For the two primary in-depth terms, we isolate three elements of the legislative calendar that political scientists agree are of fundamental importance: decisions on budgetary legislation, necessary for all manner of government activity to proceed; debates on constitutional reform and responses to constitutional crises; and protection of the integrity of the territory the state purports to control (e.g., Haggard and McCubbins 2001; Hallerberg 2004; Lijphart 1984; Laver and Shepsle 1996). We rely on richly detailed legislative records from 1996–2001 Italy and 1993–1995 Russia to home in on periods of intense policy bargaining on the applicable domains with special weight: handling of the annual budget (both Italy and Russia); constitutional reform (debated only during the Italian term); and security matters entailing a constitutional crisis (internal warfare only in Russia). To demarcate these policy stages, we refer to clear markers of the start and end of decision-making activity such as, respectively, the executive's transmittal of the annual budget bill to the legislature and the legislature's approval of the annual budget. With this finely grained operationalization, multiple policy substages appear during the parliamentary cycle, as Tables A4.1 and A4.2 illustrate (see Appendix A for Chapter 4 at the end of book). For the secondary in-depth terms, we simplify and code stage C as the period when the legislature is officially in session – when it can be engaged in any policy making at all.

As listed in the bottom row of Table 4.1, stage D (Dormant) is simply all periods other than stages A, B, and C – a residual set of intervals between the active stages. All stages save D can overlap or coincide in time.

For only one of the two primary in-depth cases, 1996–2001 Italy, is it possible to observe systematically nonlegislative elections held during the national legislative term and thus to operationalize nonlegislative electoral stages. During the 1996–2001 Italian term, five phases of electoral competition for a broad array of subnational offices occurred. One phase coincided with elections to the European Parliament. We delimit each of these five Italian electoral stages as starting 90 days before and ending 30 days after the nonparliamentary contest in question.[5] In Russia, the relatively few nonlegislative elections held during the

---

[4] Our coding of the executive stage B follows the coding of government formation in the authoritative Comparative Parliamentary Democracy Data Archive (CCPD 2011; Strøm, Müller, and Bergman 2008, esp. 6, 88–89).
[5] We resort to this simple rule of thumb because a total of seven distinct electoral systems structured Italy's electoral arenas during the 1996–2001 term (Corbetta and Parisi 1997, 14). For details on the timing of Italian nonlegislative electoral stages, see Table 4A.1 in Appendix A.

Duma's brief first term preclude any operationalization of such electoral stages; it was only after the election to the second Duma, in December 1995, that most of the first post-communist subnational elections were held (e.g., Golosov 2003). The opposite problem arises for the thirty-three secondary in-depth terms: the abundance and variable timing of nonlegislative elections across all 1,200 months of these terms create near-insurmountable challenges for coding.

4.1.2 Elaborating the Hypothesis on Timing Moves to Seize Gains

Our first hypothesis, on *timing moves to seize gains*, holds that individual legislators should change party only during active stages of the parliamentary cycle. We develop several corollaries, all of which express the idea that incumbents who time switches to reap benefits should attune their partisan strategy to the particular stage in progress. The different stages of the parliamentary cycle offer different mixes of incentives to MPs and make some payoffs more salient and immediate at some times than at others. Hence, legislators should *heed which stage* is under way. MP partisan behavior should vary by active stage.

If any legislator jumps party in stage A, she should be lured above all by the office perks linked to affiliation with the new party. Likewise, if an incumbent switches in stage B, the chief inducement should be office benefits. Policy motives should not disappear during stage A or stage B because office serves as an instrument to affect policy (cf., e.g., Laver and Shepsle 1996). Yet, when present, office goods should be the proximate motivation for MPs' choices to switch or stay with their original party. Because office-driven moves should predominate in stages A and B, MPs elected as independents should evince the greatest propensity to switch: it is then that this set of MPs, in particular, can exploit the perks and benefits of office tied to party membership.

Given incumbents' keen concentration on policy during stage C, any decision to change party should aim at shaping policy and acquiring agenda control. This means, in turn, that those MPs who, by virtue of seniority or other distinction, are most able to influence policy – notables – should have the greatest propensity to move in stage C. Moreover, legislators who switch in stage C should tailor their action for maximum policy effect, for instance, by targeting the center of the policy space (cf., e.g., McKelvey and Schofield 1987; Schofield 2009).

In sum, the expectation that incumbents should heed which stage is under way means that who switches and to what effect should vary by active stage. This discussion may be distilled into several corollaries to the first hypothesis.

- *H1A:* As distinct goals come to the fore in distinct stages of the parliamentary cycle, sets of MPs should differ in propensity to change party across stages. Independents should be most likely to move in stages A and B and notables in stage C.

Legislators' Pursuit of Benefits 59

- *H1B:* Stage C moves should aim for clear policy effect. Legislators who switch in stage C should seek the center of the policy space, grab agenda advantage, or break the government.
- *H1C:* New parliamentary groups formed in stage C should locate at the center of the policy space. Because political entrepreneurs strive for policy goals during stage C, any new groups they establish then should stake out the most advantageous position: the center.

Another corollary may be tested for the 1996–2001 Italian term alone, given our ability to observe nonlegislative electoral contests. We have stressed that the literature on change in party systems concentrates overwhelmingly on change as a product of the electoral arena. Moreover, we assume that legislators strive to compete for votes. MPs might seek advantage by changing party when the approach or aftermath of nonlegislative elections reveals information about shifts in popular support for one party or another. Precisely because their own seats are not immediately at stake, national-level MPs may be free to respond to interim signals from nonlegislative races, and free to switch in the hope of longer-run benefit to their careers (cf. Heller and Mershon 2005). This logic could apply whether or not the national-level MPs aim for reelection to the national legislature.[6]

- *H1D:* National-level incumbents should change party in proximity to nonlegislative elections. In the quest to advance their careers, national MPs should switch during nonlegislative electoral stages, in response to nonlegislative electoral pulls.

To falsify the first hypothesis, MPs' switching behavior would exhibit no or very little variation across different stages of the parliamentary cycle. Likewise, the null for these corollaries would hold that no or very little variation should appear across stages in the propensity of different sets of incumbents to change party, in mobile MPs' attempts to influence policy, and in the location of newly founded parliamentary groups. Further, national MP interparty mobility should not vary as proximity to nonlegislative elections rises and falls. We now inspect evidence bearing on these claims and counterclaims, turning first to the two legislative terms we have chosen for microscopic investigation.

4.2 INDUCEMENTS AT THE GRANULAR LEVEL: 1996–2001 ITALY AND 1993–1995 RUSSIA

Our analysis of these two terms begins with a justification of case selection. We next compare incumbents' changes of party affiliation across stages of the

---

[6] In contrast with our prior work (Mershon and Shvetsova 2008a,b; 2009c), here we treat only electoral phases associated with nonlegislative races as inducing national MPs to jump party. The large-N analysis in Part Three examines the rival arguments that the run-up to national legislative elections should inhibit national MPs from switching or prompt them to do so.

parliamentary cycle, grouping together all substages of the same type (e.g., aggregating all policy stages into a single stage C) and also distinguishing MPs by mode of election. We then disaggregate stages and examine MP interparty mobility across the discrete substages punctuating the parliamentary cycle.

4.2.1 Rationale for Selection of Two Primary In-Depth Terms

Our selection of 1996–2001 Italy and 1993–1995 Russia as the two primary in-depth terms affords a comparison of two quite different countries with remarkably similar electoral institutions (e.g., Katz 1994; Moser 2001; Shugart and Wattenberg 2001). For these two terms, Italy and Russia both used hybrid laws combining proportional representation (PR), thresholds for PR, and plurality in single-member districts (SMDs). The major difference in the electoral rules has to do with the linkage between tiers. In Italy, SMD wins were compensated in the PR tier; and Italy from 1993 to 2005 required that every SMD candidate be associated with at least one party list on the PR ballot, whereas independents could compete in Russian SMDs.[7]

The greatest weight here lies with the similarities. Moreover, those commonalities are essential to discerning the imprint of timing on legislators' decisions to change party. As political scientists of all stripes expect, formal institutions constrain and channel the choices of political actors. Given the institutional parallels, we would be able to reject the first hypothesis and its corollaries with confidence if differences in MP interparty mobility appeared – unless some feature of rules differed too. Similarities in incumbent partisan behavior would be equally valuable evidence, corroborating our reasoning.

We select the legislative term in both countries that has the highest number of switches for any term so far. The total number of moves in the 630-member 1996–2001 Italian Chamber stood at 295, and moves totaled 241 for the 450 member 1993–1995 Russian Duma. This choice might seem problematic because in the first post-communist Duma legislators might have still been learning to understand and respond to institutional incentives (Kaminski 2002; Kunicová and Remington 2005). It is also possible that the Italian deputies we study were operating under unusually high levels of uncertainty; the hybrid rules were first applied in 1994, and the share of neophytes elected in 1996 was relatively high (Verzichelli 1996; Zucchini 2001, 172). We see these possibilities as assets in our design, however: if we find that, even during the relatively uncertain first Duma and 1996–2001 Chamber, interparty mobility varies by stage, then we are likely to find elsewhere that legislative party system change varies by stage in the parliamentary cycle.

Another element of the rationale for case selection regards attributes of voter preferences. We assume that voters identify with the party of the candidate for

---

[7] Russia had equal shares of SMD and PR MPs, and in Italy about 75 percent of MPs came from SMDs. Proportional representation thresholds were 5 percent in Russia and 4 percent in Italy.

Legislators' Pursuit of Benefits 61

whom they vote and that they care about the partisan constancy of their elected representatives, preferring, other things equal, that their representatives display steadfast partisanship. Survey findings from Russia in the early to mid-1990s, despite variation in question wording and timing, suggest relatively limited and tentative party attachments at the mass level (e.g., Colton 2000; Evans and Whitefield 1995; Miller, Reisinger, and Hesli 1998; Miller, White, and Heywood 1996; White, Rose, and McAllister 1997; cf. Colton 2000, 104, 137, on the "contingent, ... labile, restive partisanship of the transition period" in Russia). We thus have less confidence in characterizing the Russian electorate of the early to mid-1990s as approaching the assumptions we set out. For Italy in the mid-1990s and early 2000s, in contrast, surveys indicate that major segments of the electorate could locate themselves in a left-right policy space, could meaningfully locate extant parties, reported that they decided on their vote well in advance of the election, and expressed partisan sympathies (e.g., Baldassarri 2005; Baldassarri and Schadee 2004; 2005; ITANES 1996; 2001; Zucchini 1997, 98). By 1996, the overwhelming majority of Italian respondents understood the workings of the hybrid electoral system introduced in 1993: in 1996, 86.2 percent of respondents correctly answered that SMD votes were cast for a candidate from an electoral alliance of parties; and 96.1 percent stated that PR votes went to a party list (Zucchini 1997, 120). One merit of the case selection for the primary in-depth terms is the capacity to assess the import of variation in the degree to which voter preferences over the partisanship of their representatives may be said to be well defined.

4.2.2 Variations in Incumbent Changes of Party across Aggregated Stages

Table 4.2 compares MPs' changes of partisan affiliation in Russia and Italy by aggregated stage in the parliamentary cycle. We examine mean weekly moves per 100 MPs, using a standardized measure because, as noted, the lower houses vary substantially in size.[8] Observe first, as the top row of Table 4.2 displays, that the opening weeks of the term, when newly elected deputies must choose parliamentary group affiliation (stage A), exhibit the highest aggregate rate of moves in both Italy and Russia. In both hybrid electoral systems, it is SMD MPs who show the strongest tendency for joining a parliamentary group different from their electoral label.

Yet, in stage A, among all MPs, the Russian switching rate is more than twice the Italian rate and, among SMD MPs, the Russian rate is more than five times the Italian. The stark contrasts stem from the behavior of Russian independents,

---

[8] This standardization does not reflect the idea that each incumbent is equally likely to move in an active stage. At any given time, we believe, some subset of legislators is likely to be open to venturing into a new party. And, at any time, leaders of legislative parties are likely to view a subset of legislators as worthy recruits. The subset involved is unlikely to constitute a fixed portion of MPs (i.e., unlikely to depend on the size of the legislature).

TABLE 4.2 *Mean weekly moves per 100 members of parliament (MPs) by type of stage and by MPs' mode of election, 1996–2001 Italian Chamber and 1993–1995 Russian Duma*

	Italian Chamber					Russian Duma			
								SMD	
Stage	Aggregate N Weeks	All MPs	SMD	PR	Aggregate N weeks	All MPs	All	Party[a]	Independent[a]	PR
A	4	1.03	1.32	0.16	7	2.74	5.36	2.07	6.68	0.19
B	9	0.35	0.25	0.67	12	0.21	0.31	0.27	0.32	0.11
C	109	0.20**	0.18	0.27	25	0.89**	1.31	0.97	1.45	0.49
D	95[b]	0.10	0.11	0.08	61	0.17	0.17	0.29	0.13	0.16
E	94[b]	0.21	0.20	0.27	0[b]	–	–	–	–	–

Key to stages: A, Affiliation; B, Benefits; C, Control of policy; E, Electoral (Italy only; see text); D, Dormant, i.e., all periods other than A, B, C (and other than E for Italy)
MP, members of parliament; PR, proportional representation; SMD, single-member district.
Sources: For dates and numbers of switches: Camera dei Deputati (2008a); Duma Statistical Services (INDEM, 2000). For detailed documentation needed to code stages: Camera dei Deputati (2008b); INDEM (2000); Italy, Istituto Cattaneo (2010); Italy, Ministero dell'Interno (2008); Pasquino (1999).
** $p < 0.05$ test for differences of means across dormant and active stages, all MPs, assuming unequal variances
[a] Independents are elected as a subset of SMD MPs only in Russia, as discussed in the text.
[b] Only for the 1996–2001 Italian term is systematic observation possible of non-legislative elections, as discussed in the text.

Legislators' Pursuit of Benefits 63

who won almost two-thirds of Russian SMDs in 1993, reflecting not only the electoral rules and weakly institutionalized party system but also the compressed campaign, a product of Yeltsin's decision to call the parliamentary elections on short notice and in conjunction with the constitutional referendum. These independents, having earned SMD seats, engaged in frenetic party shopping and hopping in the Russian stage A.[9]

All Italian deputies who changed affiliation in stage A entered the motley Mixed Group, and both electoral institutions and internal parliamentary rules influenced these moves. In Italy, no independents figured in stage A, and, in fact, no independents were elected because all SMD candidates, again, had to link to at least one PR party list. All but two SMD switchers in stage A competed as part of the center-left electoral cartel. Cartel leaders in 1996 bargained SMD candidacies among member parties so as to allot districts in proportion to expected party strength (e.g., Corbetta and Parisi 1997; Di Virgilio 1997, esp. 91–135; 2002). Candidates of such small center-left parties as the Greens were thus able to earn SMD seats, and they went to the Mixed Group in the Chamber, given the standing orders on the minimum size of parliamentary groups (twenty deputies).[10] Also among the mobile SMD center-leftists in stage A were several candidates who, in the 1996 race, mounted broad appeals and who, once in Parliament, opted for the Mixed Group instead of joining the legislative group of the largest party named on their electoral label and linked PR list or lists (Di Virgilio 1997; 2002). Only one stage A switcher was elected on a PR party list and then abandoned that label to sit in the Mixed Group.

When office benefits are allocated (stage B, second row in Table 4.2), mean weekly moves per 100 MPs are roughly similar for the full lower house across Russia and Italy. The rate of Russian switching in stage B is almost three times higher among legislators originating from single-member districts compared to multi-member districts. Independents, in particular, rushed to join parties, for membership in a party made them eligible for internal legislative office. In Italy, the proportion is flipped, with PR MPs defecting almost three times as often as their colleagues. This pattern largely traced to the choices of a subset of PR MPs who split from their parliamentary party to compete for seats on the Committee for Constitutional Reform, as detailed later.

Switching in the aggregated policy control stage (C) is more than four times more frequent in Russia than in Italy. The rate in proximity to Italian non-legislative elections, the aggregated stage E, roughly matches that registered in

---

[9] Independent MPs elected in SMD districts we code as switching in stage A if they declared factional membership with any of the Duma parties, and as not switching if they declared independent status (Smyth 2006). This coding of independents in stage A differs from our treatment in earlier work (Mershon and Shvetsova 2008a).

[10] Exceptions can be made for parties competing in a specified minimum number of districts and winning a specified minimum of votes (Art. 14.2). Articles 14 and 15 of the internal rules provide that the Mixed Group enjoys much the same rights and privileges as do party groups.

the Italian policy stage C. Once more, we cannot observe stage E for the brief first Duma.

Mean weekly moves per 100 MPs drop to their lowest rate in the full house for both Italy and Russia in the aggregated stage D (dormant), after initial affiliations are announced, when neither benefits are allocated nor major questions of policy control dominate the agenda – nor, for Italy, elections to offices outside the national legislature loom near. The differences in mean moves across active and dormant stages attain statistical significance for both terms, as Table 4.2 reports. For both Italy and Russia, interparty mobility in stage D dies down. By these data, the null hypothesis fails.

Overall, Table 4.2 allows for an assessment of our reasoning. For these terms, at least, MPs do indeed change party when their goals are best served by such action: during active, not dormant, stages of the parliamentary cycle. This evidence also lends some support to the notion that interparty mobility varies by active stage: the fact that Russian MPs elected as independents move often in stages A and B aligns with H_1A. Yet Russian independents are also prone to change parties in the aggregated policy stage C. To investigate further whether and how incumbents attune their partisan strategy to the particular active stage under way, we now scrutinize substages in these primary in-depth terms.

4.2.3 MP Interparty Mobility Disaggregated by Substage

Figures 4.1 and 4.2 portray mean weekly rates of switching per 100 MPs in all substages of the parliamentary cycle in the 1993–1995 Duma and the 1996–2001 Chamber, ordering the substages chronologically. The figures distinguish the behavior of SMD MPs from that of all incumbents. The behavior of PR MPs, as the remaining category, can be imputed. Tags identify those substages with relatively high rates and, in Italy, all electoral substages.

Looking first at Figure 4.1, the frequency of switching among Russian SMD MPs in the Duma's first affiliation stage (stage A.1) is an outlier. This is, by a large margin, the highest rate in any substage for either subgroup of deputies (SMD or PR) in the two legislatures. During the Russian A.1, which lasted only one week, SMD (but not PR) deputies were asked to declare factional (i.e., parliamentary group) membership. Whereas any party qualifying for PR seats automatically received official Duma faction status, additional groups of SMD incumbents could be formed and could obtain the same rights enjoyed by factions, as long as the group met the minimum size of thirty-five members. Seizing the opportunity to affiliate, SMD legislators leapt across groups with abandon and also formed an entirely new faction during A.1. Proportional representation incumbents could not create new groups during A.1, which ended when the Duma shifted its focus to internal institutional matters, committee assignments, and other office-related votes (stage B). Only after the extant groups had successfully monopolized committee and leadership posts did they write rules permitting new groups to form, with the approval in March 1994 of

Legislators' Pursuit of Benefits

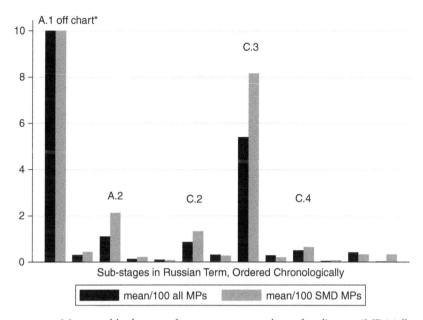

FIGURE 4.1 Mean weekly changes of party per 100 members of parliament (MPs) (all and single-member districts [SMD]), by sequential substage in term, 1993–1995 Russian Duma.

Vertical axis is truncated to clarify scale for other stages. See Appendix A, Tables 4A.1 and 4A.2 for keys to active substages. Substages with relatively high rates of interparty mobility are tagged.

*A.1 is outlier: mean/100 all MPs = 27.8; mean/100 SMD MPs = 55.6.

the law on registration of Duma factions. This law opened Russia's second affiliation stage (A.2) and enabled PR MPs to change parties, too. Even in A.2, however, SMD MPs – in particular, those elected as independents – evinced a higher rate of partisan mobility. Switching in the single benefits stage was not as great as in the two affiliation stages, but MPs elected as independents provided most of the moves in B as well. Corollary $H1A$ thus finds additional corroboration.

Legislators' policy disputes dealing with the second major campaign of the Chechen War (classified as policy stage C.3, near the midterm) generated the second highest mean weekly rate of moves per 100 MPs in the 1993–1995 Duma. Relatively high rates appeared in two other policy stages we define, one involving the first Chechen War and subsuming legislative deliberations on the 1995 budget (C.2) and the other comprised of legislators' efforts to contribute to managing the Budennovsk crisis, when Chechen insurgents held hostage an entire hospital full of patients and medics, resulting in numerous deaths (C.4). These stage C moves created new parliamentary factions and redefined agenda setting, consistent with corollary $H1B$. The new factions, Russia and Stability, positioned themselves near the center of the policy space (INDEM 2000), in line

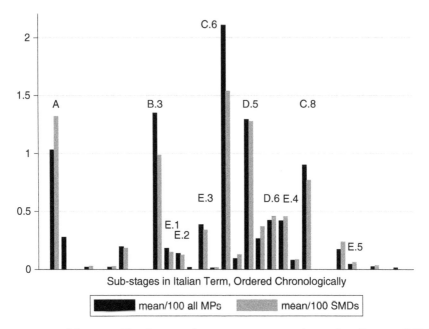

FIGURE 4.2 Mean weekly changes of party per 100 members of parliament (MPs) (All and single-member districts [SMD]), by sequential substage in term, 1996–2001 Italian Chamber.

See Appendix A, Tables 4A.1 and 4A.2 for keys to active substages. Substages with relatively high rates of interparty mobility, along with all electoral sub-stages, are tagged.

with H_1C.[11] Moreover, as the term unfolded, a number of SMD MPs originally elected as independents emerged as notables within the Duma, able to exert strong policy influence, so that the moves they executed in stage C may be interpreted as supporting corollary H_1B.

The 1993–1995 Duma thus saw substantial interelectoral party system change through the formation of start-up party groups. Four new parliamentary factions were created during the two years; one faction, the Liberal-Democratic Union, also ended during the term, having existed only from April to December 1994 (Korguniuk and Zaslavskii 1996). MP moves were so widespread that they brought about the erosion and crumbling of extant parties. MPs also switched as part of strategic delegation and deployment: the Communists helped keep the Agrarians above the thirty-five-member threshold required for valuable agenda-setting powers in the Duma (Shvetsova 2002).

Turning now to Italy, the rate of incumbent interparty mobility is highest in a policy stage near the middle of the term, as Figure 4.2 exhibits. In October

---

[11] We draw information from INDEM 2000 for the placement of newly founded parliamentary groups in policy space; INDEM placements are in turn based on roll-call voting in the Duma.

Legislators' Pursuit of Benefits 67

1998, during stage C.6, the Prodi government made a vote on the 1999 budget a matter of confidence, lost, and resigned. Communist Refounding (RC), not in the executive but until then routinely in its legislative majority, split on the confidence vote. The dissidents entered the Mixed Group, unable to form a separate legislative party due to rules on minimum size. The pro-government rump majority of the RC moderated and established a distinct parliamentary group with a new name, the Communist Group (*Corriere della Sera* [*CdS*], October 8, 1998; October 10, 1998; October 12, 1998; October 15, 1998; Pasquino 1998). The RC's fission and its effect comport with corollary $H1B$ and, given the leanings of the larger of the new groupings, corollary $H1C$ as well.

The second-highest peak in Italian interparty mobility arose in a benefits stage, B.3, when seats and leadership posts on the large Bicameral Committee on Constitutional Reform were allocated. The Prodi government made constitutional reform one of its top priorities. Because the choice of rules carried profound consequences for policy outcomes (e.g., Riker 1982), appointments to the Bicameral Committee were intrinsically linked to high-stakes policy. The bulk of moves in B.3 involved deputies from the Christian Democratic Center-United Democratic Christians (CCD-CDU), the leftmost group in the center-right bloc. The moves were made en masse, as the CDU portion of what began as the unified CCD-CDU group split off and entered the Mixed Group; the CDU contained an unusually large share of PR MPs. The day after the CDU bolted, its leader was named to the Bicameral Committee (Italy, Camera dei Deputati 2011).

Events in stage B.3 march with corollary $H1A$, on the distinctive behavior of particular sets of MPs at particular times. Office and policy motives, bound together here, drove decisions to defect (*CdS*, February 4, 1997; February 6, 1997; February 7, 1997). Many of the mobile MPs had allied with the CCD on PR lists in the 1996 elections, so that the CDU and CCD together could surpass the 4 percent barrier. Such cooperation, suited to electoral competition, was inopportune once authoritative legislative offices came up for assignment. The moves that CDU MPs carried out in stage B.3 guaranteed separate, proportional allocation of committee seats to the CDU component of the Mixed Group, in accordance with the Chamber's internal rules (Arts. 19–22).

Relatively high rates of interparty mobility distinguished the run-up to and aftermath of the May 1998 subnational elections, stage E.3. As discussed in Chapter 2, in March 1998, life Senator and former President Francesco Cossiga launched a new party, the Union of Democrats for the Republic (UDR). As the electoral campaign proceeded and overlapped with a policy stage, Cossiga articulated the UDR's positions on budgetary and constitutional debates and targeted the center of the Italian policy space. As Cossiga maneuvered for policy influence in spring 1998, he also sought to build the electoral appeal of the UDR (*CdS*, March 14, 1998; March 15, 1998; March 26, 1998; April 10, 1998; April 29, 1998; May 1, 1998; May 27, 1998; Donovan and Newell 2008; Istituto Cattaneo 2010; Pasquino 1998, esp. 127–128). Cossiga's initiatives and the switching he spurred in the Chamber support corollaries $H1A$ (on notables moving in stage C), $H1B$ (clear policy goals in stage C), and $H1C$ (new centrist groups in stage C). The timing of the moves he prompted also aligns with $H1D$, on nonlegislative elections.

After the peak in policy stage C.6, a string of stages appeared with relatively pronounced rates of interparty mobility. The single week classified as D.5 occurred in October 1998, between decisions on benefits in the D'Alema I cabinet (which replaced the ill-fated Prodi I) and the resumption of committee handling of the 1999 budget; all but one of the MPs in D.5 moved from the UDR to the Mixed Group. Stage D.6 preceded the electoral stage defined by the June 1999 subnational and European Parliament elections (E.4).

In February 1999, as Chapter 2 noted, MP and former Premier Romano Prodi created the Democrats-Olive Tree (Dem-U). In early February, a key player in Prodi's venture described the strategy: "We cannot bring on board heterogeneous troops. We want to put together only deputies who identify with the political project. ...If we do not add up to twenty, fine, that means we will belong to the Mixed Group" (Rino Piscitello, as quoted in *CdS* February 8, 1999). Although the founding of the Dem-U occurred during stage D.6, its relatively few initial adherents thus sat in the Mixed Group until the Dem-U recruited additional MPs and met the size criterion for a separate parliamentary group in late March 1999, in stage E.4. Other partisan moves, executed in the wake of the June 1999 elections, still in E.4, created the Democratic Union for Europe (UDEur) as an organized component of the Mixed Group and as the successor to the UDR, also led by Cossiga. Chamber membership in the UDEur swelled sufficiently during policy stage C.8 to qualify it as a legislative group, and stage C.8 witnessed debates on finance so fierce that, two days after the 2000 budget bill won approval, the government resigned. Together, these episodes feature moves responding to notables' initiatives and coinciding with policy controversy and electoral campaigns. Given the timing of D.5 and D.6 relative to benefit, policy control, and electoral phases, the changes of affiliation in these two substages of the generally calm stage D do not upset the first hypothesis on *timing moves to seize gains* and even buttress it.

In sum, evidence from the primary in-depth terms indicates that Italian and Russian legislators do time changes of affiliation in order to seize parliamentary gains. We also find support for our expectation that incumbents tailor their partisan strategy to the ongoing stage. Moreover, the timing of partisan moves in the run-up to and aftermath of the May 1998 and June 1999 nonlegislative elections in Italy, during stages E.3 and E.4, comports with our reasoning on MP responsiveness to pulls from nonlegislative electoral contests (cf. Heller and Mershon 2005). As Figure 4.2 displays, stages E.1, E.2, and E.5 evince lower rates of incumbent interparty mobility as compared to the phases associated with electoral contests toward the middle of the legislative term. This relative reluctance to switch during early and late nonlegislative electoral stages could be

Legislators' Pursuit of Benefits

construed as support for the second and third hypotheses. Chapter 5 explores this possibility further as it weighs the incentives and disincentives to switch party arising from electoral competition.

4.3 ENLARGING THE VIEW: MP INTERPARTY MOBILITY BY STAGE

The evidence we have mustered so far gives comfort to the first hypothesis on *timing moves to seize gains*. A more robust appraisal would incorporate additional legislative terms. We thus now expand the investigation to the thirty-three secondary in-depth terms in Italy, Romania, the United Kingdom, and the United States, for a total of 1,200 monthly observations. In taking up the latter legislatures, we trade some degree of evidentiary detail to achieve breadth, yet retain the capacity to observe MP partisan strategies across distinct stages of the parliamentary cycle.

Table 4.3 compares incumbent changes of affiliation by aggregated stage of the parliamentary cycle. We standardize the measure of MP behavior, given variation in the size of the assemblies. The first finding is that stage D is indeed dormant, contrary to the null hypothesis and in line with the hypothesis on *timing to moves to seize gains*. For no country here do mean moves per 100 MPs in the aggregated stage D bottom out at zero. All evince limited interparty mobility in stage D, however, relative to the rate observed in at least a few of the active stages. The differences in means across dormant and active stages are statistically significant for all of these systems, albeit only at the generous 0.10 level for Romania. When an extreme outlier appearing in the Romanian stage C is omitted, the Romanian means across dormant and active stages attain significance at standard levels.

The cross-national differences in the active stages may be plausibly interpreted as stemming at least in part from political institutions.[12] Note the impact of electoral and parliamentary rules in the affiliation stage. As shown on the top row of Table 4.3, not a single move occurred during these terms in stage A in Romania and the United Kingdom, whereas the index of mean monthly switches per 100 MPs is 0.07 for the A stages in the United States and 1.35 for those in Italy. The switchers in the U.S. stage A were almost all elected as independents or on a minor party label, and then, once they won their seats, joined one of the two major parties with which they may or may not have had a prior association.[13]

---

[12] To be sure, the analysis of the full dataset in Part Three permits stronger inferences about the determinants of cross-national variation in legislative party system change.

[13] Because we count moves between elections and the convening of Congress, we include U.S. switchers whose behavior is not captured in the authoritative Poole-Rosenthal roll-call vote database (cf. Nokken and Poole 2004). That said, because we focus on choices made while politicians hold national legislative office, our U.S. data omit a few changes of partisanship examined by Nokken (2009).

TABLE 4.3 *Mean monthly moves per 100 members of parliament (MPs) by type of stage, electoral system, and regime, thirty-three terms.*

	List PR				SMD			
	Open, Parliamentary		Closed, Semi-Presidential		Parliamentary		Presidential	
	Italy 1963–1994		Romania 1996–2004		UK 1970–2001		US 1970–2000	
Stage	Mean	Mo	Mean	Mo	Mean	Mo	Mean	Mo
A	1.35 (2.74)	16	0.00 (0.00)	4	0.00 (0.00)	16	0.07 (0.16)	30
B	0.68 (2.43)	56	0.13 (0.24)	7	0.00 (0.00)	16	0.09 (0.17)	30
C	0.38 (2.55)	332	1.02 (5.64)^a	77	0.03 (0.14)	290	0.01 (0.06)	285
D	0.02 (0.09)***	27	0.02 (0.07)^b	18	0.01 (0.04)**	80	0.01 (0.03)**	45

Key to stages: A, Affiliation; B, Benefits; C, Control of policy; D, Dormant, i.e., all periods other than A, B, C.
PR, proportional representation; SMD, single-member district.
Test for differences of means across dormant and active stages, assuming unequal variances:
** $p < 0.05$ for US and UK
*** $p < 0.01$ for Italy
^{a} If outlier of 162 moves (June 2001) is excluded, mean = 0.38 and SD = 0.63.
^{b} If outlier of 162 moves is excluded, test for differences of means across dormant and active stages, assuming unequal variances: $p < 0.01$.
Numbers between parentheses are standard deviations. For each system, the right column reports total months per stage. See Appendix B on operationalizing MP changes of parliamentary party group and MP formation of new parliamentary parties.
Sources: For numbers and dates of switches: *Ballot Access News* (2001a,b); Butler and Butler (2000, 248–249; 2006, 112–114); Italy, Camera dei Deputati (2008a); Timothy Nokken (personal communications, June 2006 and July 2008); Romania, Parlamentul României (2008c); United States, Congressional Biographical Directory (2008). For stages: Butler and Butler (2006); Constitutional Change and Parliamentary Democracies CCPD (2011); Strøm, Müller, and Bergman (2008); *CQ Weekly* (various dates, e.g., November 19, 1983, 2403; December 8, 1984, 3051; February 2, 1985, 177; February 17, 1990, 437; November 12, 1994, 3222; December 3, 1994, 3427; December 23, 1995, 3863; November 28, 1998, 3218; January 16, 1999, 156–157); Italy, Camera dei Deputati (2008a); Romania, Parlamentul României (2008a); United Kingdom Parliament (2008); United States House of Representatives, Office of the Clerk (2008); United States House of Representatives, Office of the Majority Leader (2008).

It is only in the United States that the use of a primary system in SMDs opens a side door through which a few independents enter the lower house, as, for example, challengers who have lost in primaries run – and win – as independents in a three-way race in the general election. In the other three countries, independents' access to legislative office is extremely restricted. In the United Kingdom, party organizations choose candidates for SMD races (on the near absence of independents winning seats in the Commons, see Butler and Butler 1986, 176; 2006, 72). In Romania and pre-1993 Italy, party-list PR gives party leaders great control over candidate selection (cf. Birnir 2004, esp. 144–146, on Romania; Wertman 1977 on Italy). Hence, the contrast emerges between, on the

Legislators' Pursuit of Benefits

one hand, the completely quiescent stage A in Romania and the United Kingdom, and, on the other, the United States, where the relatively few independents and minor party candidates who win tend to join one of the major parties in stage A so as to avail themselves of the benefits of party affiliation. Under the rules in the U.S. Congress, newly elected incumbents recognize the advantages of belonging to one of the two major parties and act accordingly.

Interparty mobility in the Italian stage A reflects the formation of the Mixed Group, as shaped by electoral and parliamentary rules. Under the highly proportional electoral laws in effect from 1946 to 1993, tiny parties (earning less than 1.5 or even 0.5 percent of the national vote) could and did win Chamber seats. The Chamber's standing orders on parliamentary group size, once again, required that deputies from small parties enroll in the Mixed Group. Starting in the 1980s, MPs from small parties proliferated as electoral support waned for what were long Italy's two largest parties, the Christian Democrats (DC) and Communists (PCI). Consider, too, party strategy in the electoral arena: the PCI included nonparty candidates (often intellectuals) on its party lists in an effort to broaden its electoral appeal, with the understanding that such candidates, if elected, were free to join the Mixed Group (cf. Hellman 1977). As it turned out, in the 1972, 1976, and 1979 A stages, such MPs, upon entering the Chamber, discarded the PCI electoral label and chose the Mixed Group. In the 1983 and 1987 A stages, such MPs met the numerical threshold for a separate parliamentary group and saw advantage in establishing the Independent Left (SI).[14]

Institutions likely influence cross-national differences in interparty mobility for other stages in the parliamentary cycle. The highest rate of interparty mobility in stage B (benefits) here appears in the parliamentary system using PR rules, 1963–1994 Italy. About two-thirds of the Italian interparty moves observed in stage B occurred in an overlapping policy (C) stage. The event that dominates the Italian stage B datum and also enters into stage C traces to the split of the briefly reunified Socialists into the Italian Socialist Party (PSI) and the Italian Social Democratic Party (PSDI), discussed in Chapter 1. The split was precipitated by sharp intraparty disputes over government policy and ruptured the ruling coalition (Di Scala 1988, esp. 161–165). Politicians of the PSI and PSDI merged in 1966 and split in 1969, confident that their implementation and reversal of the fusion carried no adverse consequences for their survival, given relatively pure PR, and for their long-term participation in the executive, given DC dominance of the party system (Mershon 1994; 2002).

In semi-presidential Romania, stages B and C also overlap at times, and it is only during the overlap that any B stage incumbent interparty mobility is registered. Switches to independent status, as expected, predominated in this span. In fact, the vice-chair of a ruling party became an independent amid disagreements over the budget that triggered a change in government (BBC

---

[14] The Chamber's rules found somewhat different application in different legislatures. On the rules and the reforms of 1971, the 1980s, and 1997–1998, see Capano and Giuliani (2003, 12–15).

1998). Note that MPs' behavior was constrained by the standing orders of the Romanian Chamber, which stipulate that MPs cannot enter a parliamentary party that has not already earned seats in elections (Chiva 2007, 203–204; Romania, Parlamentul României 2008b). Moves to join (or found) splinter parties or start-ups are impossible under these rules. We return to such institutional constraints later.

Patterns of switching during the benefits stage for the two SMD systems suggest the impact of legislative institutions and regime design. In our span of study, British politicians never jumped party when offices in one-party majority executives were decided or when posts on relatively weak legislative committees were distributed. Looking beyond the secondary in-depth terms, British MPs made not a single move during benefits stages from 1945 to 2005. In the U.S. presidential system, executive positions are obviously not at stake in the legislative stage B. Instead, seats and leadership offices on the most specialized, most powerful set of legislative committees in the world are allocated in the U.S. benefits stage. This stage engenders the highest mean monthly switches per 100 legislators of any stage in the United States. Granted, the mean in this institutional environment is very low – well below that recorded for Italian and Romanian legislators in some other aggregated stages. The fact remains that if U.S. legislators change party, they are likely to do so when either office benefits are awarded, in stage B, or the perks of party affiliation are available, in stage A.[15]

In the control of policy (C) stage, 1996–2004 Romania exhibits the highest mean monthly moves per 100 MPs across these thirty-three legislative terms. The Romanian mean is dominated by the extreme outlier observed in June 2001, when the Party for Social Democracy in Romania (PDSR), one of Romania's several successor communist parties, merged with the noncommunist Social Democratic Party of Romania (PSDR) to create the Party of Social Democracy (PSD). The merger stemmed in part from institutional incentives and constraints: as a response to the summer 2000 increase of the PR threshold (from 3 to 5 percent), the PDSR and PSDR agreed on an electoral alliance for the November 2000 parliamentary elections. The official fusion, although delayed by internal party deliberations, built on the electoral alliance (Lovatt and Lovatt 2001; Pop-Eleches 2008; Project on Political Transformation 2008). This party merger aside, for these terms, legislators in the two PR systems switch party at about the same rate in stage C.

When we draw within-nation comparisons, rates of MP interparty mobility are highest in the aggregated stage C for Romania and the United Kingdom.

---

[15] Sometimes U.S. party leaders start to woo likely recruits in stage A. In 1994, immediately after the election, Republican leaders were reported to be conferring with "as many as eight House Democrats about switching" (*CQW*, November 19, 1994, 3358). Five actually converted to the Republicans, and four of these recruits gained office benefits in the form of appointments to key committees (*CQW*, July 1, 1995, 1894; March 16, 1996, 682; June 10, 1995, 1612; January 6, 1996, 67).

Legislators' Pursuit of Benefits

These within-nation maxima reflect the founding of new parliamentary groups, discussed further later. For now, note that this pattern supports H_1B, in that the new parties aimed for an impact on policy in stage C. The Romanian PSD styled itself a natural "party of government" (Lovatt and Lovatt 2001) and pursued a "market-embracing social-democratic approach" (Pop-Eleches 2008, 469–470). The British Social Democratic Party (SDP), initiated in a 1981 policy stage, sought to pull votes from both Labour and Conservatives and to identify a middle ground in programmatic terms as well (e.g., Crewe and King 1995, esp. chapter 23).

The evidence from the secondary in-depth terms supports the notion that different groups of incumbents tend to change party at different times (H_1A). Recall, for instance, the role of independents in the U.S. A stages and the Romanian B, as well as the nonparty candidates elected on Communist lists in Italy who formed their own group in stage A. This evidence also corroborates the claim that legislators who swap party labels in stage C aim to wield an impact on policy (H_1B). To judge from these data, incumbents adapt strategy on party membership to stage of the parliamentary cycle.

Still another overall lesson from the evidence arrayed in Table 4.3 is that shifts in party systems between elections are relatively infrequent occurrences. Seismic events disrupting the legislative party system happen, although rarely, in both Romania and Italy, as suggested by the large standard deviations reported in Table 4.3 for at least one active stage in those countries. That upheavals fall in active, not dormant, stages of the parliamentary cycle marches with the hypothesis on *timing moves to seize gains*. In the United Kingdom and the United States, even small adjustments to the interelectoral legislative party system are uncommon. The relative stability where candidate-based electoral rules are used favors the hypothesis on *move to the law*.

Figure 4.3A probes further the prevalence of stability and occasions of change across distinct stages, comparing the percentage of months per stage with particular counts of interparty moves. The figure powerfully reinforces the earlier finding that these legislative party systems remain steady in stage D: for all countries examined, more than 96 percent of all months in stage D evince not a single interparty move. Figure 4.3A demolishes the null hypothesis of no difference in legislator partisan strategy across stages of parliamentary cycle. What is more, the figure highlights findings that otherwise might go unremarked. Whereas any change arising in the U.S. legislative party system during stage A is the product of one or several members of congress (MCs) entering a new camp, the shifts in the Italian A stages are of an entirely different order of magnitude. The flux in the Romanian legislative party system registered in stage C reflects not only the one-shot, large-scale merger of two parties but also many smaller scale movements.

Eighty-five percent of the months making up the thirty-three legislative terms studied in Figure 4.3A display not a single switch. Figure 4.3B redefines the unit of analysis and compares parliamentary terms. As it shows, no MP interparty moves characterize 12.1 percent of these interelectoral legislative party systems. The degrees of interelectoral change in the remainder of the systems undercut the conventional wisdom that legislative parties and party systems are fixed from one legislative election to the next.

The evidence exhibited in Figure 4.3 points to spikes in incumbent interparty mobility marking splits and mergers of extant parliamentary parties and the start-up of new parliamentary parties. We now assess evidence from both primary and secondary in-depth terms that bears on corollary H_1C, which holds that parties established in policy stages should locate at the center of the policy space.

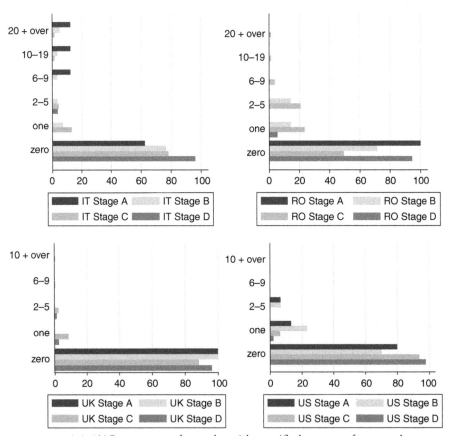

FIGURE 4.3(A) (A) Percentage of months with specified counts of moves, by stage of parliamentary cycle, thirty-three terms; (B) Percentage of legislative terms with specified totals of moves.

For differences in counts of moves (in country-specific figures), Pearson χ^2 within stages: *** $p < 0.01$ Italy stage C, U.S. stages A and B; ** $p < 0.05$ Italy stage B, Romania stages C and D, U.S. stage C

Legislators' Pursuit of Benefits

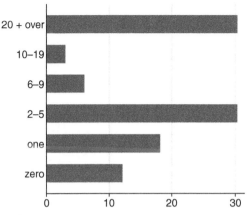

FIGURE 4.3(B) (cont.)

4.4 THE FORMATION OF NEW PARLIAMENTARY PARTIES

As Table 4.4 illustrates, 82.6 percent – nineteen of twenty-three – of the parliamentary parties created in these thirty-five terms were inaugurated while the legislature was in session for policy making, during stage C. Of the new players arriving on the scene in a policy stage, 73.7 percent – fourteen of nineteen – were either centrist or more center-leaning than their predecessor party or parties.[16] For instance, along with the cases of the Romanian PSD and the British SDP already discussed, in a 1976 Italian policy stage, deputies from the neo-fascist Italian Social Movement (MSI) broke away to establish the less extremist Constituent Right-National Democracy parliamentary group (e.g., Ignazi 1989, 174–180). During a policy stage in 1988, the SDP and the Liberals in Britain concluded talks on a merger and launched the centrist Liberal Democrats (Crewe and King 1995, chapter 21). During a policy stage in 1991, the PCI completed its transformation into the Party of the Democratic Left (PDS), moderating its policies along the way (e.g., Bull 1991; Ignazi 1992; Hopkin and Ignazi 2008). And, in a 1994 policy stage, engulfed by official investigations into corruption, the DC at its last party congress became the Popular Party (PPI), which qualified as more centrist than its predecessor, since center-right elements dropped away (e.g., Newell and Bull 1995; Wertman 1995).

We acknowledge the richness and variety of the events involved in the founding of these new parliamentary parties. Fewer than forty people negotiated

---

[16] We count the SI twice, as it formed on two distinct occasions. As in Chapter 2, we use party leader policy declarations and secondary sources based on such declarations to locate newly founded parliamentary parties in policy space (Birnir 2004; Bull 1991; Newell and Bull 1995, 76–77; Chiva 2007; Crewe and King 1995; Di Scala 1988; Drucker 1977; Hopkin and Ignazi 2008; Ignazi 1989; 1992; Korguniuk and Zaslavskii 1996; Lovatt and Lovatt 2001; Morlino 1996; Newell and Bull 1997; Pasquino 1998; Wertman 1995).

TABLE 4.4 *New parliamentary parties, by type of stage, electoral system, and regime, thirty-five terms*

	List PR		SMD		Hybrid	
	Open, Parliamentary	Closed, Semi-Presidential	Parliamentary	Presidential	Parliamentary	Semi-Presidential
Stage	Italy 63–94	Romania 96–04	UK 70–01	US 70–00	Italy 96–01	Russia 93–95
C	PSIUP[a] PSU[b] PSI[a] and PSDI[a] CD-DN[a] SJ[a] Com-PDS[a] DP-Com[b] DC-PPI[a] and CCD[a]	*PSD*[b]	SLP[a] *SDP*[c] *LibDem*[b]	No new party	UDR[c] *UDEur*[c] GC[a,d]	*Ross*[c] *Stab*[c]
Non-C	SJ[a]			No new party	*DemU*[c,d]	LDS[c] N-96[c]

[a] Fission
[b] Fusion
[c] Start-up
[d] Stage C under simpler operationalization used for secondary in-depth terms (see Table 4.1).

Entries are acronyms of parties, ordered chronologically by type of stage and by country. Acronyms in italics indicate a new party that is either centrist or more center-leaning than its predecessor(s). See Appendix B on operationalizing member of parliament (MP) changes of parliamentary party group and MP formation of new parliamentary parties; note that some instances of fission do not generate new groups under parliamentary rules and under our operationalization.

PR, proportional representation; SMD, single-member district.

Key to party group acronyms (year founded): CCD, Christian Democratic Center (1994); CD-DN, Constituent Right-National Democracy (1976); Com-PDS, Communists-Party of Democratic Left (1991); DC-PPI, Christian Democracy-Italian Popular Party (1994); DemU, Democrats-Olive Tree (1999); DP-Com, Proletarian Democracy-Communists (1991); GC, Communist Group (1998); LDS, Liberal Democratic Union of December 12 (1994); LibDem, Liberal Democratic Party (1988); N-96, New Regional Policy – Duma 96 (1993); PSD, Social Democratic Party (2001); PSDI, Italian Social Democratic Party (1969); PSI, Italian Socialist Party (1969); PSIUP, Italian Socialist Party of Proletarian Unity (1964); PSU, Unified Socialist Party, Italy (1966; name changes disregarded here); Ross, Russia (1995); SDP, Social Democratic Party (1981); SJ, Independent Left (outside Stage C in 1983; C in 1987); Stab, Stability (1995); UDR, Union of Democrats for the Republic (1998); UDEur, Democratic Union for Europe (1999)

Legislators' Pursuit of Benefits 77

the Lib Dems into existence in four months (Crewe and King 1995, 416). The creation of the PDS was fiercely debated throughout the PCI's organization and was put to two congress votes over fifteen months. Yet the point is that, whether the genesis was short or long, attended by few or many, almost three-quarters of the new parliamentary groups that formed in stage C gravitated to centrist locations in the policy space, as held in corollary H_1C.

Even those parliamentary groups arising in stage C that run counter to H_1C disclose the workings of centripetal forces. For example, the Italian Socialist Party of Proletarian Unity (PSIUP) split from the PSI in January 1964, during a policy stage, to oppose the policy moderation entailed in the Socialists' December 1963 entry into the executive (Di Scala 1988, chapter 10; Ginsborg 1989, 370–371). When the merger of the Italian Socialists and Social Democrats came to an acrimonious end in 1969, the reconstituted PSI was leftist relative to the Social Democrats and to the fusion that had failed; a phase of "confusion" in PSI policy ensued as DC control of government continued undisturbed (Di Scala 1988, 165). The short-lived, miniscule Scottish Labour Party split to protest Labour's failure on devolution (Butler and Butler 1986, 171; Drucker 1977, 44–63). The Italian Proletarian Democracy-Communist group (DP-Com) joined deputies on the far left in 1991, uniting the DP with erstwhile Communists who repudiated the PCI's rebirth as the more moderate PDS. MPs from the center-right minority of the embattled DC constituted the Christian Democratic Center (CCD), leaving the majority PPI firmly situated in the center (Wertman 1995).

The record of the few parliamentary parties founded outside stage C bolsters the accumulated evidence in favor of H_1C. Two new groups in the 1993–1995 Russian Duma were created when independents sought to reap the rewards of group affiliation during the tumultuous stage A. Both of these entrants originated in an affiliation stage and located on the periphery of the policy space. In accordance with H_1C, then, when legislative parties were founded during a policy stage, they tended to adopt centrist or center-leaning policy positions. Parliamentary groups established outside policy stages were more likely to locate away from the center.

The Italian Dem-U was launched soon after the midterm peak in switching during a policy stage, and it qualified as a parliamentary group in an electoral stage. If the simplified operationalization of stages for secondary terms were applied to the 1996–2001 Italian term (so that any months when a legislature meets would be counted as stage C), the creation of the Dem-U would fall in a policy stage. In this light, Prodi's contest for the center, narrated in Chapter 2, supports corollary H_1C, along with H_1A and H_1B.

Table 4.4 presents further suggestive evidence on the impact of institutions. Among these legislatures, fission recurs only in the Italian Chamber, which from the end of World War II to 1993 featured a highly permissive form of PR and, from 1993 to 2005, used a hybrid system deliberately designed to preserve small parties (e.g., Warner and Gambetta 1994). The products of party fission in Italy could realistically hope to survive, given the electoral rules. Romania witnessed only one fusion over the eight years studied, reflecting the constraints imposed by the legislative standing orders and the incentives to coalesce under the 2000 electoral laws. The United Kingdom experienced one start-up, the Social Democrats (SDP); one fusion, the Liberal Democrats; and one fission, Scottish Labour. Under SMD rules, political entrepreneurs should strive to avoid fission. In the case of the SDP, they succeeded, in that the party drew legislators with multiple affiliations – not only Labour MPs but also, in the 1979–1983 term alone, two MPs with Independent Labour status, one Conservative MP, and one Conservative Peer (Butler and Butler 2000, 248–249; Crewe and King 1995, 114, 478). The utter absence of new parties in the 1950–2000 U.S. Congress may be interpreted as a consequence not only of the constraints of SMD competition but also of the need for parties to mount nationwide presidential contests.

The relative abundance of start-ups in the two systems using hybrid electoral laws also deserves comment. Under the Italian variant of hybrid laws, even small units in electoral competition could hope to earn legislative seats, due both to the mechanics of the linkage between SMD and PR races and to the parties' strategic construction of electoral cartels and strategic nomination of some candidates from small parties in SMDs (e.g., D'Alimonte and Bartolini 2002; Di Virgilio 1997; 2002). Moreover, small parties could hope to survive in electoral contests using pure PR, such as European Parliament elections.

The unlinked PR and SMD tiers in the Russian hybrid laws slowed the process of party system institutionalization and invited political entrepreneurs to create and change parties with ease (cf. Shvetsova 2003; 2005). MPs created four entirely new parliamentary parties during the 1993–1993 Duma. The membership of some parliamentary parties crumbled, and the Communists strategically delegated MPs to the ideologically proximate Agrarians in order to enhance agenda control. Two of the start-ups occurred in stage C and one other in stage A, and strategic delegation began in stage A and continued throughout the term to compensate for ongoing attrition in Agrarian membership due to MP moves.

4.5 CONCLUSION

Our theory relies on the assumption that legislators are strategic actors who view party affiliation as a strategic choice – as a means to an end. Starting from this premise, we expect politicians' behavior to track and respond to evolving opportunities. In this perspective, any choice to change parties signifies that a new allegiance has become more advantageous than the old one, given changed opportunity structures. Thus, if legislators change party affiliation, the timing of their moves conveys information about their chief motivation: when they switch tells us why they switch.

The empirical investigation conducted in this chapter lends substantial support to our claim that incumbents should time moves among parties to seize benefits. We can clearly reject the null hypothesis of no difference in incumbent partisan strategy between the dormant stage and active stages of the parliamentary cycle.

Legislators' Pursuit of Benefits

We have adduced abundant evidence that legislators time transfers of party allegiance to reap office and policy gains. What is more, our case studies indicate that legislators pursue a strategy on partisanship that is suited to the particular stage under way: independents are most likely to take on a party label in stages A and B, MPs who jump party in stage C look for policy influence, and new parliamentary groups established in stage C lean to the center of the policy space.

Our detailed examination of 1996–2001 Italy and 1993–1995 Russia has also uncovered a peak in switching behavior at roughly the middle of the legislative term. This finding poses the question: when incumbents introduce change to the parliamentary party system, how do they weigh their decisions relative not only to stages of the parliamentary cycle but also to the distance from one legislative election to the next?

The next chapter addresses that question. There, we investigate the forces that might inhibit legislators' responses to inducements to move from one party to another and thus put a brake on interelectoral change in parliamentary party systems.

5

Avoidance of Electoral Costs and Stability in Parliamentary Parties

We now have evidence in hand that legislators can secure office and policy gains by changing party affiliation. Yet we have also found that, for the legislatures studied thus far, incumbents' moves among parties are relatively rare events. Although incumbents do introduce change in legislative party systems between elections, continuity prevails much of the time. We would not wish to conclude, however, that whatever continuity is observed in legislative parties and party systems reflects merely the absence of inducements to change. We suspect that, as we just discovered, as there are stimuli to party system change, there are also forces that actively operate to favor party system stability. An inquiry into the roots of systemic stability should center on isolating and analyzing those factors that counter individual legislators' temptation to change parties.

What might constrain change in legislative party systems between elections? The model advanced in Chapter 3 hinges on the notion that voters' preference for partisan loyalty prevents members of parliament (MPs) from defecting from their electoral labels. Hence, voters and their preferences impart stability to legislative party systems between elections, just as voters and their choices generate change at election time. Yet, at the level of theorizing, such a constraining influence is but an assumption, albeit an eminently reasonable one.

This chapter brings diverse evidence to bear on our claims about MPs' efforts to avoid the electoral costs of partisan disloyalty. To pave the way for the intensive case study analysis, the first section of the chapter revisits the hypotheses on preference-based deterrents to change in legislative party systems. The second part examines evidence from the primary in-depth legislative terms, 1996–2001 Italy and 1993–1995 Russia. The third section expands the investigation to the secondary in-depth terms. The conclusion takes stock of the granular evidence on the mechanisms working to disrupt and reinforce party system stability between elections.

5.1 REVISITING THE LOGIC ON INCUMBENT AVOIDANCE OF ELECTORAL COSTS

Recall that the second hypothesis, *stay put when elections loom*, maintains that MPs should become more wary of moving among parties as the legislative term unfolds. The importance that voters assign to their representatives' partisan identity and reputation should depress party system change toward the end of the term. The third hypothesis, dubbed *wait to jump ship*, holds that the more candidate-centered the system, the more reluctant MPs should be to defect from their electoral label immediately after an election. In relatively candidate-centered systems, then, we should find the conditional midterm effect. According to the fourth hypothesis, *move to the law*, switching should be relatively infrequent under candidate-focused laws. To appraise these hypotheses, we analyze monthly observations of incumbent behavior across our set of secondary in-depth terms – and, in subsequent chapters, in the large-N dataset as well.

The finely detailed evidence from 1993–1995 Russia and 1996–2001 Italy affords the most thorough inspection of our claims. For these legislative terms, we can assess the individual-level fifth hypothesis on *limiting moves*, according to which most incumbents who switch should move only once. For these terms, moreover, we can probe the extent to which an MP's responsiveness to electoral deterrents might vary with the strength of her connection to a party. This question speaks to basic features of our reasoning: again, we assume that the fact of party membership endows a partisan candidate with relatively low perceived policy variance in the voter's eyes, and we show that a voter's utility of voting for an incumbent depends on the incumbent's history of party membership during a legislative term. Given this logic, we would expect representatives elected as independents to pursue affiliation strategies distinctive from the strategies of their colleagues who enter office as partisans. It is also possible that MPs with relatively weak links to party labels (e.g., those who are serving in national legislative office for the very first time) make choices in affiliation less attuned to the needs of electoral competition than do their counterparts firmly associated with party brand names.

5.2 THE CLOSEST SCRUTINY OF DETERRENTS TO CHANGING PARTY: 1996–2001 ITALY AND 1993–1995 RUSSIA

We first take up evidence on the timing of MP interparty moves relative to elections. We next compare sensitivity to electoral deterrents across different groups of incumbents. We then juxtapose the record of change in parliamentary parties, on the one hand, and, on the other, the evidence on party system continuity between elections.

5.2.1 A First Look at the Timing of Interparty Moves Relative to Elections

Despite clear differences in incumbent partisan behavior across 1996–2001 Italy and 1993–1995 Russia, interparty mobility declines near the end of the term in both legislatures, as shown in Figures 5.1A and B. Figure 5.1A plots two measures of incumbent interparty mobility – the number of moves per 100 MPs and the log of 1 plus the raw count of switches – for every week of the Italian term. Figure 5.1B does the same for the shorter Russian term. The log is informative because it reduces the pull of outliers while retaining information on all variation; it thus brings variation at lower levels into clear view. Because the Italian lower house is larger than the Russian by half, we standardize the number of moves. We highlight dominant trends in the data with locally weighted scatterplot (LOWESS) smoothing.[1]

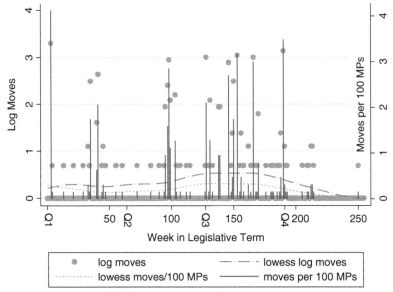

FIGURE 5.1(A) (A) Log of raw number of member of parliament (MP) moves and number of moves per 100 MPs, by week in the legislative term, Italy 1996–2001 (LOWESS smoothing).

Here and in B, the horizontal axis includes markers for the start of each quarter of the legislative term. Q3 thus denotes the midterm; that is, the week that opens the third quarter; (B) Log of raw number of MP moves and number of moves per 100 MPs, by week in the legislative term, Russia 1993–1995 (LOWESS smoothing). The horizontal axis includes markers for the start of each quarter of the legislative term. Q3 thus denotes the midterm.

---

[1] The bandwidth for the smoothers is set at 0.50. In both Figures 5.1A and B, the horizontal axis includes markers for the start of each quarter of the term; Q3 thus denotes the week in which the third quarter starts; that is, the midterm.

Avoidance of Electoral Costs

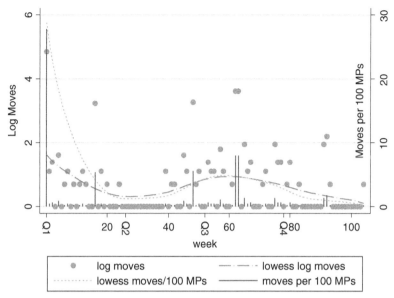

FIGURE 5.1(B) (cont.)

As Figure 5.1A illustrates, a spike in interparty mobility appears in the first few weeks of the Italian term, as discussed in Chapter 4. Even taking into account that early surge, the trend lines oscillate around a fairly stable central tendency until the second quarter of the term, when switching begins to rise. Comparing the first quarter of the Italian term with the steeper downward slope of the smoother in the last quarter, we find support for the notion that legislators retain party loyalties when the next election is near. The prospect of elections dampens party system change, in accord with the second hypothesis. The smoothers also show support for the third hypothesis that incumbents wait until after elections to introduce change to the party system. The early burst aside, in the weeks featuring the greatest switching, legislators acted collectively to rupture extant parliamentary party groups and create new ones, as noted (cf. Mershon and Shvetsova 2008a; 2009b). Weeks with the greatest number of moves per 100 MPs cluster toward the middle of the term. Likewise, the trend lines evince a peak about halfway through the term. Evidence of a midterm effect thus appears for the 1996–2001 Italian Chamber.

As Figure 5.1B exhibits, in Russia, the frequency of switching is extremely high when the legislature opens and then declines during the first quarter of the term. As discussed in Chapter 4, this turbulence at the very start of the Russian term does not contradict our argument that association with party labels induces stability immediately after an election, because it captures not the behavior of partisan MPs but instead independents' early rush to join parties (cf. Mershon and Shvetsova 2008a). Indeed, 85 percent of MPs who switched in the week launching the term were elected as independents. In the last quarter of the Russian term, despite some flurries, MP moves wane relative to earlier spikes. In this sense, the Russian evidence marches with the second hypothesis that incumbents stay put when elections loom. Moreover, attending specifically to partisan legislators, the Russian evidence comports with the third hypothesis on waiting to move. Among partisan legislators, as detailed below, we can observe a midterm peak in the 1993–1995 Duma.

For the two legislatures elected under similar rules, the prospect of voter scrutiny at the next election diminishes MP interparty mobility: relative to the maxima established in each system, incumbents change party with declining frequency as the term draws to a close. This basic commonality deserves attention. Yet the magnitude of change in the Russian party system between elections far exceeds that in Italy, as demonstrated in the vertical axes of Figures 5.1A and 5.1B. The magnitude of change in the last quarter of the term is also greater in Russia than in Italy. To the extent that that Russian voters have relatively weakly defined preferences over the partisanship of their representatives, as is reasonable to assume, these outcomes align with our argument. Given the attributes of the electorate, we expect, and we find, relatively great interelectoral party system change and relatively limited MP sensitivity to the proximity of elections in Russia.

We now drill down to the individual-level behavior underlying the patterns discerned so far. We begin with the basic question of how many incumbents remained loyal or instead shifted allegiance to a new party.

5.2.2 Timing and Limiting Moves: Comparisons across Groups of MPs

As the top panel of Table 5.1 shows, one-quarter of deputies switched in the 1996–2001 Italian Chamber. One move was the mode for mobile Italian representatives, in line with the fifth hypothesis. Legislators elected in single-member districts (SMDs) and those elected on party lists under proportional representation (PR) rules displayed little variation in whether and how often they jumped party. These similarities are understandable, given the formal linkage between the two tiers of the Italian mixed electoral system noted earlier. Analysts have also highlighted the "proportionalization" of centralized interparty negotiations on SMD candidacies within the center-right and, especially, center-left electoral cartels (e.g., D'Alimonte 2001; Di Virgilio 1997; 2002).

As the bottom panel of Table 5.1 depicts, in 1993–1995 Russia SMD legislators were much more likely to change affiliation than their PR counterparts. Whereas 80 percent of party list representatives stuck to their label, almost 60 percent of those elected in SMDs changed allegiance. This difference in propensity to switch between PR and SMD deputies in Russia attains statistical significance. One move was the mode among mobile Russian legislators, whether PR or SMD. Yet the mean number of moves was somewhat higher

Avoidance of Electoral Costs 85

TABLE 5.1 *Percentage of members of parliament (MPs) with specified numbers of interparty moves, Italian and Russian MPs, by mode of election.*

Mode of Election	% all 0	% among mobile MPs only 1	2	3	>3	mean	T MPs
Italian MPs Elected in 1996							
PR	72.90	50.00	21.43	21.43	7.14	1.93	155
SMD	75.79	47.83	24.35	21.74	6.09	1.91	475
All MPs	75.08	48.41	23.57	21.66	6.37	1.92	630
Russian MPs Elected in 1993							
PR	80.27	75.00	22.73	2.27	0.00	1.27	223
SMD	41.67***	68.25	20.63	7.94	3.17	1.46*	216
All MPs	61.28	70.00	21.18	6.47	2.35	1.41	439

Administrative difficulties prevented all 450 Russian MPs from being successfully elected in mid-December 1993, as discussed in note 2.
To left of table, for fact of switching across subgroups, Pearson χ^2: *** $p < 0.01$
To right, test for differences of means between PR and SMD, unequal variances: * $p < 0.10$
PR, proportional representation; SMD, single-member district

among SMD deputies than among party list ones. The difference in means is statistically significant, albeit at a generous level.[2]

Table 5.2 focuses on the behavior of first-time representatives in the Italian Chamber and of independents in the Russian Duma. Only for 1996–2001 Italy can we observe variation across legislators in length of legislative career. Conversely, independents gained access only to the first post-communist Duma. Indeed, as seen, independents abounded in Russia as a result of the unlinked hybrid electoral rules, weak parties, and nonpartisan gatekeepers in the first, hastily convened post-communist legislative election (e.g., Colton 2000; Moser 2001; Smyth 2006).

The top panel of the table, on Italy, discloses that novice deputies roughly resembled their more experienced counterparts in whether and how often they swapped party label. Statistically significant differences appeared in *when* in the term the two sets of MPs tended to move: on average, as revealed along the right side of the table, neophytes carried out their first move about ten months after veterans and their last move about six months afterward.[3] This evidence is

---

[2] In the first post-communist legislative election, administrative difficulties prevented the full set of 450 Duma members from taking their seats in the first week of the legislative session (e.g., Sakwa 1995). Furthermore, several MPs left the Duma for the cabinet early in the term. Thus, here, we include only the 439 Russian MPs successfully elected on December 12, 1993 and sitting at the very start of the legislature because those entering the Duma later did not have the same range of opportunities to switch.

[3] In contrast, Italian SMD and PR legislators differed little in timing of first and last moves. The *Week of last move* variable captures the timing of the switch closest to the election ending a term. It thus includes both the week of the last move for MPs switching multiple times and the week of the only move for MPs switching once.

TABLE 5.2 *Percentage of members of parliament (MPs) with specified numbers of moves, and mean weeks of first and last moves, by set of MPs, Italy 1996–2001 and Russia 1993–1995.*

		Among mobile MPs only							
	% all	%				Mean	Mean week of move		T
Set of MPs	0	1	2	3	>3	Moves	First	Last[a]	MPs
Italian MPs Elected in 1996									
Veteran	77.09	51.22	23.17	19.51	6.10	1.84	79.29	115.73	358
Novice	72.43	45.33	24.00	24.00	6.77	2.00	102.11[**]	140.44[**]	272
All MPs	75.08	48.41	23.57	21.66	6.37	1.92	90.19	127.54	630
Russian MPs Elected in 1993									
All partisan	78.25	69.35	27.42	1.61	1.61	1.35	48.31	56.44	285
Independent	29.87[***]	70.37	17.59	9.26	2.78	1.44	25.14[***]	39.70[***]	154
All MPs	61.28	70.00	21.18	6.47	2.35	1.41	33.59	45.81	439

[a] This variable captures the timing of the switch closest to the election ending a term (see note 3). The Italian term lasts 256 weeks (midterm at 128), and the Russian, 105 (midterm at 52.5).
To left of table, for fact of switching across two subgroups, Pearson χ^2:
*** $p < 0.01$
To right, test for difference of means across two subgroups, assuming unequal variances:
** $p < 0.05$
*** $p < 0.01$

consistent with the idea that representatives new to the Chamber are last in line for the potential and actual benefits that might accompany changing party. The evidence also suggests that new deputies were less likely than their more party-branded counterparts to stay put as election time neared.

The bottom panel of Table 5.2 illustrates the distinctiveness of deputies elected as independents in Russian SMDs. Almost 70 percent of MPs entering the Duma as independents changed affiliation at least once during the term. In stark contrast, almost 80 percent of all partisan representatives – both those elected on party lists and partisan candidates in SMD races – hewed to their original party label throughout the term. This difference between MPs originating as independents and as partisans attains statistical significance. The two groups of legislators also evince statistically significant differences in the timing of interparty mobility. Among those partisan MPs who switched, the first and last moves on average fell near the middle of the Duma's 105-week term. Independents instead leapt early to new affiliations.

We now turn to the task of examining the electoral fortunes of incumbents who sought reelection. Addressing this task is possible only for the Italian 1996–2001 Chamber, given the churning in the Russian party system during – and since – the mid-1990s (e.g., Colton 2000; Löwenhardt 1998; Moser 2001). We emphasize that we observe incumbents who sought reelection without knowing why they self-selected and were selected into (and out of) races for reelection: politicians have strong incentives to paint their career decisions in the best possible light, and

TABLE 5.3 *Percentage of members of parliament (MPs) winning reelection, by number of moves and quartiles of first and last moves among MPs running for reelection, Italy 1996–2001.*

Set of MPs	N Interparty Moves (% won) 0	1	>1	Mobile Only: When Moved (% won) Quartile First Move Lower	Upper	Quartile Last Move[a] Lower	Upper
All MPs	74.02	61.11	59.09**	71.43	41.67**	72.73	50.00[†]
SMD	74.80	60.53	51.61***	68.18	40.91*	69.57	33.33**
PR	71.60	62.50	76.92	83.33	50.00	80.00	83.33
Novice	66.90	53.85	50.00	66.67	37.50	61.54	46.15
Novice right	85.51	66.67	50.00*	NA	0.00[b]	60.00	40.00
Elected right	84.80	66.67	63.64**	66.67	33.33	73.33	50.00

Cell entries are percentages of deputies winning reelection.
[a] This variable captures the timing of the switch closest to the election ending a term.
[b] Only one novice elected on a right label in 1996 and seeking reelection in 2001 switched outside the interquartile range on *Week of first move*.
For whether won as function of number of moves (*left panel*) and as function of moving in lower vs. upper quartile on *Week first* and *Week last* move (*right panel*), Pearson χ^2:
[†] $p \approx 0.10$; * $p < 0.10$; ** $p < 0.05$; *** $p < 0.01$

the processes by which party leaders negotiate candidacies and party lists are far from transparent. Caveat issued, we track who won and who lost among those deputies who competed in the 2001 Italian elections to the Chamber.[4]

Table 5.3 gives the success rates – the percentage of MPs winning – among all those deputies seeking reelection in a given category. As the top row demonstrates, among all incumbents who ran in the 2001 race, the more moves an MP carried out, the less likely she was to return to the Chamber. The drop in the success rate attains statistical significance and accords with our argument. The pattern holds and retains significance for SMD deputies, although not for PR ones: in this sense, the linked party-list tier afforded electoral protection to Italian switchers. This finding, too, aligns with our argument. Neophyte legislators were less likely to win reelection if they switched ($p < 0.10$, Pearson χ^2); yet, given their relatively low success rates overall, the percentage of rookies winning fell only moderately as the number of their moves rose. The bottom two rows of Table 5.3 concentrate on deputies elected on right labels in 1996, because parliamentary groups based on those labels were in opposition throughout the term and also because the right-wing electoral alliance won the 2001 race. Both for neophytes and for all MPs originating on the right in 1996, success rates in 2001 declined significantly with the number of switches executed.

---

[4] Among Italian incumbents elected in 1996, those who switched were somewhat less likely than loyalists to contest the 2001 elections ($p < 0.10$, Pearson χ^2). Deputies who moved more than once were even less likely to run for reelection ($p < 0.05$, Pearson χ^2).

The right side of Table 5.3 investigates success rates as a function of when the mobile MP pursuing reelection chose to move. We create two dummy variables based on the interquartile range of the *Week of first move* and *Week of last move*, identifying whether an MP swapped labels earlier than did three-quarters of her mobile colleagues (in the lower quartile) or later than three-quarters (upper quartile). As the top two rows of the table reveal, among all deputies and among SMD deputies contesting the 2001 race, the closer to the upcoming election the incumbent switched, the more likely she was to meet electoral punishment. These differences are statistically significant for SMD incumbents for the quartile of the first and last move, and for the full set of incumbents for the quartile of the first move. Changes of party timed relatively late tended to bring electoral retribution among non-SMD deputies as well, but such differences do not attain statistical significance. Proportional representation incumbents mark a partial exception to this pattern. Given very sparse data (one datum!), no inference about success rates can be drawn about novices elected on a right label in 1996, seeking reelection, and switching outside the interquartile range on *Week of first move*.

We have assessed varied evidence from the two primary in-depth terms that incumbents are mindful of electoral deterrents as they pursue strategy on partisanship. We now seek to integrate the lessons on MP pursuit of parliamentary benefits and aversion to electoral costs.

5.2.3 Finding a Balance? Averting Electoral Costs Yet Reaching for Parliamentary Benefits

Figures 5.2 and 5.3 plot the running totals of the raw count of weekly interparty moves over time in the term for 1993–1995 Russia and 1996–2001 Italy, respectively. The figures portray the duration of each substage of the parliamentary cycle, the switching in that phase, and the timing of that phase – with switching – relative to elections. The figures convey in a novel way what are by now familiar themes. Incumbents introduce change to the parliamentary party system above all toward the middle of the parliamentary term. This pattern holds even in light of the tumultuous opening of the Russia Duma. MP interparty mobility flattens out toward the end of the term. Change is registered in what we code as active stages, whether stage A (Affiliation), B (Benefits), or C (Control of Policy). Nevertheless, the distribution of switching over time stands independent of the researcher-imposed coding of stages.[5]

In sum, evidence on weekly observations of MP behavior from the two primary in-depth terms favors the second and third hypotheses and discloses

---

[5] The two legislatures obviously differ in the length of active versus dormant stages. On the Italian Parliament as handling a relatively high volume of legislation, see, for example, Capano and Giuliani (2001a,b); Di Palma (1977); Zucchini (1997). On the Russian Duma, even after its first term, see, for example, Remington (2001).

Avoidance of Electoral Costs 89

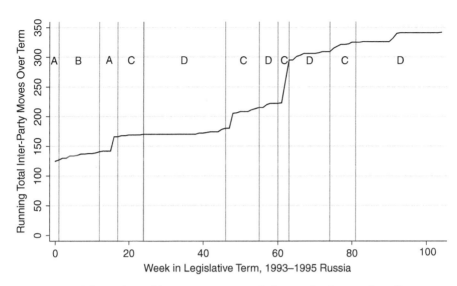

FIGURE 5.2 The timing of interparty moves relative to elections and parliamentary benefits, 1993–1995 Russia.

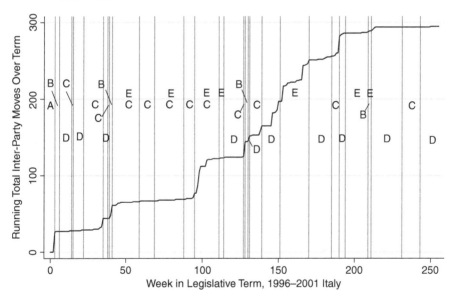

FIGURE 5.3 The timing of interparty moves relative to elections and parliamentary benefits, 1996–2001 Italy.

maxima in party switching near the middle of the term. When we shift the level of analysis to individual MPs, our findings strengthen the inference that the electoral connection operates as the mechanism buttressing party system stability between elections. Incumbents limited the moves they made, in that the modal number of switches among mobile deputies in Italy and Russia was one. Across all Italian MPs, the mean week of first move and the mean week of the last move occurred roughly near the midterm. The same may be said for Russian partisan MPs. The timing of switches among incumbents with relatively weak links to partisan representation (neophytes in Italy and those elected as independents in Russia) instead suggests relative insensitivity to electoral deterrents. Notably, Russian MPs who entered the Duma as independents dashed to change affiliation early in the term. Additional findings at the individual level comport with our theory: Italian voters spurned MPs running for reelection whose records included multiple switches and who timed a switch relatively close to the upcoming election. Weekly aggregates of switching, in the form of running totals of raw counts, provide further evidence that, on balance, MPs switch party when the parliament actively decides on office and policy benefits and stay loyal when the prospect of penalties at the next election nears. Finally, compared to MPs in the 1996–2001 Italian Chamber, incumbents in the 1993–1995 Russian Duma strove to recreate the party system between elections. This finding is understandable in that the Russian electorate had relatively weakly defined preferences for incumbent partisan loyalty.

The next step in gauging the internal validity of our argument is to open up the inquiry to additional legislatures. Whereas we control for type of electoral law in the primary in-depth terms, we expand the range of institutional variation in the secondary in-depth terms.

5.3 EXPANDING THE INVESTIGATION OF ELECTORAL DETERRENTS

To weigh incumbent strategy on the timing of interparty moves relative to elections, we examine switching in one term from each country here and next compare all legislatures of similar duration among the secondary in-depth terms. We then survey all secondary in-depth terms, comparing MP interparty mobility across quarters of the term.

5.3.1 A First Cut at Locating Moves in Time

For Table 5.4, we select one term from each country that features some discernible shift in the legislative party system between elections. To the extent possible, we also control for term length, focusing on legislatures from Italy, Romania, and the United Kingdom that last roughly four years, double the unusually short U.S. duration.[6] Table 5.4.A reports mean monthly moves

---

[6] The criteria for selecting terms for this first cut ease comparison. Given the rarity of switching in the United Kingdom and the United States, however, few terms there meet the first criterion; setting term length to double the U.S. length excludes multiple Italian terms. Of the four-year Italian terms, we chose the one for Table 5.4.B that most *dis*advantages our argument.

TABLE 5.4 *Mean monthly moves per 100 members of parliament (MPs), by type of stage and by six-month span in the legislative term, select terms and subset of terms based on length.*

A

Legislature	Stage A	Stage B	Stage C	Stage D
IT 79–83	1.27 (1.80)	0.25 (0.80)	0.10 (0.38)	0.00 (0.00)
RO 00–04	0.00 (0.00)	0.00 (0.00)	1.74 (8.21)	0.03 (0.09)
UK 79–83	0.00 (0.00)	0.00 (0.00)	0.13 (0.35)	0.03 (0.07)
US 104th	0.00 (0.00)	0.00 (0.00)	0.05 (0.10)	0.08 (0.13)

B

Legislature	0–6	7–12	13–18	Months in Legislative Term 19–24	25–30	31–36	37–42	>42
IT 79–83	0.36 (0.96)	0.00 (0.00)	0.03 (0.06)	0.05 (0.08)	0.05 (0.08)	0.03 (0.06)	0.05 (0.08)	0.13 (0.21)
RO 00–04	7.43 (18.58)	0.15 (0.26)	0.41 (0.74)	0.20 (0.25)	0.20 (0.37)	0.46 (0.63)	0.31 (0.47)	0.12 (0.17)
UK 79–83	0.02 (0.06)	0.00 (0.00)	0.00 (0.00)	0.37 (0.76)	0.21 (0.37)	0.21 (0.24)	0.05 (0.08)	0.03 (0.06)
US 104th	0.03 (0.09)	0.11 (0.13)	0.04 (0.09)	0.00 (0.00)	–	–	–	–
All ~48-month terms	0.98[a] (6.03)	0.09 (0.38)	0.33 (1.87)	0.09 (0.27)	0.09 (0.21)	0.12 (0.27)	0.12 (0.50)	0.06 (0.18)

[a] This datum includes Romanian extreme outlier (count of 162 moves in June 2000). If that outlier is excluded, mean moves per 100 MPs = 0.25, SD = 1.26. Eleven of the thirty-three secondary in-depth terms have a length of approximately forty-eight months. IT, Italy; RO, Romania; UK, United Kingdom; US, United States

per 100 MPs for each aggregated stage of the parliamentary cycle, and Table 5.4. B reports that index for each six-month span of the term.

It might seem that the temporal units in the top and bottom halves of the table amount to proverbial apples and oranges. After all, as emphasized, the stages of the parliamentary cycle are not consecutive, can recur, and are often of unequal length; furthermore, one active stage can overlap with another. Yet the juxtaposition of stages and six-month spans brings into unified view the extent to which incumbents, on the one hand, change party to obtain parliamentary benefits during active stages and, on the other, switch at some remove from election time. The table serves as a simple but effective device to assess, simultaneously, posited forces for change in legislative party systems and posited forces for stability. This illustration complements the more powerful analyses of Part Three.

First, consider MP interparty mobility in the Italian 1979–1983 legislature. As the top row of Table 5.4.A displays, the affiliation (A) stage witnessed relatively many moves. A few deputies also switched in benefits (B) and control of policy (C) stages. The dormant (D) stage saw party stasis in the 1979–1983 Italian Chamber. The top row of Table 5.4.B indicates how the evolution of parliamentary parties unfolded relative to the timing of elections. Change was pronounced in the first six months of the term, incorporating the A stage. Limited movement occurred in all but one of the other six-month segments, as several representatives elected on diverse labels chose to enter or (more rarely) exit the Mixed Group. An uptick in switching occurred during the last six months of the term, as disputes within a small libertarian party, the Radicals, matured into departures for the Mixed Group (De Vito 1982; Melega 1982).

In the Romanian 2000–2004 legislature, change in the parliamentary party system fell almost exclusively in policy stages, as shown in Table 5.4.A. Negotiations on the merged Party of Social Democracy came to fruition and reached their conclusion in the sixth month of the 2000–2004 term, not in the first month or two. Legislators carried out solo moves with a fair degree of frequency throughout the term. Despite the constraints from parliamentary rules noted in Chapter 4, this weakly institutionalized system saw relatively great switching in the last several six-month spans of the term.

We now take up the U.K. House of Commons from 1979 to 1983. This legislative term is well known as the first in which Margaret Thatcher held the post of prime minister. It is recognized, too, for the split in the Labour Party, when, in March 1981, four prominent leaders founded the Social Democratic Party (SDP). Less often appreciated is the timing of the decisions of those Labour MPs who followed the so-called "Gang of Four." As the third row of Table 5.4.A indicates, almost all of the exits from Labour occurred in policy stages. The third row of Table 5.4.B reveals timing relative to elections: switchers traveled to the SDP in several waves, which, despite some spread, were clustered near the midterm. Meetings of Labour MPs willing to "think the unthinkable" of abandoning the party "at some indefinite time in the future" began in December 1980

Avoidance of Electoral Costs 93

(Crewe and King 1995, 72–84, quote from 79). Most recruits to the SDP jumped in March 1981, soon after the party was launched, and in October–December 1981.

Table 5.4 also conveys the decisions of those legislators who did not enter the SDP. The first switcher of the term journeyed from one minor party to another. The last migrant, an erstwhile Labourite, left the SDP for a minor party. According to Crewe and King (1995, 479), about forty MPs who figured as potential recruits chose to stay with Labour.[7] Consider Conservatives as well. In a January 1981 television interview, just before the SDP's founding, a "wet" Conservative backbencher estimated that twenty of his colleagues might join a center party (Crewe and King 1995, 114). In autumn 1981, SDP leaders held discussions about prospective membership with several Conservative MPs and Peers. Yet, after a turning point in winter 1981–1982, such interest in the SDP ebbed away (Crewe and King 1995, 114–116). The sole Conservative MP who entered the SDP made the leap in the heady days of March 1981.

Now observe the U.S. 104th Congress, when, as discussed in Chapter 2, the House saw a total of five switches (cf. Nokken and Poole 2004). Recall from the last chapter that change in the U.S. legislative party system generally occurs in stages A and B. As the last row of Table 5.4.A suggests, in this Congress, four of the five moves took place in policy stages. The sole member of congress (MC) who became Republican in stage D jumped on the heels of "feverish" work on spending bills, the centerpiece of the policy agenda of the "Republican Revolution" (*CQ Weekly* [*Congressional Quarterly Weekly, CQW*], July 29, 1995; August 12, 1995). As highlighted in the penultimate row of Table 5.4.B, the first MC to defect did so five months after the election, in April 1995. Two representatives next crossed the aisle in, respectively, June and August 1995. The last two switched at roughly midterm, in November and December 1995.

The bottom row of Table 5.4 examines mean monthly moves per 100 MPs by six-month span across all secondary in-depth terms that lasted roughly four years, which constitute one-third of the secondary in-depth terms. The differences in means across all countries do not attain statistical significance, either with or without the spectacular Romanian outlier. In a suggestive but hardly definitive finding, the rate of switching declines toward the end of these terms.

5.3.2 What Time Tells about MP Efforts to Curb Electoral Costs

Turning now to all thirty-three secondary in-depth legislatures, Table 5.5 compares mean monthly moves per 100 incumbents by quarter of the legislative term. As listed on the top row, the rate of switching in the first quarter is

---

[7] Crewe and King (1995) identify potential recruits on the basis of four types of evidence: interviews, press reports, a key October 1971 vote in the Commons on what was then the European Economic Community, and signed support for September 1980 reforms of party structure.

TABLE 5.5 *Mean monthly moves per 100 members of parliament (MPs), by quarter of term, thirty-three legislatures.*

	Quarters of Term			
Legislatures	Q1	Q2	Q3	Q4
IT 1963–1994 [371]	0.35 (1.33)	0.22 (1.50)	0.49 (2.99)[a]	0.43 (3.44)[a]
RO 1996–2004 [97]	2.37 (10.07)[b]	0.24 (0.40)	0.27 (0.40)	0.38 (0.78)
US 1970–2000 [360]	0.04 (0.11)	0.02 (0.06)	0.01 (0.04)	0.01 (0.04)[**]
UK 1970–2001 [372]	0.01 (0.05)	0.03 (0.20)	0.05 (0.13)	0.01 (0.05)[*]
All 33 secondary in-depth terms [1,200]	0.30 (2.87)	0.10 (0.85)	0.19 (1.67)	0.18 (1.99)[c]

Number of monthly observations appears between brackets in leftmost column.
[*] $p < 0.10$;
[**] $p < 0.05$ Wald χ^2, James' approximation
[a] If two extreme outliers (count of 156 moves in February 1991, 207 in January 1994) are excluded, mean moves per 100 MPs in Q3 = 0.23, SD = 1.57; in Q4 = 0.07, SD = 0.28.
[b] If extreme outlier (162 moves) is excluded, mean moves per 100 MPs in Q1 = 0.32, SD = 0.68.
[c] If three extreme outliers identified above are omitted, mean moves per 100 MPs in Q1 = 0.14, SD = 0.76; in Q3 = 0.11, SD = 0.88; in Q4 = 0.06, SD = 0.30; differences in mean moves are significant at 0.10 level.
IT, Italy; RO, Romania; UK, United Kingdom; US, United States

relatively high in Italy, reflecting in part the rule-driven changes of affiliation in stage A. The means reported after the midterm hinge on two extraordinary events that spelled the end of the Italian party system as it operated from the end of World War II to the early 1990s: the February 1991 split of the Communist Party and the January 1994 split of the Christian Democrats, both discussed in Chapter 4. When the two outliers are deleted from the monthly data, mean moves per 100 MPs fall to 0.23 in the third quarter and to 0.07 in the last: it would seem from this evidence that Italian MPs, otherwise available to respond to opportunities to switch, remain faithful to their parties when elections are near at hand. Yet, overall, the differences in rates of incumbent switching across quarters lack statistical significance, whatever the treatment of the two outliers.

Our study includes two legislatures from post-communist Romania. Even when the merger creating the Party of Social Democracy is disregarded, the rate of interparty mobility is higher in the first quarter of the Romanian terms than in the two middle quarters. The rate of switching does not dampen down but instead escalates in the last quarter. The differences in means across quarters are not statistically significant. By the light of these data, Romanian incumbents display limited sensitivity to the electoral deterrents to changing party.

Rates of MP interparty mobility in the United Kingdom are low in all quarters of the term and lowest in the first and last quarters. These patterns support both the hypothesis that MPs wait until after the initiating election to abandon their electoral party and the hypothesis that MPs stay put when the upcoming elections loom. For the British parliamentary party system, then, a midterm effect appears. The differences in means across quarters attain statistical significance, albeit at generous levels.

In the United States, as in the United Kingdom, legislative incumbents rarely change party. Any change in the United States, however, is concentrated in the first quarter, as a few independents affiliate with one of the two major parties in stage A and a few MCs cross the aisle for office benefits in stage B. In the last two quarters of the U.S. legislative term, representatives stick with their party label. In fact, only two of the total of thirty-three switches among U.S. MCs from 1946 to 2000 in our dataset occurred after mid-March of a term's second year. One of two late switchers faced an autumn primary (United Press International 1984) and saw that his district had, like him, "become more Republican" (Gillespie in Hickey 2003). He won reelection as "part of the Reagan landslide" (his post-switch campaign manager, quoted in *Frontline* 2005). The other late switcher met defeat in a March primary and did not run for reelection (*Los Angeles Times* February 23, 2000; June 6, 2000; July 27, 2000). Hence, the U.S. evidence shores up the second hypothesis on legislator loyalty with the approach of the next election. The differences in mean moves per 100 incumbents across quarters of the term are statistically significant.

We now have evidence in favor of the fourth hypothesis on the impact of electoral laws. Table 5.5 sends this message and Figure 5.4 drives it home by charting, for each quarter of the term and each country, the percentage of months in which legislators carried out specified counts of interparty moves. Observing gradations of change and imputing the percentage of months when stability reigned, we see that, at least among the secondary in-depth legislatures, elected representatives in candidate-based electoral systems change party less often than do their counterparts in party-list systems.

Figure 5.4 also offers evidence reinforcing the second hypothesis that incumbents refrain from switching when elections loom. True, deviations from this expectation appear in Romania, where voter preferences are weakly defined relative to voter preferences in Italy, the United Kingdom, and the United States. The deviations are unsurprising and even heartening. Among our secondary in-depth cases, Romania is where we expect electoral deterrents to be the weakest. Evidence on relatively substantial Romanian switching near the end of the term thus aligns with our argument. What is more, Figure 5.4 yields findings in support of the third hypothesis: legislators in the two SMD systems here, compared to their counterparts in the two party-list systems, wait after the initiating election to jump the party ship.

5.4 CONCLUSION

This chapter and Chapter 4 have closely tracked the partisan strategies of sitting legislators. We have discovered that timing matters both for incumbents' moves

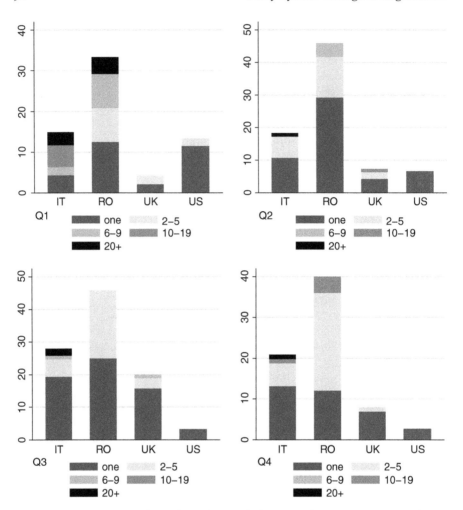

FIGURE 5.4 Percentage of months with specified counts of moves, by quarter of term, thirty-three terms.

among parties and for the forces curbing their moves. We can now be reasonably confident that incumbent legislators change parties to obtain parliamentary benefits. We can be confident as well that legislators who face relatively partisan electorates retain party loyalties in an effort to avoid electoral penalties. The investigation has demonstrated the analytical leverage of the mechanism we posit: the legislator who decides whether to stay true to her original party or transfer to another party considers not only what benefits and costs hang in the balance, but also when she is most likely to acquire benefits or incur costs.

Our analysis is based on the assumption that legislative incumbents in all democracies are essentially of the same type. Hence, legislators omitted

Avoidance of Electoral Costs

from our intensive case studies should act as do the MPs studied here and in Chapter 4 – unless other factors come into play that alter the posited self-interested responses to incentives and constraints. The combined findings of the chapters in Part Two thus serve as a platform for Part Three and its appraisal of institutional incentives to – and preference-based brakes on – parliamentary party system change in a broader range of empirical settings.

PART THREE

GENERALIZING IN A BROADER EMPIRICAL SETTING

Part Three expands the range of countries and parliaments studied in order to demonstrate the broad applicability of our claims. These extensive comparisons are essential. Testing our argument in variegated contexts and conditions enables us to discern the generalizability of our theory. Moreover, there are a number of hypotheses that can only be assessed against the large-N dataset.

The intensive analyses conducted earlier and the extensive comparisons made later complement and reinforce each other. Our scrutiny of parliamentary party systems at the granular level, in 1996–2001 Italy and 1993–1995 Russia, yields evidence in accord with our argument. The same can be said for our study of the secondary in-depth terms. Equally important, investigation of both sets of in-depth terms permits us to gauge whether the causal mechanisms we posit actually whir along to produce the outcomes we observe.

The time has now come to widen our field of vision still further. The next several chapters trade depth for breadth, yet, in conjunction with preceding chapters, they also *combine* breadth and depth. Hence, the study as a whole is equipped to evaluate both the general applicability of the theory we advance and the operation of the causal mechanisms we posit.

Chapter 6 prepares the way for the statistical analysis of our time-series cross-national dataset by discussing how we operationalize our hypotheses and rival hypotheses on the determinants of flux and continuity in parliamentary party systems. Chapter 7 uses the large-N dataset to appraise our theoretical argument on institutional inducements and electoral deterrents to change in interelectoral party systems. Chapter 8 is rooted in a thought experiment: what if there were an alternative to the world we posit theoretically and examine empirically in the first seven chapters of the book? What would happen, for example, if voters did *not* punish politicians' partisan disloyalty? Or, what if there were laws in effect that limited incumbents' freedom to move among parties? Exploring this and other possibilities brings the empirical analysis to additional country cases, including Brazil, Malawi, and Thailand. The insights offered by our framework even when key assumptions are relaxed further demonstrate its power and reach.

6

Setting Up the Analysis of One Hundred and Ten Parliaments

In our theory, institutional inducements tempt sitting members of parliament (MPs) to introduce change in party systems between elections, whereas preference-based deterrents put a brake on change. The incentives for incumbents to adjust partisan strategy arise sporadically over the course of the parliamentary cycle. Conversely, the deterrents to transfers of allegiance evolve smoothly, as the election initiating a given term becomes more remote in time and as the election ending the term approaches. Thus, at some moments, the incumbent reasons that reaching out for benefits near at hand will likely incur few costs, and she walks over to a new party. At other moments, the legislator expects that voter attention is most acute, so that a switch will likely punish her electorally; the MP then remains within the party that won her election.

If we are right, then the basic pattern we posit should materialize despite variation in such contextual features as social cleavage structures. Ascertaining the explanatory power of the argument across diverse settings requires large-N statistical analysis, and this chapter both sets up that analysis and characterizes the dataset analyzed, which spans eight countries, 110 parliamentary terms, and 4,072 monthly observations.[1]

The first part of the chapter treats measurement of the dependent variable in the large-N estimations, incumbents' moves among parties during legislative terms. This is, of course, the central phenomenon of interest throughout our study. We devote particular attention to measurement here precisely because of the special opportunities and challenges entailed in the statistical analysis. The remainder of the chapter operationalizes explanations for incumbent interparty mobility. The second part further specifies measures of and expectations about

---

[1] When the analysis encompasses Spain, in Chapter 8, we have a total of 116 terms and 4,324 monthly observations.

institutional inducements to interelectoral change in parties and party systems. The third section addresses measures and expectations for the constraints on change we posit. The fourth part details controls and indices for alternative hypotheses. We close by taking stock of our expectations at the same time that we look ahead to the analyses conducted in Chapter 7.

6.1 MEASURING INCUMBENTS' CHANGES OF PARTY

Broadly speaking, the dependent variable in our statistical analyses is legislative incumbents' mobility among parliamentary parties (or to or from independent status) in a given month in a given legislative term in a given country. Note that this statement combines three points: what constitutes an incumbent's change in partisan strategy, what time interval we use for aggregating observed incumbent behavior, and what we can and cannot observe. We address each in turn.

As stated at the outset, we adhere to the accepted definition of a politician's party switch as "any recorded change in party affiliation on the part of a politician holding or competing for elective office" (Heller and Mershon 2009b, 8). Our subject of study, specifically, is the politician holding legislative office, the sitting MP. As argued and illustrated, the decisions of individual incumbents to adopt new partisan affiliations can change parliamentary party systems. The incumbent's choice to move among parties is how change is enacted. This choice is also how change is chronicled – entered and preserved in parliamentary documents.

Settling on our definition is thus necessary but not sufficient to the task of measuring incumbents' changes of party. Is a move to be counted as occurring on a particular day or, as for the close-ups of 1993–1995 Russia and 1996–2001 Italy, during a particular week? The best we can do, given variable record-keeping across countries and across time within one country, is to opt for the same monthly aggregation of individual interparty moves that we use for the secondary in-depth terms in Chapters 4 and 5. This monthly time interval allows our study to encompass a wide range of parliamentary terms.

We emphasize that we deal in observed – executed – moves among parties, not potential moves that MPs weighed and then discarded as unworkable alternatives.[2] No perfect way could be invented to capture the recurring calculus on partisanship that we theorize. Even if we had asked each MP in one or more legislatures about her calculus on partisanship, it would have been unrealistic to believe that none would have strategically misrepresented the truth. Even if we had kept a machine continuously hooked to each legislator's brain throughout a

---

[2] For the in-depth terms, we can identify some potential switchers who ended up staying put. Recall, for example, the British Labourites who considered but rejected joining the Social Democrats. The potential moves we detect are but the tip of the iceberg; that we can spot any at all attests once more to the strength of the research design.

Setting Up the Analysis

term, the indices of activity would not have revealed the kinds and content of reasoning we posit.

Precisely because we observe steps taken, not strategies contemplated, it is vital to adopt multiple measures of the dependent variable in our statistical estimations. The principle of triangulation is fundamental to all social research. In our study, the multiple measures of incumbent behavior per monthly time interval enhance our confidence that we adequately tap the phenomenon we seek to explain: parliamentary incumbents' readiness to change their party allegiance as that readiness might vary with varying circumstances. Moreover, if the multiple measures of the dependent variable were to generate consistent findings in favor of our hypotheses, we would have greater confidence in our theoretical argument than would be the case if we had relied on a single operationalization.

First, we examine the absolute number of MPs' interparty moves, $Move_j$, during the month of observation j.[3] As Appendix A, Table 6A.1 shows, the raw count of incumbent moves has a mean of 0.547 and a maximum value of 207 across the 4,072 months in the comprehensive dataset. In 87.3 percent of monthly observations, zero moves occur, and in 8.3 percent, one MP jumps party, as listed on the penultimate row of Appendix A Table 6A.1. Yet, when the view shifts to parliamentary terms, as on the bottom row, we see stasis in 20.9 percent of terms and varying degrees of interelectoral party system change in the remaining 79.1 percent of the terms in the dataset. A very few extreme outliers exist among the monthly observations, when relatively large new parliamentary parties form between elections. Together, the seven observations of more than fifty switches per month provide 38.5 percent of the 2,226 incumbent interparty moves observed across the entire dataset. In our estimations in Chapter 7, we deal with this imbalance by capping the monthly number of switches at fifty (setting the maximum value at fifty, even for those seven observations where more than fifty moves took place) rather than by omitting the outliers. We thus retain the substantive and much of the numerical weight of these outliers while allowing the remainder of the data to come into fuller play in the analysis.

Second, faced with the reality that incumbents change party relatively infrequently, we adopt a dummy variable for the fact of switching, $Fact_j$. This variable is coded 0 in the absence of switching in a given month and 1 when any moves, of any number, occur in the month in question. After all, differences in the incentives to jump party might well be exaggerated by the measure of the absolute number of monthly moves when the comparisons sweep from the United States, where legislative party switching is quite uncommon, to Germany, which has on occasion evinced substantial interelectoral party system change. Even a single move signifies that change in the parliamentary party system has transpired. Moreover, under some configurations of the party

---

[3] For details on rules for coding incumbents' changes of affiliation, see Appendix B, Table B.1. Data on incumbents' changes of party are drawn from the legislatures directly or indirectly (authoritative sources using data from legislatures are, e.g., Butler and Butler [2006]).

system, one move suffices to tip the partisan balance of power, with profound consequences for agenda setting and policy outcomes, as the case of Senator Jim Jeffords, discussed in Chapter 2, illustrates so well. The fact of switching is thus a crucial item in our battery of measures of the dependent variable.

Our third measure, $Category_j$, is designed to tap the qualitative difference between two distinct strategic circumstances in which MPs change party allegiance: solo defection and coordinated action when a new parliamentary party is founded during the term. We believe that our basic theory about inducements and deterrents to change in parliamentary party systems applies equally under both conditions, although the magnitude of MP interparty mobility and thus of interelectoral system change differs. To capture the distinction between individual responses to opportunities and collective events, we create an ordered categorical dependent variable, which takes the value of 0 when no incumbent changes party allegiance in the given legislative month, the value of 1 when between one and nineteen switches take place, and the value of 2 when twenty or more occur. The last category roughly corresponds to instances in our dataset when parliamentary parties split, merge, or start up entirely anew.

6.2 INDUCEMENTS TO MP MOBILITY AMONG PARTIES

In our theory, the chief forces that explain variation in incumbents' readiness to move among parties distill, in a word, to *time*. The incentives that tempt MPs to change party arise at particular times – stages – of the parliamentary cycle. The disincentives that counter any impulse to change and reinforce MP partisan loyalty are grounded in voter preferences, reach maximal levels at election, and diminish as the distance in time from elections increases.

Even a simple slice into the comprehensive dataset reveals how time matters for change in parliamentary party systems. Table 6.1 reports the mean number of MP interparty moves by year elapsed in the parliamentary cycle, distinguishing systems by electoral law and isolating active stages of the parliamentary cycle. Although Germany, with mixed laws, does not enter directly into either of the columns on electoral laws, the evidence on non-proportional representation (PR) systems (i.e., single-member district [SMD] plus Germany) and likewise non-SMD ones can be inferred. The table omits the United States, given its extremely short, fixed term. U.S. congressional terms, like clockwork, run always and exactly to twenty-four months, whereas without the United States, the eighty-three terms in our dataset last 41.3 months on average and vary in length from seven to sixty-two months. Even these crude comparisons across the broad swath of the full dataset disclose that incumbents avoid moves late in the term, when elections loom near. A peak in interparty mobility appears toward the middle of the term. In addition, PR systems evince a relatively great frequency of moves. Furthermore, these comparisons attest to relatively pronounced change in interelectoral party systems during active stages of the parliamentary cycle.

Setting Up the Analysis

TABLE 6.1 *Mean monthly moves per year elapsed in term, by electoral system and active vs. dormant stage (United States excluded).*

Year (N months) in term	All non-U.S. terms Stages All	All non-U.S. terms Stages Active	SMD (non-U.S.) Stages All	SMD (non-U.S.) Stages Active	PR Stages All	PR Stages Active
0 to 11[a]	0.49 (983)	0.53 (865)	0.22 (648)	0.22 (566)	1.99 (155)	2.18 (142)
12 to 23[a]	0.39 (912)	0.45 (774)	0.17 (577)	0.19 (483)	1.29 (155)	1.43 (140)
24 to 35	0.40 (786)	0.45 (659)	0.24 (469)	0.27 (388)	0.49 (144)	0.52 (126)
36 to 47[a]	0.79 (557)	0.90 (466)	0.49 (289)	0.56 (239)	1.72 (130)	1.97 (112)
≥ 48	0.38 (183)	0.46 (145)	0.18 (119)	0.22 (93)	0.77 (62)	0.88 (52)

The United States is excluded given its extremely short, fixed term. Each cell shows between parentheses the total number of observations (i.e., months) in the given category.

[a] The table excludes the three observations with more than 150 moves. The top row omits the Romanian extreme outlier of 162 moves in June 2000, the second row omits the Italian extreme outlier of 207 moves in January 1994, and the third row omits the Italian extreme outlier of 156 moves in February 1991.

PR, proportional representation; SMD, single-member district

This broad, albeit rough, look at MP switching behavior in active stages introduces the first class of explanatory factors we identify, time-specific institutional inducements to legislators' switches of party. Once more, the rules and procedures structuring legislative activity demarcate the temporal boundaries of the stages of the parliamentary cycle, and the relative prominence and immediacy of different inducements to change party vary across these stages. And, again, the first hypothesis holds that incumbents, if unchecked by deterrents, should time any moves they make among parties so as to realize concrete gains that are particular to the stage of the legislative term.

We construct our measures of stages for the large-N analysis as follows. We include a dummy variable capturing the predictably occurring stage of the parliamentary cycle, stage A (Affiliation). This variable takes the value of 1 for the first two months of a legislative term (stage A), and 0 otherwise; dates of legislative elections come from the highly respected Constituency-Level Elections Archive (CLEA, Kollman, Hicken, Caramani, and Backer 2011, appendix I). In stage A, MPs have the chance to alter the label under which they won election – when they declare party group membership for the legislative session. Our coding here for the comprehensive dataset replicates that used for the secondary in-depth terms.

Two additional dummy variables tap the unevenly occurring active stages of the parliamentary cycle, stages B (Benefits) and C (Control of policy), which leaves the nonactive stage D (Dormant) as the residual category. As noted, active stages may overlap or coincide.

To designate stage B, we assign the value of 1 to the first month that the newly elected legislature is in session, to mark the allocation of legislative committee and leadership posts. The stage B for internal legislative offices thus hinges on coding when the legislature is in session, stage C, discussed later. For the U.S. presidential system, we code the first month after the election as entering into stage B, backdating to 1946 the regularity observed for the U.S. in-depth terms. We also code as 1 any month in which cabinet(s) are negotiated for executive benefits in semi-presidential and parliamentary systems. All other months of the term are coded 0 on the stage B dummy. For the executive stage B in semi-presidential and parliamentary systems, we use data on cabinet formation from the authoritative Comparative Parliamentary Democracy Data Archive (Constitutional Change and Parliamentary Democracies [CCPD] 2011).[4]

To locate stage C, we incorporate information retrieved from legislative records for the in-depth terms to show when legislatures in those terms are officially in session. For the other terms in the comprehensive dataset, we use patterns discerned in the in-depth terms to create a rudimentary algorithm for when legislatures are likely to be in session and deciding on policy in stage C: the first month after an election and then all months except August and September, with three exceptions. In Australia, summer recess tends to fall in December and January (Australia, Parliament 2011). For the U.S. fixed terms, the House convenes in January of its first year and typically meets save for August of both years and October of the second year, when the race for the next election is near at hand. Last, outside Australia, we code September as the first month of the legislative session when an election is held in either July or August, a rare occasion in our dataset. For stage C, then, we accord the value of 1 to any month that the legislature is (likely to be) in session; all other months receive the code of 0.

With the stages thus coded, we expect positive and significant coefficients on the dummies for the active stages of the parliamentary cycle and a negative and significant coefficient on the dummy for the dormant stage. We grant that the rough coding outside the in-depth terms introduces noise into our estimations. It is vital that any bias introduced into the analysis works *against* generating the posited patterns. If findings march with expectations, our confidence in inferences is untouched by this source of bias.

Table 6.2 reports preliminary evidence that the active stages as we code them do offer incentives to incumbent interparty mobility. Distinguishing among the active stages of the parliamentary cycle, the table illustrates that Benefits stages most often generate the fact of switching. The table also documents statistically significant differences in the occurrence of switching between all active stages and the dormant stage for SMD systems, non-SMD systems, and all systems studied. One question probed in the large-N estimations is the extent to which

---

[4] The CCPD database does not cover Australia and Canada, for which we use another well-regarded source, Kam and Indridason (2005). To update the CCPD and supplement the Kam-Indridason 1957–2001 data, we rely on the Yearly Data Handbooks of the *European Journal of Political Research* and parliamentary websites (Australia 2011; Canada 2011). Our criteria for coding new executives are those of the CCPD (Strøm, Müller, and Bergman 2008, esp. 6, 88–89).

Setting Up the Analysis

TABLE 6.2 *Fact of switching, by electoral system and stage of parliamentary cycle.*

Electoral system	Active Stages				Stage D	All Stages
	A	B	C	All Active		
SMD	0.12	0.14	0.09	0.10	0.07	0.09
	(0.32)	(0.34)	(0.29)	(0.30)	(0.25)**	(0.29)
Non-SMD	0.23	0.24	0.22	0.22	0.09	0.20
	(0.43)	(0.43)	(0.41)	(0.41)	(0.29)***	(0.40)
All	0.15	0.18	0.14	0.14	0.07	0.13
	(0.35)	(0.38)	(0.34)	(0.34)	(0.26)***	(0.33)
N obs.	220	310	3,321	3,479	593	4,072

Cell entries are percentage of months in which the fact of switching (any occurrence of switching) is observed. Standard deviations appear between parentheses.
Key to stages: A, Affiliation; B, Benefits; C, Control of policy; D, Dormant.
SMD, single-member district
For differences in means between all active stages and dormant stage, Pearson χ^2:
** $p < 0.05$
*** $p < 0.01$

the occurrence of switching continues to be associated with active stages when we weigh other factors that might affect incumbent partisan behavior.

6.3 DETERRENTS TO MP MOBILITY

Disincentives to incumbents' moves constitute the second major class of explanations that we evaluate for interelectoral change and stability in parties and party systems. These disincentives, we contend, are created by voter preferences for low policy variance.

Because we posit that voters are particularly wary when an MP hops to a new party close to an impending election, time remaining until the end of the term is a key independent variable that taps expected voters' aversion to the current move come the next election. Because we claim that the adverse impact of a switch on a legislator's reelection decays through time, we expect the *Time left in term* variable to be positively and significantly associated with MP switching behavior. This variable takes its maximum value (the total months that the legislature serves) at the start of the term, dwindles by one with each month of the term, and reaches zero at term's end.

A second time-based independent variable, *Time since start of term*, captures what we expect to be the declining electoral cost to an incumbent from abandoning her initial label as time elapses since the previous election. As argued, if an MP abandons her electoral party very soon after entering office, that act upsets voters' beliefs about her policy position and reduces voters' utility from supporting her in the next election. Because voters seek to learn about MPs' steadfastness from the durability of their association with one label, the longer an MP sticks with her electoral party, the more informative and variance-reducing her fact of partisanship should be. The *Time since start of term* variable is a counter, increasing by one with each month of the legislative term.

Because increases in both *Time since start of term* and *Time left in term* reduce the electoral costs to MPs of defecting from their party, we expect both variables to be positively related to incumbents' willingness to execute interparty moves. These two time-based variables, in their linear specifications, will offset each other if applied to a single term. We emphasize that in the large-N dataset of 110 legislative terms of varying lengths, the two measurements of time are not strongly correlated and thus can enter the estimations together.[5] This is one clear advantage of the pooled dataset. We use linear and quadratic specifications of *Time since start of term* and *Time left in term* in the analysis in Chapter 7. Note, too, that our argument suggests that it is the actual number of months separating a switch from an election – the absolute distance in time – that counts for voters. For example, a switch made five months before the end of a term of twenty-four months should bring as much electoral damage to the switcher as one made five months before the end of a sixty-month term. The data bear out this notion.

Ideally, we would incorporate into our analysis direct measures of voter preferences for incumbents' party loyalty. In the theoretical model, we use the variable α to emphasize the impact of variation in electoral rules, and we posit that legislative party systems should be relatively stable under candidate-focused electoral institutions because under such rules voters should heed relatively closely candidates' policy positions and should use permanence of the party label to appraise candidates' policy variance. Pragmatically, we forego the quest for capturing gradations in the candidate-centeredness of election laws and, in our empirical estimations, treat variation in rules as a dichotomy. We focus on proportional versus other (single-member district [SMD] and hybrid) rules in our statistical models because this key institutional feature allows us to separate voter attention to a party slate versus to individual candidates (see, e.g., Shvetsova [2003], on Germany's hybrid system). In this sense, incorporating electoral laws centrally in our statistical specifications affords a close fit between the theory and the statistical models. As one key step, we use the dummy variable *Proportional*, which has the value of 1 where and when legislative elections use proportional representation and 0 otherwise. We expect a positive and significant coefficient on the *Proportional* dummy.[6]

[5] The Pearson correlation between *Time left in term* and *Time since start of term* is -0.585. Data for the two time-based variables, as implied earlier, are drawn from CLEA (Kollman, Hicken, Caramani, and Backer 2011, appendix I).

[6] As Table 6.2 suggests, candidate-centered SMD systems prevail in the dataset, providing 67.5 percent of monthly observations; 15.9 percent of observations come from PR systems and 16.5 percent from the German hybrid system. In Chapter 8, the estimations expand to include another PR system, Spain. The SMD systems help ensure variation in the dataset on the institutional attributes of federalism and, especially, presidentialism.

Setting Up the Analysis 109

Having operationalized for large-N analysis the testable implications of our formal model, we now turn to the next step in setting up estimations of statistical models: selecting and operationalizing controls and indices for rival alternative hypotheses.

6.4 ALTERNATIVE INFLUENCES AND CONTROLS

Our argument is strengthened to the extent that we can adduce empirical evidence supporting it while taking into account other potential influences on interelectoral party system change. To avoid the proverbial kitchen sink approach, we identify other factors and controls by drawing guidance from prominent schools in the study of party competition, electoral change and persistence, and democratic institutions and development (e.g., Aldrich 2006; Boix and Stokes 2007; Cheibub 2006; Chhibber and Kollman 2004; Duch and Stevenson 2008; Ferree 2010; Lichbach and Zuckerman 1997; Powell 2004; Przeworski, Alvarez, Cheibub, and Limongi 2000; Strøm, Müller, and Bergmann 2008). We group the additional independent variables we consider into four categories: party system properties, attributes of democratic institutions, sociological and structural conditions, and cultural factors and salient issues. To increase confidence in the inferences we make, we rely on widely used sources of data and adopt time-specific measures as much as possible.

6.4.1 Party System Properties at the Most Recent Election

We first control for the number of parties winning seats at election time, at the very start of the given legislative term, before incumbents might make any within-term moves. Following standard practice, we use both the raw number and the effective number of parliamentary parties (e.g., Herron and Nishikawa 2001; Laakso and Taagepera 1979; Taagepera 1997; 1999; Taagepera and Shugart 1989). In one light, it makes intuitive sense that the greater the number of parties, the greater the number of options open to MPs as they engage in an ongoing calculus of affiliation. Indeed, political scientists from multiple schools suggest that the nature and dynamics of party competition vary according to the number of parties in the party system (e.g., Powell 2000; Sartori 1976; Schofield and Sened 2006; cf. other works cited in Chapter 1). Yet, in formal and computational analysis, Laver and Benoit (2003) show that the intuition makes more sense under some conditions than others: under office-seeking assumptions, legislative party systems with larger numbers of parties are relatively likely to change between elections; under policy-seeking assumptions, however, substantial change can occur even in party systems composed of three parties. Moreover, our treatment in Chapter 2, based on assumptions of mixed motivations, illustrates that interelectoral change can occur for party systems with relatively few parties. Hence, if the intuitive argument held, the coefficient for the raw and effective *Number of Parliamentary Parties* at election

TABLE 6.3 *Mean monthly moves during term, by raw number of parliamentary parties and effective number of parliamentary parties at outset of term.*

Raw N parties	Moves (SD)	Obs	ENPP	Moves (SD)	Obs
<4	0.07 (0.38)	1,477	<2	0.05 (0.25)	809
4	0.19 (0.91)	604	≥2 <3	0.36 (2.51)	2,167
5	0.12 (0.64)	452	≥3 <4	0.97 (7.65)	803
≥6 <9	0.84 (7.00)	713	≥4 <5	1.53 (10.97)	247
≥9	1.64 (10.87)***	826	≥5	9.46 (42.11)***	24
All systems	0.55 (5.76)	4,072	All systems	0.55 (5.76)	4,072

Cell entries are mean monthly moves, with standard deviations between parentheses.
Tests of means across groups with cutpoints as defined above, allowing for heterogeneity:
*** $p< 0.01$

t would be positive and significant. There are also good reasons to believe that the coefficient should be insignificant.[7]

As recorded in Table 6.3, simple bivariate comparisons indicate that the greater the number of parliamentary parties at the outset of the term, the higher the mean monthly interparty moves observed during the term. Mean switching does not increase monotonically with the raw number of parties. Even so, with the cutpoints identified as in the table, the relationships between mean monthly moves and both the raw and effective number of parliamentary parties attain statistical significance.

It is also important to evaluate the potential impact of electoral volatility, which, as discussed, captures the aggregate shift in shares of the vote among parties from one legislative election to the next (e.g., Pedersen 1979; 1983; Katz 1997; Mainwaring and Zoco 2007). We are interested in volatility at the election inaugurating the given legislative term, election t, as parties' vote shares depart from the results registered at the previous election $t - 1$. It is possible that relatively high electoral volatility at the election initiating a given term would, all else equal, relax the electoral constraints that otherwise operate to bind incumbents loyally to their status-quo parties throughout that term. That is, when the electorate has shifted support among parties, the penalties for incumbents who swap party labels might become less severe (cf. Bartolini and Mair [1990] on party system change and stability in the electoral arena). If this logic applied, the coefficient on *Electoral Volatility* would be positive and significant.[8]

---

[7] Data on effective numbers of parliamentary parties come from the highly regarded Carey and Hix dataset (2008; 2010, who in turn rely on Golder [2005] and Gallagher [2008; 2011]); as needed, we supplement with Gallagher (2008; 2011). For raw numbers of parties, we draw on the authoritative Cheibub (2006) dataset, updated by Canada (2011).

[8] Our data on electoral volatility come from Scott Mainwaring (Mainwaring, Gervasoni, and España-Nájera 2010). Our deep thanks to Mainwaring for sharing his data and codebook.

Research on weakly institutionalized party systems implies that, in such systems, the electoral deterrents to partisan moves may falter or fail altogether because voters may not believe that stable partisanship diminishes a candidate's policy variance and enhances her quality as their representative (e.g., Mainwaring 1998; 1999; Mainwaring and Scully 1995; 2008; Mainwaring and Torcal 2006). We sidestep the complexities of measurement here because only one country in the comprehensive dataset may be said to have loosely defined voters' beliefs and expectations with regard to parties. We use the fixed effect for Romanian observations as a crude control for weak party system institutionalization. As we observed in Chapter 3, the implication would be that $H2$ through $H4$ should not hold for weakly institutionalized party systems; this reasoning offers a variant of the null hypothesis.

6.4.2 Democratic Institutions

While our theory assigns a key place to electoral systems, we appraise several other institutional features of democratic regimes as potential influences on continuity and change in interelectoral party systems. First, consider federalism. Whereas we uncover electoral inducements to incumbents' partisan loyalty, research on federalism points to conditions under which electoral inducements to disloyalty might operate. In particular, the distinctive subnational arenas of partisan competition and voter attachment in federal systems might bring national MPs to consider or even opt for new party affiliations (cf. Chhibber and Kollman 2004; Filippov, Ordeshook, and Shvetsova 2004). This logic holds that, as candidates compete for and serve in the authoritative, autonomous, and constitutionally protected subnational offices characteristic of federal systems, voters should come to define concerns and loyalties that are at least partly distinct from those they have in the national arena. National MPs in federal systems should heed the distinctiveness of subnational constituencies because they likely have climbed steps on the career ladder unavailable to legislators in unitary systems. Hence voters' partisan attachments at the subnational level may draw the national MP away from the party label under which she won her seat in the most recent national election and lead her to join the party more recently favored by voters in subnational elections. Because the institutional architecture of federalism splits voter loyalties, the reasoning runs, the national MP may switch party to stay loyal to her subnational voters. We operationalize the control for federalism as a dummy coded 1 where the system is federal or highly regionalized, and 0 where unitary. If this reasoning is right, the coefficient on *Federalism* should be positive and significant.

Prominent scholarly work has examined the impact of gradations in district magnitude on the shape of national party systems (e.g., Amorim Neto and Cox 1997; Benoit 2001; Carey and Hix 2011; Carey and Shugart 1995; Cox 1997; Ordeshook and Shvetsova 1994). Although these analysts have trained attention on parties in the electoral arena and candidate strategies at election time, the

TABLE 6.4 *Mean monthly moves during term, by mean and median district magnitude in elections.*

Mean Magnitude	Moves (SD)	Obs	Median Magnitude	Moves (SD)	Obs
1	0.20 (1.92)	2,694	1	0.20 (1.90)	2,750
>1 ≤5	0.32 (0.64)	56	>1 ≤5	–	0
>5 ≤15	2.65 (16.46)	97	>5 ≤15	0.99 (9.84)	274
>15 ≤20	2.03 (13.05)	552	>15 ≤20	0.17 (0.80)	399
> 20	0.43 (2.09)***	729	> 20	2.06 (12.19)***	649
All systems	0.55 (5.76)	4,072	All systems	0.55 (5.76)	4,072

Cell entries are mean monthly moves, with standard deviations between parentheses.
Tests of means across groups with cutpoints as defined above, allowing for heterogeneity:
*** $p < 0.01$

work has implications for the behavior of parliamentary incumbents. The inference would be that the greater the number of representatives elected per district, other things equal, the weaker the ties binding legislators and voters and thus the greater the freedom that legislators should have to alter party affiliation. We measure both mean and median district magnitude in election t (data from Carey and Hix 2008; 2010). The logic here suggests a positive and significant coefficient on *Mean (Median) District Magnitude*.

The bivariate comparisons summarized in Table 6.4 support that logic. The higher the mean and median district magnitude, the more interparty moves incumbents execute during the parliamentary term. With cutpoints as defined in the table, these relationships are not monotonic. Nonetheless, differences in mean monthly moves across both sets of groups are statistically significant.

We contend that as the time nears for the election ending a given legislative term, an incumbent should grow more reluctant to change party. A robust test of this argument should control for the rival hypothesis that with the approach of a new election, the drive for reelection comes to the fore and MPs switch party in efforts to jockey for electoral advantage (cf. Mershon and Shvetsova 2008a; 2009c). To operationalize the run-up to national legislative elections, we create a dummy variable, coding the last six months of the legislative term as 1 and all other months as 0. If the rival hypothesis on preelectoral positioning applies, then the coefficient on *Election Run-Up* should be positive and significant.

Our next control reflects scholarly debates about partisan dynamics under presidentialism. Whereas some comparativists assert that presidential democracies tend to suffer from undisciplined parties, fragmented legislative party systems, and decisional deadlock (e.g., Linz 1990; Linz and Valenzuela 1994; Stepan and Skach 1993; Valenzuela 2004), others maintain that no such systematic tendencies set apart presidential regimes once additional factors are taken into account (e.g., Cheibub 2007; Cheibub and Limongi 2002; Filippov, Ordeshook, and Shvetsova 1999). Of special relevance is the claim advanced by the adherents of the first school that "direct election of the president ... is

Setting Up the Analysis 113

TABLE 6.5 *Mean monthly moves during term, by institutional design.*

Territorial Governance	Executive-Legislative Relations (Semi-)Presidential	Parliamentary	All
Federal	0.05 (0.25)	0.55 (6.23)***	0.43 (5.46)
Unitary	1.77 (11.46)**	0.60 (4.63)	0.80 (6.35)
All	0.48 (5.78) [n = 865]	0.56 (5.75) [n = 3,207]	[n = 4,072]

Cell entries are mean monthly moves, with standard deviations between parentheses. Numbers of observations appear between brackets.
Among presidential systems, difference in means between federal and unitary:
** $p < 0.05$
Among federal systems, difference in means between presidential and parliamentary:
*** $p < 0.01$

typically associated with less cohesive parties, both as electoral organizations and as parliamentary groups" (Shabad and Slomczynski 2004, 153). In light of these debates, we control for presidential design, coded 1 for presidential and semi-presidential systems, and 0 otherwise. The coefficient on *Presidentialism* should be positive and significant if the claim just cited were to hold.

Preliminary evidence on that claim appears in Table 6.5. As the table shows, relatively high switching emerges in those (semi-)presidential systems that are also unitary, and relatively low switching occurs in federal (semi-)presidential systems; that difference attains statistical significance. Among federal systems, a statistically significant difference in incumbent interparty mobility separates presidential and parliamentary regimes. For all countries studied, however, the difference between presidentialism and parliamentarism fades into insignificance. The large-N estimations in the next chapter sort out these and other influences on MP partisan behavior.[9]

We control as well for the age of the democratic regime, as tapped by the number of uninterrupted months since the first democratic national election was held in a given country. It is possible that the greater the entrenchment of democratic electoral practices, as indexed by time, the more voters develop partisan attachments (cf. Converse 1969; but see Mainwaring and Torcal 2006; Mainwaring and Zoco 2007). Hence, the longer the electorate's exposure to democratic rules, the more voters demand that their representatives remain faithful to electoral labels and the more likely that they punish incumbents for partisan disloyalty. If this holds true, then the coefficient on the *Age of democracy* variable should be negative and significant.[10]

---

[9] Recall that, because our dataset covers relatively few countries, multiple institutional variables easily become de facto country effects, thus muddying inferences. Thus, for instance, the United States is the single federal, presidential system we study. We return to this issue in Chapter 7.
[10] The starting point for our monthly coding on this variable is drawn from the CLEA archive (Kollman, Hicken, Caramani, and Backer 2011, appendix I), already cited; we regard a score of

6.4.3 Ascriptive Cleavages and Economic Factors

According to multiple schools in political science, social cleavages leave a profound imprint on party systems in the electoral arena (e.g., Amorim Neto and Cox 1997; Caramani 2004; Franklin, Mackie, and Valen 1992; Lipset and Rokkan 1967; Ordeshook and Shvetsova 1994; Rokkan 1970). In addition, a prominent theme sounded by many researchers is that economic conditions powerfully influence voter choices (e.g., Anderson 1995; 2000; 2007; Duch and Stevenson 2008; Lewis-Beck and Stegmaier 2000; Powell and Whitten 1993). We thus examine the social and economic context in which voters evaluate candidates for legislative office and candidates compete for such office.

A range of arguments about ethnic heterogeneity advise investigating its role. Scholars have analyzed the impact of ethnic heterogeneity on such phenomena as electoral volatility (e.g., Ferree 2010), tax compliance (e.g., Lassen 2007), public goods provision (e.g., Habyarimana, Humphreys, Posner, and Weinstein 2007), patronage (e.g., Arriola 2009), economic growth (e.g., Posner 2004; Rodrik and Wacziarg 2005), and civil war (e.g., Bhavnani and Miodownik 2009; Blimes 2006; for overviews, see Chandra 2008; Chandra and Wilkinson 2008). Most pertinent here, classic comparative research has found that ethnic heterogeneity interacts with district magnitude to determine the number of electoral parties and the number of parliamentary parties at the start of the term (Amorim Neto and Cox 1997; Ordeshook and Shvetsova 1994). To capture the cleavage structure underpinning a party system, we adopt the three indices developed by Alesina et al. (2003; 2011), which distinguish among ethnic, language, and religious fractionalization as of the late 1980s to 2001 and whose values range from 0 to 1 and are invariant for each country across time.[11] To the extent that ethnic heterogeneity leads voters to cast votes expressive of their identity, regardless of whether particular candidates display or betray partisan loyalty, then controlling for *Fractionalization* should deprive our temporal and institutional measures of electoral deterrents to MP interparty mobility of significant effect. Conversely, deep societal divisions might lead voters segmented along ethnic lines to punish disloyal incumbents relatively harshly; if so, the coefficients on the *Fractionalization* variables would be negative and significant.

Still another set of variables taps economic conditions at or near election time. The reasoning would be that voters decide to reelect (or reject) an incumbent on the basis of good (or poor) economic conditions, not on the record of partisan loyalty (or disloyalty) that the incumbent compiles during a given legislative term. To assess this reasoning, we include three measures of economic context: mean three-year growth in gross domestic product (GDP, averaged for two years

---

+6 or above on the widely used Polity IV index as denoting a democratic regime (cf. Carey and Hix 2008; 2010, among others).

[11] For Alesina et al. (2003; 2011), the measure of fractionalization is the inverse of the effective number of groups.

Setting Up the Analysis

before a given legislative election t and in the year of election t, with the value at t reproduced monthly until election $t+1$), GDP per capita (GDP per capita divided by 1,000, in the year of election t, with value at t reproduced until election $t+1$), and the widely used Gini coefficient of income inequality (in election year t, with value at t reproduced until election $t+1$).[12] To the extent that incumbents believe that "it's the economy" driving electoral outcomes, to echo U.S. political consultant Jim Carville, then the addition of economic controls should also deprive our measures of electoral deterrents of significant effect.

6.4.4 Cultural Factors and Salient Issues

A first set of cultural arguments focuses on the role of formal education in shaping citizen preferences. One line of reasoning would be that the more educated voters are, the more likely they have relatively ample access to information and the more likely they are to assign relatively greater weight to candidates' policy promises (cf. Desposato 2006b). Thus, the higher the mean level of schooling completed by voters, all else equal, the more likely that MPs face electoral penalties if they break promises by switching. In short, better educated voters should imply greater deterrents to MP changes of party. The counterclaim is implied, however, by those who contend that the spread of education among contemporary electorates has weakened partisan attachments (e.g., Dalton 2000; Dalton and Wattenberg 2000). Our measure is the mean education level for the national population aged fifteen and above. The coefficient on the *Education* variable should be negative and significant if the first argument holds, and positive and significant if the second holds.[13]

We also control for the Cold War era as a way of exploring whether some issues might become so prominent that they override the operation of the mechanisms we propose. We give the value of 1 to all months from February 1947, when the Truman Doctrine was announced, to December 1991, when the Soviet Union was officially dissolved; this dummy variable otherwise is coded 0. The context of the Cold War might be envisioned as working something like a toggle, turning either off or on the electoral deterrents to incumbent interparty mobility. On the one hand, perhaps the stark confrontation between world powers deflected voter attention from incumbent partisan disloyalty in the domestic sphere; what drove voter concerns was the issue of national security in the perilous international environment, so much so that considerations of MP partisan loyalty fell away. On the other hand, perhaps, given the rigidity of the international balance of power, partisan stances on foreign policy formed an integral part of the policy package that voters endorsed at election time, so that

---

[12] All of these data are drawn from Carey and Hix (2008; 2010).
[13] Our source for these data, whose values vary every five years, is Barro and Lee (2010; 2011). We use a new value on this variable at the month of the first election for which it is available and reproduce that value monthly until the next election, when a new value is available.

incumbents who weighed the option of undoing that package and discarding one partisan label for another should have anticipated electoral losses and refrained from switching. We are agnostic on the direction of the potential effect and acknowledge the stream of research showing that the impact of foreign policy issues on voter choices is conditional (e.g., for the United States, Aldrich, Sullivan, and Borgida 1989; Aldrich, Gelpi, Feaver, Reifler, and Sharp 2006). Our expectations for the impact of this and other variables discussed in this chapter are summarized in Appendix A, Table 6A.2.

6.5 CONCLUSION

At the outset here, we presented multiple measures of the phenomenon to be explained in the large-N estimations – incumbents' changes of party. We also discussed how we tap three categories of potential explanations for change and stability in parliamentary party systems: posited time-specific inducements to incumbents' interparty mobility, posited time-specific deterrents to change, and other explanatory variables. We aim to assure isomorphism between our formal models and statistical analyses. The next chapter shows how that effort plays out in practice, as we turn to the statistical estimations and the findings they generate across the comprehensive dataset.

7

Institutional Inducements and Preference-Based Deterrents to Legislative Party System Change

Building on the foundations laid in Chapter 6, this chapter appraises the general explanatory purchase of our argument about the evolution of interelectoral party systems. The comparisons encompass eight countries, 110 parliamentary terms, and more than 4,000 monthly observations of legislator behavior. The first section introduces the basic form of the statistical models. The next three sections present findings from estimations using different measures for sitting legislators' mobility among parties. The second part examines the absolute number of interparty moves as the dependent variable. The third section looks at the fact of switching, and the fourth, at the category of switching – at whether members of parliament (MPs) stay put, change party alone or in small groups, or move en masse. The fifth section focuses on the relationship between stability and gradations of change in a legislative party system on the one hand and voters' choices at the election ending a legislative term on the other.

7.1 INTRODUCING THE STATISTICAL MODELS

In the large-N statistical estimations, as in the case studies, the hypotheses we evaluate center on institutional inducements and preference-based deterrents to change. We seek to gauge the extent to which, on the one hand, the availability of benefits as structured by political institutions might *induce* individual incumbents to change party affiliation, and, on the other, the expression of voters' preferences at the last and next elections might *deter* MPs from moving among parties. We thus ask: to what extent do these two sets of forces, taken together and controlling for other potential influences, drive variations across space and time in interelectoral party system change?

This overarching question finds natural translation in statistical models that take the following form:

$$\text{Mobility}_j = k + \beta_1 \text{ Stage} + \beta_2 \text{ Time left in term} + \beta_3 \text{ Time since start of term} + \beta_4 \text{ Institutions} + \beta_5 \text{ Controls} + \varepsilon$$

where

> *Mobility_j* is MP mobility during month *j* of the term (measured three ways),
> *Stage* is a vector tapping stages of the parliamentary cycle,
> *Time left in term* is the number of months from the end of the term (or its square in an alternative specification),
> *Time since start of term* is the number of months from the start of the term (or its square),
> *Institutions* is a vector of institutional variables, including, for example, electoral laws and the age of the democratic regime, and
> *Controls* is a vector of (noninstitutional) controls and variables capturing rival hypotheses.

The statistical model thus captures inducements to MPs' moves (posited in *H1*) via *Stage*. The model taps deterrents (*H2* and *H3*) via *Time left in term* and *Time since start of term*, respectively, and candidate-centered systems (*H4*) within the *Institutions* vector. Recall that the additional hypotheses and controls we investigate fall into four groups: party system attributes, sociological and structural conditions, cultural factors, and controls for region and era. In separate specifications, we replace the combinations of institutional and control variables with country fixed effects to probe the robustness of the hypotheses on MP propensity to discard or keep their party label depending on temporal stages and temporal distance to elections.

When we use the non-negative integer count of interparty moves as the measure for the dependent variable, a Poisson regression model is the appropriate specification for the statistical analysis. When the dependent variable is the fact of switching, we estimate probit models. For the ordered dependent variable, the category of switching, we estimate ordered probit models.

An integral part of introducing the statistical models is discussing the implications of the most-different systems design for the analysis. Specifically, country case selection for the comprehensive dataset deliberately maximizes institutional variation. This design enables a strong test of our hypotheses: if the analyses reveal that, even under different institutional conditions, MPs adjust partisan strategy as posited, responding to incentives and disincentives unfolding over time in the parliamentary term, we can have confidence in the broad applicability of the argument here. Along with this crucial advantage comes a drawback, however: given the relatively small number of countries in the dataset, particular mixes of institutional features can easily become synonyms for particular countries – that is, become country effects. This means that the statistical analysis cannot examine fine institutional distinctions, such as the difference between majority rule and simple plurality rule among single-member district (SMD) systems. Consider, too, that the statistical analyses are based on the premise that

Inducements and Deterrents to Change

all parliamentary terms in all countries in the dataset evince essentially similar dynamics: our expectations about the impact of stimuli and restraints on MP behavior should withstand scrutiny under the most-different systems design. This approach obviously abstracts from the reality of cross-national specificities. Applying our theory alone and neglecting context is bound to capture only a portion of the variance in interelectoral party system change. Yet, to discern the explanatory purchase of our claims, we must do just that, stripping the theory to its basics and applying it alone, at least as a first step; the estimations reported in Tables 7.1, 7.6, and 7.7 take precisely that step. The rich data at hand equip us to venture further: in additional steps, the analysis looks at incumbent behavior as shaped by federal institutions, economic conditions, societal cleavages, and so forth. Tables 7.3 and 7.4, among others, explore this territory.

7.2 EXPLAINING THE ABSOLUTE NUMBER OF MONTHLY MP MOVES

We now turn to the task of accounting for the magnitude of interparty mobility, measured as the raw number of monthly changes of party affiliation carried out by sitting legislators. Because this measure is a count of occurrences, a non-negative discrete number in any given month, we estimate Poisson regression models (e.g., Long 1997, 242–249; 2006). The absolute number of monthly switches displays substantial cross-national variation and also substantial variation over time within the parliamentary term, as suggested by Table 6.2 and, for a subset of the data, by Chapters 4 and 5. The temporal variation in MP interparty mobility is essential to evaluating our theory of inducements and constraints.

Yet, can the analysis rest on the assumption that this temporal variation is the same across all parliamentary terms studied? The answer, according to our own argument, is no. If Hypothesis 3 were right – if the election launching a term were to relatively strongly bind MP interparty mobility in candidate-centered systems – then an estimation incorporating party-list systems alongside candidate-centered ones would violate the assumption of the same temporal dynamic across all terms.

Moreover, the magnitude of incumbent mobility differs markedly between SMD and non-SMD systems, with no MP switches at all in 90.7 percent of SMD monthly observations. To account for the difference in the two data-generating processes posited between electoral systems, we use a "with zeros" Poisson model, which permits distinct expectations for the overall magnitude of party system change in two types of settings (e.g., Long 1997, 242–243; Mullahy 1986). We include a zero-inflation step (with a logit link) in the estimation to address the idea that, in line with Hypothesis 4, switching should be relatively rare in SMD systems; we use the SMD dummy variable as the inflation parameter.[1]

---

[1] As discussed, we cap at fifty the count of monthly switches. Setting the bound at thirty produces quite similar results; details are available from the authors. Models in which $Moves_j$ is operationalized as the log of switches plus one also yield similar results.

7.2.1 The Basic Model and the SMD–PR Divide

The simplest and most direct test of our theory examines the extent to which time-based stimuli and restraints, along with electoral institutions, affect interelectoral party system change. In our argument, time-specific institutional inducements to change should occur unevenly over the course of the parliamentary cycle. We identify three phases of heightened incentives to switch party – affiliation, benefits, and policy stages – along with the dormant stage, when the status quo should reign. Recall from Chapter 6, however, that outside the secondary in-depth terms we are forced to rely on a rough coding of stages. Given that imprecision, the estimations that follow enter one stage at a time.[2]

We expect that temporal proximity to elections deters legislators from changing party. Recall that the *Time left in term* variable has its maximum value (total term length in months) at the term's start, shrinks by one with each month, and arrives at zero at term's end. The *Time since start of term* variable, a counter, stands at zero when the term opens and rises by one with each month of the term. Because both increases in *Time left in term* (according to H_2) and increases in *Time since start of term* (H_3) diminish the electoral costs to MPs of abandoning their party, we expect both variables to be positively related to representatives' willingness to carry out interparty moves.

Lacking direct measures of voter preferences for incumbent partisan loyalty, we home in on candidate-centered rules, used in SMD and mixed systems (e.g., Shvetsova [2003] on the German hybrid system), as magnifying voter attention to individual candidates' behavior after the initiating election. Our expectations are distinct for proportional representation (PR) systems. We adopt the interactive variable, *Time since start of term under PR*, in an effort to detect whether MP interparty mobility differs structurally between candidate-centered and party-list systems. As Table 7.1 displays, models 1 through 6 also include a dummy variable for PR systems, *Proportional*. Both *Time since start of term* and *Proportional* should have positive coefficients, whereas *Time since start of term under PR* should have a negative coefficient, reflecting the notion that, for the reference group of non-PR systems, coded zero on the interactive variable, MP interparty mobility early in the term should be quite low.

The first three columns of Table 7.1, reporting on models 1 through 3, demonstrate that these expectations are all upheld. The last three columns, on models 4 through 6, which include squared variants of the time-based measures for deterrents, yield analogous results. We find support for the notion of a conditional midterm effect, as indicated by the sign and significance of the coefficient on the interactive term, *Time since start under PR*. MPs elected on party lists, unlike those elected in candidate-centered systems, are not averse to

---

[2] Again, any bias in the estimations works against producing the posited results. If findings align with expectations, our confidence in inferences is unaffected by this source of bias.

TABLE 7.1 *Explaining the absolute number of switches (cap of fifty) with stages and time in term; zero-inflated Poisson regression.*

	(1)	(2)	(3)	(4)	(5)	(6)
Time left in term	0.02***	0.02***	0.02***	—	—	—
	(0.00)	(0.00)	(0.00)			
Time left in term, squared	—	—	—	0.0003***	0.0003***	0.0004***
				(0.0000)	(0.0000)	(0.0000)
Time since start of term	0.02***	0.03***	0.02***	—	—	—
	(0.00)	(0.00)	(0.00)			
Time since start of term, squared	—	—	—	0.0002***	0.0003***	0.0002***
				(0.0000)	(0.0001)	(0.0001)
Proportional	1.46***	1.37***	1.43***	1.13***	1.07***	1.03***
	(0.10)	(0.10)	(0.10)	(0.08)	(0.08)	(0.09)
Time since start of term × PR	−0.02***	−0.02***	−0.03***	—	—	—
	(0.00)	(0.00)	(0.00)			
Time since start of term, squared × PR	—	—	—	−0.0003***	−0.0003***	−0.0002***
				(0.0001)	(0.0001)	(0.0001)
Stage A	0.80***	—	—	0.61***	—	—
	(0.09)			(0.09)		
Stage B	—	1.09***	—	—	1.00***	—
		(0.07)			(0.06)	
Stage D	—	—	−0.61***	—	—	−0.59***
			(0.14)			(0.15)
Constant	−0.42*	−0.65***	−0.16***	0.20*	0.08	0.24**
	(0.15)	(0.14)	(0.15)	(0.08)	(0.08)	(0.08)

TABLE 7.1 (cont.)

	(1)	(2)	(3)	(4)	(5)	(6)
Inflation factor (logit)						
SMD	0.76***	0.73***	0.79***	0.80***	0.78***	0.79***
	(0.10)	(0.10)	(0.10)	(0.10)	(0.10)	(0.10)
Constant	1.25***	1.22***	1.25***	1.26***	1.23***	1.25***
	(0.07)	(0.07)	(0.07)	(0.07)	(0.08)	(0.07)
Vuong z	6.15	6.41	6.23	6.22	6.41	6.27
Prob > z	0.000	0.000	0.000	0.000	0.000	0.000
Observations	4,072	4,072	4,072	4,072	4,072	4,072
Nonzero obs.	519	519	519	519	519	519

Robust standard errors in parentheses; *$p < 0.05$; **$p < 0.01$; ***$p < 0.001$
PR, proportional representation; SMD, single-member district

Inducements and Deterrents to Change 123

defecting from their electoral label early in the term. That the inflation model and the inflation variable are statistically significant throughout buttresses *H4*: as expected, the inflation factor inflates the appearance of zero switches in the monthly observations.

The estimations also assess inducements to change. As Table 7.1 records, the affiliation and benefits stages bring individual MPs to switch party and introduce change to the legislative party system, whereas the dormant stage dampens interelectoral party system change. The coefficients on all variables attain statistical significance. *H1* is corroborated in this basic test.

7.2.2 Inducements, Deterrents, and Country Effects

Having established that the central explanatory forces in our argument operate as anticipated, we now dig deeper, first by submitting this finding to the most challenging test of searching for country effects. Numerous other factors could well influence representatives, parties, and parliaments in addition to the ebb and flow of inducements and constraints on which we focus. The data-generating process underlying change and stability in parliamentary party systems may even be unique to each country, if each is uniquely characterized by some mix of variables capable of strongly affecting the evolution of the interelectoral party system. The question is: once we identify countries, letting country names stand for the specificities in each nation, what shared traits remain, if any, to explain party system change in their parliaments?

Table 7.2 answers that question by reporting on models 7 through 12, all estimations with country fixed effects. The continuing explanatory power of our chief independent variables shows that the argument here is robust to this check. Even while acknowledging country contexts, the coefficients on all of our key variables retain their expected signs along with statistical significance. Above and beyond the particulars of each country, the models disclose the common imprint of MP responsiveness to inducements and deterrents to changing party affiliation. As the listing of countries in the lower half of the table suggests, the omitted category in these estimations is the United States; Romania is the excluded category among the PR systems.

Table 7.2 thus demonstrates that our hypotheses survive a fundamental test. In a most-different systems design, with country fixed effects incorporated into the analysis, the results show that incumbents' decisions to move among parties and redefine legislative party systems depend on the temporal stages of the parliamentary cycle and the temporal distance to elections. We again find evidence of a conditional midterm effect, as indicated by the sign and significance of the coefficient on the interactive term, *Time since start under PR*. Representatives elected on party lists are relatively open to leaving their original party early in the term.

TABLE 7.2 *Absolute number of switches (cap of fifty) with stages, time in term, and fixed effects.*

	(7)	(8)	(9)	(10)	(11)	(12)
Time left in term	0.01* (0.003)	0.01* (0.003)	0.01* (0.003)	—	—	—
Time left in term SQ	—	—	—	0.0001*** (0.0000)	0.0001** (0.0000)	0.0003*** (0.0000)
Time since start of term	0.01* (0.004)	0.01** (0.004)	0.00 (0.004)	—	—	—
Time since start of term SQ	—	—	—	0.0001 (0.0001)	0.0001 (0.0001)	0.0001 (0.0001)
Proportional	3.03*** (0.23)	3.01*** (0.23)	2.94*** (0.24)	2.75*** (0.23)	2.79*** (0.22)	2.50*** (0.23)
Time since start of term × PR	−0.02*** (0.003)	−0.02*** (0.003)	−0.02*** (0.004)	—	—	—
Time since start of term SQ × PR	—	—	—	−0.0003*** (0.0001)	−0.0002*** (0.0001)	−0.0002*** (0.0001)
Stage A	0.70*** (0.09)	—	—	0.68*** (0.09)	—	—
Stage B	—	1.02*** (0.07)	—	—	0.99*** (0.07)	—
Stage D	—	—	−0.75*** (0.14)	—	—	−0.75*** (0.14)
Australia	−0.45 (0.31)	−0.39 (0.31)	−0.47 (0.31)	−0.41 (0.31)	−0.33 (0.31)	−0.48 (0.31)
Canada	1.89*** (0.22)	1.89*** (0.22)	1.99*** (0.22)	1.96*** (0.22)	2.00*** (0.21)	1.93*** (0.22)
France	2.27*** (0.24)	2.30*** (0.24)	2.35*** (0.24)	2.25*** (0.24)	2.35*** (0.23)	2.11*** (0.24)
Germany (mixed)	2.25*** (0.22)	2.24*** (0.22)	2.27*** (0.22)	2.31*** (0.22)	2.35*** (0.21)	2.20*** (0.22)

Italy	0.39***	0.29**	0.51***	0.39***	0.30***	0.45***
	(0.09)	(0.09)	(0.09)	(0.09)	(0.09)	(0.09)
U.K.	1.12***	1.20***	1.11***	1.22***	1.36***	1.06***
	(0.24)	(0.24)	(0.24)	(0.23)	(0.23)	(0.23)
Constant	−1.58***	−1.74***	−1.37***	−1.44***	−1.57***	−1.30***
	(0.22)	(0.21)	(0.21)	(0.20)	(0.20)	(0.20)
Inflation factor (logit)						
SMD	0.17	0.14	0.17	0.17	0.16	0.18
	(0.11)	(0.11)	(0.11)	(0.11)	(0.11)	(0.11)
Constant	1.33***	1.31***	1.31***	1.33***	1.32***	1.31***
	(0.07)	(0.07)	(0.07)	(0.07)	(0.07)	(0.07)
Vuong z	6.20	6.49	6.27	6.22	6.45	6.23
Prob > z	0.000	0.000	0.000	0.000	0.000	0.000
Observations	4,072	4,072	4,072	4,072	4,072	4,072
Nonzero obs.	519	519	519	519	519	519

Robust standard errors in parentheses; *$p < 0.05$; **$p < 0.01$; ***$p < 0.001$
PR, proportional representation; SMD, single-member district

7.2.3 Inducements and Deterrents with Institutional, Economic, and Cultural Conditions

With confirmation in hand that our hypotheses continue to find support even in view of country effects, the next set of steps is to explore other potential influences on change and stability in interelectoral party systems. As Chapter 6 discussed, we heed extant research to identify the additional hypotheses that we examine. The measures capturing a few of such hypotheses are time-invariant for any given country yet vary across countries, such as ethnic heterogeneity, whereas other measures vary both within and across countries, such as economic growth. Because the analyses in Tables 7.1 and 7.2 establish that use of the linear and squared specifications of the measures for time-based deterrents generates similar results, only quadratic models appear in the next several tables; the similar linear estimations are available from the authors.

The analysis summarized in Table 7.3 opens the investigation of additional hypotheses by bringing in a range of institutional factors, measures tapping economic circumstances, and education as a cultural factor shaping voter preferences. Observe first that the coefficients on all indicators for inducements and constraints maintain their expected signs and statistical significance. Our hypotheses continue to be upheld even when varying institutional, economic, and cultural conditions come into play.

The findings on institutions sustain some contentions in the literature and undermine others. Contrary to some arguments about presidentialism, the interelectoral party systems in (semi-)presidential regimes here are not particularly subject to flux. When the United States is included in estimations, as in Table 7.3, legislative party systems under presidentialism are relatively stable; when U.S. observations are removed, the coefficient on *(Semi-)presidentialism* becomes positive and loses significance (details available from authors). In line with claims drawn from research on federalism, incumbents in federal and highly regionalized systems tend to switch relatively often. Yet, when the relatively strong inducements to MP interparty mobility during the benefits stage are considered, the coefficient on *Federalism* is statistically significant only at generous levels (model 14) or loses significance (model 17); probing further, if we omit Italy as a highly regionalized system (after 1976), the coefficient on *Federalism* takes on a negative sign and nears statistical significance in model 17 (details obtainable from the authors). We weigh the possibility that the more entrenched the practice of democratic elections, the more likely voters demand MP loyalty to electoral labels and the more ready voters are to punish partisan disloyalty. The evidence supports this notion.[3]

---

[3] Recall that *Age of democracy* varies over time and space, as illustrated by the United States, the oldest democracy in the world (minimum of 1,642 months and maximum of 2,266 in the dataset), and Romania (minimum 0, maximum 96).

TABLE 7.3 *Explaining the absolute number of switches (cap of fifty) with quadratic time in term, stages, and institutional, economic, and cultural conditions; zero-inflated Poisson regression.*

	(13)	(14)	(15)	(16)	(17)	(18)
Time left in term, SQ	0.0004***	0.0003***	0.0005***	0.0003***	0.0002***	0.0004***
	(0.0001)	(0.0000)	(0.0000)	(0.0001)	(0.0000)	(0.0000)
Time since start of term, SQ	0.0003***	0.0003***	0.0003***	0.0002**	0.0002**	0.0002***
	(0.0001)	(0.0001)	(0.0001)	(0.0001)	(0.0001)	(0.0001)
Proportional	1.32***	1.31***	1.25***	1.49***	1.37***	1.41***
	(0.10)	(0.10)	(0.10)	(0.12)	(0.12)	(0.12)
Time since start of term, SQ × PR	−0.0003***	−0.0003***	−0.0003***	−0.0003***	−0.0003***	−0.0003***
	(0.0001)	(0.0001)	(0.0001)	(0.0001)	(0.0001)	(0.0001)
Stage A	0.44***	—	—	0.63***	—	—
	(0.10)			(0.11)		
Stage B	—	0.88***	—	—	0.89***	—
		(0.07)			(0.07)	
Stage D	—	—	−0.61***	—	—	−0.65***
			(0.16)			(0.15)
Presidential	0.17	0.08	0.21	−0.16	−0.22	−0.08
	(0.12)	(0.12)	(0.12)	(0.14)	(0.14)	(0.14)
Federal	0.32***	0.20*	0.43***	0.19*	0.13	0.35***
	(0.09)	(0.08)	(0.08)	(0.09)	(0.08)	(0.08)
Age of democracy	—	—	—	−0.001***	−0.001***	−0.001***
				(0.0001)	(0.0001)	(0.0001)
GDP per capita	0.02*	0.02*	0.01*	0.06***	0.05***	0.05***
	(0.01)	(0.01)	(0.01)	(0.01)	(0.01)	(0.01)
Gini	−0.03***	−0.03***	−0.02*	−0.05***	−0.05***	−0.04***
	(0.01)	(0.01)	(0.01)	(0.01)	(0.01)	(0.01)
Economic growth	—	—	—	0.13***	0.11***	0.12***
				(0.02)	(0.02)	(0.02)

TABLE 7.3 (cont.)

	(13)	(14)	(15)	(16)	(17)	(18)
Education	-0.11***	-0.10***	-0.11***	0.00	0.02	-0.01
	(0.03)	(0.03)	(0.03)	(0.03)	(0.03)	(0.03)
Constant	1.26***	1.46***	1.15**	0.74	0.73	0.69
	(0.38)	(0.38)	(0.37)	(0.44)	(0.44)	(0.43)
Inflation factor (logit)						
SMD	0.53***	0.50***	0.52***	0.33**	0.31**	0.33**
	(0.11)	(0.11)	(0.11)	(0.12)	(0.12)	(0.12)
Constant	1.41***	1.38***	1.40***	1.40***	1.39***	1.39***
	(0.08)	(0.08)	(0.08)	(0.08)	(0.08)	(0.08)
Vuong z	6.04	5.74	5.59	5.56	5.74	5.60
Prob > z	0.000	0.000	0.000	0.000	0.000	0.000
Observations	3,998	3,790	3,790	3,790	3,790	3,790
Nonzero obs.	500	455	455	455	455	455

Robust standard errors in parentheses; *$p < 0.05$; **$p < 0.01$; ***$p < 0.001$
GDP, gross domestic product; PR, proportional representation; SMD, single-member district

Inducements and Deterrents to Change

The state of the economy at or near the time of a given election, as measured here, matters for the evolution of the legislative party system once representatives have won their seats. As Table 7.3 exhibits, greater affluence (i.e., greater gross domestic product [GDP] per capita) and greater growth in GDP tend to accompany greater parliamentary party system change between elections. Greater income inequality, registered as higher values on the Gini index, instead tends to dampen legislative party system change. The coefficients for these economic variables have consistent signs and statistical significance in models 13 through 18. The electoral constraints on switching relax during good economic times and tighten when adversity is at hand. Yet, even when economic circumstances enter into view, the argument here finds support.[4]

As noted, researchers disagree about the impact of formal education on voters' preferences. Whereas some scholars suggest that better educated voters likely attend more closely to candidates' policy promises, implying greater deterrents on incumbent interparty mobility, others argue that widespread education weakens voter partisan attachments, which would loosen electoral deterrents. As revealed in models 16 through 18 here, once economic growth enters the picture, the mean education level of the national adult population has no effect on change and stability in the parliamentary party systems. And introducing the *Education* measure leaves our argument intact.

We are keen to discern the impact of institutions on MP partisan strategy because political scientists concur that the formal rules of political competition channel the behavior of officeholders. Our argument focuses on the role of electoral laws, and other scholars have treated presidentialism, federalism, and age of democracy as potential influences on party systems (e.g., Amorim Neto and Cox 1997; Mainwaring and Zoco 2007; Ordeshook and Shvetsova 1994). What we discover shores up the argument we advance. Yet we acknowledge that our results on the import of institutions may well be limited by the relatively small number of countries in the dataset; the findings on presidentialism and federalism just cited illustrate this point. Indeed, specific institutional features (subtypes of SMD rules, subtypes of PR, semi-presidentialism, presidentialism per se, regionalization stopping short of full federalism, and so forth) combine to create so many distinct permutations of institutional formats that the number of democratic regimes in the world might not suffice for conclusive tests. This possibility does not provide counsel for despair. Rather, it leads to the next step in the analysis.

7.2.4 Inducements and Deterrents with Institutions, Economic Conditions, and Party System Properties at the Most Recent Election

Political scientists have analyzed attributes of party systems as products, in part, of electoral laws and other institutions. In that light, our estimations

---

[4] Missing data on the economic and education measures reduce the number of observations in Table 7.3.

now incorporate the effective number of parliamentary parties at the outset of a given legislative term, immediately after an election; we exclude from consideration presidentialism and federalism so as not to overspecify the models. In models 19 through 21, to the left of Table 7.4, the coefficients on the key explanatory factors in our argument once again display the expected signs and statistical significance. The economic variables and *Age of democracy* preserve the signs and significance demonstrated earlier as well. We now learn that the higher the effective number of parties at the start of a term, the greater the degree of party system change during the term. This result holds, as do the findings in favor of our argument, when the raw number of parties replaces the effective number of parties in the estimations (details available from the authors). The greater the number of membership options open to incumbents, the more often they move among parties. This finding makes intuitive sense.

Yet it is possible that some policy questions so thoroughly permeate and transform politics that they void our theoretical argument about the evolution of parliamentary party systems between elections. We consider the Cold War as one potentially overriding political set of issues that might supersede the operation of the stimuli and restraints on MP behavior posited here. As noted, the Cold War context might have worked in one of two ways. Perhaps electoral deterrents to MP interparty mobility faded away when the harsh international confrontation deflected voter attention from legislator partisan disloyalty in the domestic sphere. Alternatively, electoral deterrents might have strengthened when the rigid international divisions injected foreign policy into domestic politics and heightened the stakes of any MP failure to toe party lines. Given the results just revealed, we examine the impact of the Cold War era in models 22 through 24, along with the number of membership options – the effective number of parties at the term's onset. Because we study Romania only after the Cold War – with those observations lacking variation on this factor – we drop Romania from the analysis.[5]

As the right half of Table 7.4 registers, the geopolitical context does not consistently exercise a statistically significant influence on the evolution of parliamentary party systems. Again, the more parties gain representation at the outset of the term, the more interelectoral party system change occurs. And, once more, legislators introduce change to parliamentary party systems during active stages of the parliamentary cycle and refrain from doing so when election time is near: our argument is sustained. Variants of models 22 through 24 using the raw number instead of the effective number of parties generate results analogous to those arrayed in Table 7.4 (details available from the authors).

---

[5] Because economic growth marks much of the Cold War era, we omit it and the other economic variables from the analysis. We also drop *Age of democracy*, which is lower during the Cold War.

TABLE 7.4 *Explaining the absolute number of switches (cap of fifty) with quadratic time in term, stages, party system attributes at start of term, economic conditions, and international context; zero-inflated Poisson regression.*

	(19)	(20)	(21)	(22) Romania excluded	(23) Romania excluded	(24) Romania excluded
Time left in term, SQ	0.0002***	0.0003***	0.0004***	0.0004***	0.0003***	0.0005***
	(0.0000)	(0.0000)	(0.0000)	(0.0000)	(0.0000)	(0.0000)
Time since start of term, SQ	0.0002***	0.0002***	0.0002***	0.0003***	0.0003***	0.0003***
	(0.0001)	(0.0001)	(0.0001)	(0.0001)	(0.0001)	(0.0001)
Proportional	1.24***	1.14***	1.14***	0.69***	0.59***	0.64**
	(0.14)	(0.14)	(0.14)	(0.10)	(0.10)	(0.10)
Time since start of term, SQ × PR	−0.0004***	−0.0003***	−0.0003***	−0.0003***	−0.0002***	−0.0003***
	(0.0001)	(0.0001)	(0.0001)	(0.0001)	(0.0001)	(0.0001)
Stage A	0.70***	—	—	0.57***	—	—
	(0.10)			(0.09)		
Stage B	—	0.91***	—	—	1.03***	—
		(0.07)			(0.07)	
Stage D	—	—	−0.64***	—	—	−0.53***
			(0.15)			(0.14)
Effective number of parliamentary parties	0.24***	0.23***	0.25***	0.40***	0.41***	0.41***
	(0.05)	(0.06)	(0.06)	(0.05)	(0.05)	(0.05)
Age of democracy	−0.0004***	−0.0004***	−0.0004***	—	—	—
	(0.0001)	(0.0001)	(0.0001)			
GDP per capita	0.05***	0.05***	0.05***	—	—	—
	(0.01)	(0.01)	(0.01)			
Gini	−0.04***	−0.04***	−0.04***	—	—	—
	(0.01)	(0.01)	(0.01)			
Economic growth	0.13***	0.12***	0.12***	—	—	—
	(0.02)	(0.02)	(0.02)			

TABLE 7.4 (cont.)

	(19)	(20)	(21)	(22) Romania excluded	(23) Romania excluded	(24) Romania excluded
Education	−0.04 (0.02)	−0.04 (0.02)	−0.04 (0.02)	—	—	—
Cold War	—	—	—	0.16* (0.08)	0.15 (0.08)	0.14 (0.08)
Constant	−0.16 (0.47)	0.18 (0.47)	0.05 (0.46)	−1.06*** (0.20)	−1.19*** (0.19)	−1.05*** (0.20)
Inflation factor (logit)						
SMD	0.32** (0.12)	0.29* (0.12)	0.33** (0.12)	0.55*** (0.10)	0.52*** (0.11)	0.54*** (0.10)
Constant	1.39*** (0.08)	1.38*** (0.08)	1.38*** (0.08)	1.41*** (0.08)	1.38*** (0.08)	1.40*** (0.08)
Vuong z	5.65	5.84	5.68	6.11	6.38	6.21
Prob > z	0.000	0.000	0.000	0.000	0.000	0.000
Observations	3,790	3,790	3,790	3,975	3,975	3,975
Nonzero obs.	455	455	455	479	479	479

Robust standard errors in parentheses; *$p < 0.05$; **$p < 0.01$; ***$p < 0.001$
GDP, gross domestic product; PR, proportional representation; SMD, single-member district

Inducements and Deterrents to Change

7.2.5 Societal Cleavages as Barriers to Change in Parliamentary Party Systems

One basic way to characterize a society is to map its ascriptive cleavages. When societal groups seek representation of their preferences in politics and through the party system, specific parties can come to articulate the interests and concerns associated with ethnic, linguistic, or religious groups (e.g., Amorim Neto and Cox 1997; Caramani 2004; Horowitz 1985; Lipset and Rokkan 1967; Ordeshook and Shvetsova 1994). Societal divisions of this sort would segment electorates and erect barriers to legislators who might wish to move among parliamentary parties. Because, as we argue, voter preferences constrain change in the parliamentary party system, it would stand to reason that voters in a sharply segmented electorate would staunchly oppose incumbents' moves out of parties "owned" by their respective societal groups. Nor would MPs be readily welcomed in parties representing constituent groups other than their own. For that matter, deputies bound to societal groups might not respond to the time-based incentives and disincentives to change posited here.

As a look at models 25 through 27 in Table 7.5 shows, of the three commonly explored lines of societal division – ethnic, linguistic, and religious – only the latter exerts a statistically significant impact on MP interparty mobility. The greater the religious fractionalization (as measured by Alesina et al. 2003; 2011), the more parliamentary party system change is suppressed. This effect increases notably during active stages (models 27 and 28), when it counteracts inducements to change that otherwise might boost switching.[6]

Just as the impact of religious fractionalization merits attention, so, too, does the corroboration of the key explanatory forces in our argument. Even while taking into account variation in the cleavage structure underpinning a party system, the coefficients on all measures tapping time-based inducements and deterrents preserve their expected signs and statistical significance in models 25 through 29. Even in societies that are relatively divided along religious lines, elected representatives react to the inducements and constraints hypothesized here.

7.3 PRESENCE OR ABSENCE OF MP SWITCHING

The inquiry so far has focused on the scale of change in parliamentary party systems and has yielded evidence bearing out our theory. We now look at the incidence of any change while disregarding its magnitude. We operationalize

---

[6] The system with the highest religious fractionalization in the dataset is the United States, followed closely by Australia. The countries with the lowest values on the religious fractionalization index are Italy and Romania. These facts point to a problem: given the relatively few countries in the dataset, the societal fractionalization measures identify country clusters.

TABLE 7.5 *Explaining the absolute number of switches (cap of fifty) with quadratic time in term, stages, and societal fractionalization; zero-inflated Poisson regression.*

	(25)	(26)	(27)	(28)	(29)
Time left in term, SQ	0.0003*** (0.0000)	0.0003*** (0.0000)	0.0002*** (0.0000)	0.0002*** (0.0000)	0.0004*** (0.0000)
Time since start of term, SQ	0.0002*** (0.0001)	0.0002*** (0.0001)	0.0002*** (0.0001)	0.0002*** (0.0001)	0.0002*** (0.0001)
Proportional	1.11*** (0.08)	1.15*** (0.08)	0.49*** (0.13)	0.29* (0.13)	0.48*** (0.13)
Time since start of term, SQ × PR	−0.0003*** (0.0001)	−0.0003*** (0.0001)	−0.0003*** (0.0001)	−0.0003*** (0.0001)	−0.0003*** (0.0001)
Stage A	0.61*** (0.09)	0.60*** (0.09)	0.71*** (0.09)	–	–
Stage B	–			1.05*** (0.07)	–
Stage D	–			–	−0.64*** (0.14)
Ethnic fractionalization	−0.10 (0.16)	–	–	–	–
Linguistic fractionalization	–	0.17 (0.20)	–	–	–
Religious fractionalization	–	–	−2.01*** (0.34)	−2.37*** (0.33)	−1.71*** (0.33)
Constant	0.24* (0.10)	0.15 (0.10)	1.56*** (0.24)	1.70*** (0.24)	1.40*** (0.24)
Inflation factor (logit)					
SMD	0.79*** (0.10)	0.80*** (0.10)	0.71*** (0.10)	0.66*** (0.10)	0.71*** (0.10)
Constant	1.26*** (0.07)	1.25*** (0.07)	1.25*** (0.07)	1.22*** (0.07)	1.24*** (0.07)
Vuong z	6.22	6.21	6.15	6.37	6.21
Prob > z	0.000	0.000	0.000	0.000	0.000
Observations	4,072	4,072	4,072	4,072	4,072
Nonzero obs.	519	519	519	519	519

Robust standard errors in parentheses; $*p < 0.05$; $**p < 0.01$; $***p < 0.001$
PR, proportional representation; SMD, single-member district

incumbents' changes of party with the *Fact of switching*, coded 0 when no legislator moves in a given month and 1 when MPs carry out any number of switches. When the magnitude is ignored, will the incentives and disincentives to incumbent interparty mobility that we posit still operate, or will they be overwhelmed by "noise" in MP behavior? And, if we encounter noise, then what factors might hold explanatory weight?

Inducements and Deterrents to Change 135

We conduct probit estimations to address these issues because we seek to explain the likelihood of interparty mobility. As listed on the left of Table 7.6, models 30 through 32 examine our theory alone. The coefficients on all time-based deterrents to switching have the expected signs and statistical significance. The sign and significance of the coefficient on the interactive term, *Time since start under PR*, again points to a conditional midterm effect. The active stages, as expected, boost the probability of MP interparty mobility, whereas dormant stages reduce the probability of any change.

We also consider whether a focus on the *Fact of switching* helps identify factors that might loosen the constraints we posit. As discussed, one school of research flags weakly institutionalized party systems as characterized by relatively malleable voter preferences; the implication is that the deterrents to change might falter in such systems. We adopt the Romanian fixed effect as a proxy for weak party system institutionalization, and we include other institutional variables in models 33 through 35, as shown to the right of Table 7.6. Whereas the effective number of parliamentary parties at the start of the term increases the probability of the incidence of switching, federalism and presidentialism exert no significant impact. Romania evinces a relatively great likelihood of interparty mobility throughout the term, as indicated by the positive and statistically significant coefficients on the fixed effect. This result on Romania emerges for the *Fact of switching*, although not for the magnitude of change (estimations analogous to those in Tables 7.1–7.5 including the Romanian fixed effect are available from the authors). Weak party system institutionalization thus seems to allow for less constrained partisan behavior on the part of incumbents. Our model overall captures the "noise" in the Romanian system not exhibited by other countries in our dataset, even though the coefficients on a few variables tapping elements of our argument fade in strength.

7.4 STABILITY, SOLO MOVES, OR MASS MOVES

Now that we have examined the overall magnitude of MP interparty mobility and the fact of switching, the next task is to investigate the potential qualitative distinction in strategic conditions between a solo switch and mass moves. It is always up to the individual legislator to decide to transfer party allegiance, and it is the choice of the individual MP that becomes part of legislative records. Yet it is possible that when many individual decisions to switch coincide at (roughly) the same time – in a given month – they can yield valuable collective outcomes for incumbents. One might even imagine that the inducements, as generated by the active stages of the parliamentary cycle, would no longer be needed to prompt change: perhaps once a sizeable group of mobile MPs gets a bandwagon rolling, even founding a new parliamentary party, additional incumbents might jump on for the ride. The accumulated MP interparty mobility in a particular

TABLE 7.6 *Explaining the fact of switching with stages, quadratic time in term, party system attributes at start of term, and institutional effects; probit.*

	(30)	(31)	(32)	(33)	(34)	(35)
Time left in term, SQ	0.0001*	0.0001**	0.0001**	0.0001	0.0001	0.0001**
	(0.0000)	(0.0000)	(0.0000)	(0.0000)	(0.0000)	(0.0000)
Time since start of term, SQ	0.0003***	0.0003***	0.0003***	0.0003***	0.0003***	0.0003***
	(0.0000)	(0.0000)	(0.0000)	(0.0000)	(0.0000)	(0.0000)
Proportional	0.67***	0.64***	0.64***	0.24*	0.20	0.20
	(0.09)	(0.09)	(0.09)	(0.11)	(0.11)	(0.11)
Time since start of term, SQ × PR	−0.0002*	−0.0001*	−0.0001*	−0.0001	−0.0001	−0.0001
	(0.0001)	(0.0001)	(0.0001)	(0.0001)	(0.0000)	(0.0001)
Stage A	0.25*	—	—	0.27*	—	—
	(0.12)			(0.12)		
Stage B	—	0.25**	—	—	0.27**	—
		(0.10)			(0.10)	
Stage D	—	—	−0.36***	—	—	−0.38***
			(0.09)			(0.09)
Effective number of parties	—	—	—	0.25***	0.24***	0.24***
				(0.05)	(0.05)	(0.05)
Romania (weakly institutionalized)	—	—	—	0.34*	0.36*	0.38*
				(0.17)	(0.17)	(0.17)

Federal	—	—	—	−0.12 (0.07)	−0.12 (0.07)	−0.11 (0.07)
Presidential	—	—	—	0.10 (0.08)	0.09 (0.08)	0.11 (0.08)
Constant	−1.58*** (0.05)	−1.58*** (0.05)	−1.53*** (0.05)	−2.10*** (0.14)	−2.10*** (0.14)	−2.06*** (0.14)
Pseudo–R2	0.06	0.06	0.06	0.07	0.07	0.08
Prob > χ^2	0.000	0.000	0.000	0.000	0.000	0.000
Observations	4,072	4,072	4,072	4,072	4,072	4,072

Robust standard errors in parentheses; *$p < 0.05$; **$p < 0.01$; ***$p < 0.001$
PR, proportional representation; SMD, single-member district

month, by itself, might furnish benefits to the additional switcher to join along. Does this scenario hold, so that mass moves arise from processes different from those driving solo or small-group moves?

The analysis summarized in Table 7.7 tackles that question. We conduct ordered probit estimations because we use an ordered categorical dependent variable. As noted, this measure is coded 0 for those months when no MP switches, 1 for those with up to nineteen interparty moves, and 2 when twenty or more moves occur; the last category captures most but not all months when new parliamentary parties emerge in the dataset. What does Table 7.7 reveal? First, and most fundamentally, our argument survives this test. The estimations registered on the left of the table (models 36 through 38) strip the theory to its basics, much as did the models in Table 7.1 and models 30 through 32. Reinforcing earlier findings, models 36 through 38 demonstrate that MPs' propensities to carry out both solo and mass interparty moves hinge on the temporal stages of the parliamentary cycle and the temporal distance to elections. The incentives supplied in active stages still motivate MPs to transfer allegiance, and the dormant stage still suppresses change in parliamentary party systems; the coefficients on these variables consistently attain statistical significance. The coefficients on all variables tapping time-based deterrents continue to display their expected signs and coefficients.

Models 39 through 41, on the right of the table, take into account key features of the party system and institutions: the effective number of parliamentary parties at the start of the term, federalism, and presidentialism. The greater the effective number of parties gaining parliamentary representation, the greater the probability of months with both solo and mass moves. Controlling for the effective number of parties, federalism and presidentialism play significant roles, with federalism somewhat reducing and presidentialism increasing the probability of solo and mass moves. The conditional midterm effect again appears, as shown by the negative and significant coefficients on the interactive *Time since start of term under PR* in conjunction with a positive and significant effect on *Time since start of term*. Yet the conditional midterm effect is less pronounced here than in the analysis of the magnitude of change.

Hence, the inducements offered in active stages instigate moves, even when many incumbents enter into the fray at (roughly) the same time. The argument about deterrents to change in legislative party systems applies to both solo and mass moves, although the impediments differ in strength: the initiating election exerts a relatively powerful check on any change in the parliamentary party system. Overall, once more, the argument is sustained.[7]

---

[7] Estimations with a threshold of thirty yield much the same results and are obtainable from the authors.

TABLE 7.7 *Explaining the occurrence of solo and mass moves with quadratic time in term, stages, party system attributes at start of term, and institutional effects; ordered probit.*

	(36)	(37)	(38)	(39)	(40)	(41)
Time left in term, SQ	0.0001**	0.0001**	0.0001***	0.0001*	0.0001*	0.0001**
	(0.0000)	(0.0000)	(0.0000)	(0.0000)	(0.0000)	(0.0000)
Time since start of term, SQ	0.0003***	0.0003***	0.0003***	0.0003***	0.0003***	0.0003***
	(0.0000)	(0.0000)	(0.0000)	(0.0000)	(0.0000)	(0.0000)
Proportional	0.70***	0.67***	0.66***	0.31**	0.28**	0.28**
	(0.09)	(0.09)	(0.09)	(0.11)	(0.11)	(0.11)
Time since start of term, SQ × PR	−0.0002**	−0.0002*	−0.0002*	−0.0001*	−0.0001	−0.0001*
	(0.0001)	(0.0001)	(0.0001)	(0.0001)	(0.0001)	(0.0001)
Stage A	0.28*	—	—	0.30*	—	—
	(0.12)			(0.12)		
Stage B	—	0.30**	—	—	0.32***	—
		(0.10)			(0.10)	
Stage D	—	—	−0.37***	—	—	−0.38***
			(0.08)			(0.09)
Effective number of parliamentary parties	—	—	—	0.26***	0.26***	0.26***
				(0.04)	(0.04)	(0.04)
Federal	—	—	—	−0.14*	−0.15*	−0.13
				(0.07)	(0.07)	(0.07)

TABLE 7.7 (cont.)

	(36)	(37)	(38)	(39)	(40)	(41)
Presidential	–	–	–	0.16*	0.17*	0.18**
				(0.07)	(0.07)	(0.07)
Cut 1	1.59	1.60	1.54	2.16	2.16	2.12
	(0.05)	(0.05)	(0.05)	(0.13)	(0.13)	(0.13)
Cut 2	3.20	3.21	3.16	3.78	3.79	3.75
	(0.09)	(0.09)	(c.09)	(0.16)	(0.16)	(0.16)
Pseudo–R2	0.06	0.06	0.06	0.07	0.07	0.07
Prob > χ^2	0.000	0.000	0.000	0.000	0.000	0.000
Observations	4,072	4,072	4,072	4,072	4,072	4,072

Robust standard errors in parentheses; *$p < 0.05$; **$p < 0.01$; ***$p < 0.001$
PR, proportional representation; SMD, single-member district

7.5 THE RELATIONSHIP BETWEEN INTERELECTORAL PARTY SYSTEM CHANGE AND ELECTORAL VOLATILITY

Our premise is that when individual MPs adopt a new party affiliation, they bring change to the parliamentary party system. MPs' decisions can result in the emergence or disappearance of parliamentary parties, and, more often and not less importantly, shifts in the sizes of existing parties. All of these, as Chapter 2 illustrated, have the potential to alter legislative outcomes: with each change introduced by the individual incumbent, the balance of power in the parliament is redefined. Not by accident, scholars in one research tradition treat parliamentary party systems as "decisive structures." The systems do stand as decisive structures, endowed with decision-making powers, predicted to and able to make different decisions depending on the array of their components. This makes every modification in parliamentary parties, no matter how small, potentially of great importance.

Yet scholars who emphasize the linkages from elections to party systems would contend that voters' decisions are paramount in settling parties' fates from one election to the next. Even more, such scholars might expect that any interelectoral parliamentary party system change might amount to a short-term failure of strict accountability, to be corrected at the next election, when voters cast their votes. To these scholars, what voters decide in the next election is the ultimate test of whether the party system has genuinely changed. These scholars would then focus on electoral volatility, which, as discussed at the outset of this study, is the measure used to assess the overall degree of change in voter support between any two successive elections. Homing in on electoral volatility, these scholars would expect voters at the next election to "restore" parliamentary party systems to the status quo established at the prior election: voters would act to undo any interelectoral change worked by sitting MPs.

Table 7.8 probes these ideas by taking the parliamentary term as the unit of analysis. The dependent variable now becomes electoral volatility in election $t + 1$, the election that follows parliamentary term w, launched in its turn by election t. A number of likely explanatory variables appear in the table: electoral volatility in election t (from election $t - 1$); the effective number of parties at t; the length of term w, separating elections t and $t + 1$ and thus giving time for voters to adjust their opinions and preferences; and the cumulative number of switches executed by incumbents in parliament w, serving between elections t and $t + 1$. Those estimations including term length (models 42 through 46) omit the United States, given its very short and fixed terms. As seen, in estimations without the United States, only the cumulative number of MP interparty moves exercises a statistically significant effect on the subsequent shift in electoral returns; that effect is positive. When the analysis extends to the United States, both electoral volatility at t and cumulative switching during term w boost volatility at $t + 1$.[8]

---

[8] The data point for France 2007 (as compared to 2002) is missing, bringing the number of term observations to 109.

TABLE 7.8 *Explaining electoral volatility in election* t + 1; *GLS.*

	(42) U.S. out	(43) U.S. out	(44) U.S. out	(45) U.S. out	(46) U.S. out	(47) With U.S.	(48) With U.S.
Volatility at election t	0.54* (0.23)	–	–	–	0.31 (0.19)	0.33* (0.16)	–
Term w's length	–	0.12 (0.08)	–	–	0.03 (0.08)	–	–
Effective N parliamentary parties at t	–	–	5.51* (2.51)	–	1.77 (1.97)	2.32 (1.39)	–
Cumulative N of switches in term w	–	–	–	0.11*** (0.03)	0.07* (0.03)	0.07** (0.03)	0.12*** (0.03)
Constant	4.93** (1.76)	5.28 (3.25)	–4.86 (6.51)	7.50*** (0.74)	–0.60 (6.34)	–1.55 (3.77)	6.28*** (0.57)
R-squared	0.19	0.04	0.18	0.37	0.41	0.47	0.40
Prob > F	0.012	0.035	0.031	0.000	0.000	0.000	0.000
Observations	79	82	82	82	79	105	109

Robust standard errors in parentheses; *p < 0.05; **p < 0.01; ***p < 0.001

Yet does this finding amount to a tautology? Might voters modify their preferences from one election to the next (t to $t + 1$ in the models), and might parliamentary incumbents during the intervening term (w) merely adapt to what voters have come to want? If that were so, the degree of electoral volatility at the next election ($t + 1$) would be a function of the flux in voter opinion and the capacity of elites to meet it: voters, not incumbents, would drive the story. To be sure, in a sense, voters must either accept or reject the alternatives that political elites place in front of them, and if new parliamentary parties participate in election $t + 1$, they will win at least a few votes. In this light, MP choices on affiliation during a term are mechanically the precursor to electoral volatility following that term (cf. Tavits 2008). It is possible that the dynamics in parliament anticipate the readiness of voters to realign. We do not have the information to refute this notion, and the question cannot be settled definitively. Although it is normatively appealing for voters to lead in this process of communication and adaptation, with MPs adjusting in advance, it is also possible that voters can become followers who validate elite players' prior choices.

That latter scenario emerges when we use the large-N dataset to explore when we would most likely see incumbent interparty moves aimed at accommodating shifts in voter preferences. If MPs wanted to meet voter opinion, they would need to move in close proximity to the next election, when they would have the most current information on which to act. Our own hypotheses suggest the opposite and are supported with the evidence adduced so far. Yet, to go the proverbial

Inducements and Deterrents to Change

extra mile, suppose it is only right before an election that politicians switch to anticipate the evolution in voter opinions. Coding the last six months before an election as the election run-up period, we test for this possibility. Analogs of the models in Tables 7.1 through 7.5 that incorporate the *Election Run-Up* dummy in place of an active stage disconfirm the notion (rivaling our *H2*) that, just before the next election, incumbents would switch for electoral advantage and in anticipation of altered voter preferences.[9]

These results buttress the interpretation we offer. We see no positive evidence either that elections reverse interparty mobility during the term or that incumbents jump party to chase voter opinion right before an election. By the light of these data, sitting legislators supply an impetus to the overall shift in vote choices: the greater (or lesser) MP interparty mobility is during a term, the greater (lesser) the electoral volatility after that term.

Assuming that this discussion resolves the tautology, and that incumbents' interparty moves prompt volatility in subsequent elections, we can track which type of MP within-term mobility spells party system change for voters. The models in Table 7.9 return to the endeavor of explaining electoral volatility at election $t + 1$, but now include as separate explanatory variables three familiar intervals in which individual MPs might alter the party system: the affiliation (A), benefits (B), and dormant (D) stages. Calculating now the cumulative total of MP moves in each type of interval for each term in our data, we obtain aggregate measures of politicians' activity or inactivity associated with the different stages. To capture another way that incumbents reshape party systems between elections, we code a new dummy variable, assigning the value of 1 when the raw number of parliamentary parties changes during the term and 0 when the number remains the same.[10] A caveat must accompany use of this dummy variable in conjunction with the cumulative number of switches, however, because switching is a necessary but not sufficient condition for a change in the number of parliamentary parties. With caution, in the estimations reported in Table 7.9, we thus use the stage-specific cumulative numbers of MP moves alongside the dummy variable of change in the number of parliamentary parties. We again include as an explanatory variable electoral volatility in election t (from election $t - 1$).

Table 7.9 discloses that what incumbents do during a term has consequences that reverberate at the subsequent election. Although the cumulative number of MP switches during a term, as an inclusive category, strongly affects volatility in

---

[9] The coefficients on *Election Run-Up* lack significance while the key variables in our argument still perform as expected (details obtainable from authors). We are prevented from using more fine-grained cutoffs for the election run-up by the within-nation variation on such cutoffs, both subnationally (e.g., United States) and over time.

[10] We code only a change in the raw number of parliamentary groups, not a change in identities; if one party splits and two others merge during a term, leaving intact the raw number of parties, this term registers no change on the dummy variable. This coding strategy biases our estimations away from the expectation of elite influence on electoral outcomes.

TABLE 7.9 *Electoral volatility in election t +1 with stage-specific cumulative switching and change in the number of parliamentary parties; GLS.*

	(49)	(50)	(51)	(52)	(53)	(54)
Volatility at election t	0.36*	0.59**	0.50*	0.51*	0.51*	0.50*
	(0.18)	(0.21)	(0.22)	(0.22)	(0.22)	(0.22)
Cumulative N of Stage A switches in term w	–	0.11 (0.12)	–	0.05 (0.12)	–	–
Cumulative N of Stage B switches in term w	–	0.05 (0.03)	–	–	0.01 (0.05)	–
Cumulative N of Stage D switches in term w	–	0.47 (0.31)	–	–	–	−0.07 (0.32)
Cumulative N of switches in term w	0.09** (0.03)	–	–	–	–	–
Change in N of parties during term w	–	–	5.92* (2.57)	5.47† (2.84)	5.74† (3.20)	6.10* (2.94)
Constant	3.80*** (1.10)	2.88* (1.27)	3.05* (1.36)	3.00* (1.36)	3.04* (1.36)	3.08* (1.34)
R-squared	0.45	0.29	0.33	0.33	0.33	0.33
Prob > F	0.000	0.000	0.002	0.005	0.002	0.002
Observations	105	105	105	105	105	105

Robust standard errors in parentheses; †$p < 0.1$; *$p < 0.05$; **$p < 0.01$; ***$p < 0.001$

the next election (model 49), the coefficients on the stage-specific totals of interparty moves have positive signs yet lack statistical significance (model 50). What is clear is that change in the number of parties during a term boosts subsequent electoral volatility (model 51). Including one of the variables tapping single-stage cumulative moves along with the dummy isolating a change in the number of parties in models 52 through 54, we discover that a change in the number of parties relatively strongly influences voters at the next election; the dummy attains statistical significance at generous levels in models 52 and 53 and at conventional levels in model 54.

Throughout our study, both theoretically and empirically, we treat the MP's decision *to move* among parties as based on beneficial opportunities that arise from parliamentary politics. The pressure of elections instead motivates the MP's decision *to stay* with her status-quo party. We have just recounted a story, based on Table 7.9, in which political elites lead voters and have the de facto discretion to do so. In discussing Table 7.8, we argued that MP interparty mobility during a term gave an impetus to change in voters' choices in the subsequent election. We now add that electoral change follows elite change in the term, in the form of both MP choices on partisanship, which modify the weights of parliamentary parties, and also, even more strongly, MP decisions to alter the number of parliamentary parties. When system change happens during the term, voters in the next election catch up.

Inducements and Deterrents to Change 145

TABLE 7.10 *Cumulative number of member of parliament (MP) moves during term, by electoral system and change in number of parliamentary parties.*

Parliamentary terms (N)	Election rule	Cumulative Number of Switches (% of terms)						N Terms
		0	1	2–5	6–9	10–19	≥20	
All terms	SMD	26.83%	25.61%	26.83%	7.32%	6.10%	7.32%	82
	Mixed	6.67	0	46.67	20.00	6.67	20.00	15
	PR	0	0	0	0	7.69	92.31	13
Only terms with change N parties	SMD	0	0	16.67	25.00	25.00	33.33	12
	Mixed	0	0	0	0	0	100	3
	PR	0	0	0	0	0	100	11

Cell entries are percentages, save for the rightmost column, where number of terms per category appear. PR, proportional representation; SMD, single-member district

The question remains: how much switching does it take for sitting legislators to alter the number of parliamentary parties? As Table 7.10 shows, the answer differs markedly depending on the system used to elect the legislature. When the number of parties changes in a parliament elected under relatively candidate-centered rules, MPs achieve this outcome relatively economically: the cumulative number of switches falls below ten in 41.7 percent of SMD legislatures witnessing a change in the number of parliamentary parties. In the German hybrid system, as in the PR systems, all terms that experience a change in the number of parliamentary parties see twenty or more cumulative interparty moves. Yet a striking contrast separates the PR and German systems, as the rightmost column reveals: 84.6 percent of PR terms undergo a change in the number of parliamentary parties, whereas the same is true for 20 percent of the German terms and 14.6 percent of the SMD terms. This evidence reinforces the finding, already established, that candidate-centered rules impart stability to parliamentary party systems.

7.6 CONCLUSION

In this chapter, we have taken a path made up of many steps. Throughout this journey, whether the theory is pruned to its essentials or other explanations are weighed, all of our hypotheses are sustained, with the coefficients on our explanatory variables displaying the expected signs and attaining statistical significance. Incumbents switch in response to inducements available during active stages of the parliamentary cycle and stay loyal during the dormant stage. The approach of the next election diminishes MP interparty mobility. The evidence shows as well that legislators elected under candidate-centered rules avoid betraying their party early in the term: conditional on use of candidate-centered rules, a midterm effect appears. Two distinct processes generate the magnitude of switching in SMD and PR systems, as indicated by the zero-inflated Poisson models. The role of electoral institutions recurs as a prominent element of the findings: overall, more incumbents move between parties in parliaments elected by PR. Our argument accounts for the incidence of any switching and accounts, too, for the occurrence of both solo (or small-group) and mass moves, with PR rules continuing to exert a positive, significant influence. We then shift the view to parliamentary terms. What incumbents do between elections to remake the parliamentary party system, as tapped by the cumulative number of switches during the term, does much to explain electoral volatility after the term – so much so that the impact of usual suspect explanations ebbs away. A change in the number of parliamentary parties during the term also has a discernable impact on electoral volatility following the term.

All steps together and by themselves support our argument. Elected representatives, pulled by parliamentary inducements, introduce change to interelectoral party systems; they are checked by electoral deterrents as well. Both forces operate to account for stability and gradations of change in parliamentary party systems. Moreover, the change that legislators bring to party systems while in parliament affects volatility at the next election.

8

Comparative Statics: Where Our Assumptions May Not Apply

Each chapter so far has contributed to the overarching argument that, on the one hand, the concerns, priorities, and preferences of voters dampen any impulse that elected representatives might have to change party affiliation, and that, on the other, political institutions define opportunities and inducements for representatives to seize the moment to switch party. The first chapter introduced the argument in the broadest strokes, the second chapter demonstrated the import of party system change between elections, and the third developed a formal model to elaborate the argument about interelectoral party system change and stability. Chapters 4 through 7 evaluated the model's testable implications via both intensive case studies and large-N statistical analyses. The findings lend substantial, consistent, and strong support to our claims.

Yet we grant that the assumptions on which the formal model is grounded – and thus the hypotheses we have extracted – are not the only way of understanding the phenomenon of incumbents' strategic choices on partisan affiliation. It is possible that, in some places and times, voter preferences do not deter incumbents from moving out of their original party and into another one. Thus, in this chapter, we imagine a state of the world that stands as an alternative to what we have posited theoretically and examined empirically.

In the first section, we spell out the elements of that alternative state of the world. The next two sections of the chapter appraise the record of incumbents' exercise of their discretion to move out of their electoral parties. The second part examines the frequency of legislative switching, and the third, the enforcement of curbs on switching. We contend and show that the enforceability of institutional curbs on incumbent interparty mobility depends in part on the nature of voter preferences.

8.1 WHAT DIFFERENCE DO ASSUMPTIONS MAKE?

Throughout the book, we have adopted commonplace assumptions about voters: that voters care to some degree about matters of public policy, and that voters prefer, other things equal, those candidates for elective office who have remained loyal to their original parties. That is, we assume that voters like what parties are and do as an institution. In a world in which voters prefer that legislators refrain from switching party, and legislators care about reelection (Mayhew 1974), strategic legislators should heed voter preferences and should stay put in their status-quo party unless there are overwhelming inducements to change. This is the world we have inhabited throughout the study.

Now consider the contrasting scenario, one in which voters might or might not care about policy but pay little attention to candidates' and incumbents' histories of party affiliation. Parties are not important to these voters and may be even perceived in a negative light. In this alternative world, voters would focus not on past loyalty to a party label but instead on such factors as candidate personality, ethnicity, or delivery of pork and local public goods. Although voters would not actively encourage representatives to hop from party to party, neither would their preferences constrain incumbent interparty mobility. In this setting, strategic legislators should feel relatively free to seize opportunities to benefit from a change of party affiliation while serving in office.

Given the assumptions about voters' preferences as we have maintained them so far, we have submitted our argument to varied tests and probed its generalizability in multiple ways. An even more robust assessment of our logic would study what happens when we relax the foundational assumption of a partisan electorate. To grasp the role and import of an assumption, we need to let it go – let it vary, not stand as a (near) constant. If removal of the condition of the relatively partisan electorate does *not* generate findings that depart from what we discover when we assume partisan voters, then either the assumption is redundant or our logic requires revision. In this chapter, then, we engage in comparative statics, comparing settings in which the basic assumption of relatively well-defined voter preferences for incumbent partisan loyalty does and does not apply.

8.2 INTERELECTORAL PARTY SYSTEM CHANGE AS A FUNCTION OF VOTER PREFERENCES

This picture of two states of the world leads to the proposition that relatively partisan electorates should inhibit incumbent switching. Conversely, where voter preferences over the partisanship of their representatives are weakly defined, incumbent interparty mobility should be relatively frequent.

Table 8.1 arrays measures of the aggregate frequency of legislator switching against depictions of voter preferences. For switching, diversity in the information available forces use of four kinds of indices. The first three pertain to legislator behavior alone: mean percentage of members of parliament (MPs) switched per year (as in, e.g., Ecuador), mean percentage of MPs switched per term (e.g., Malawi), and percentage of MPs switched at least once over a

TABLE 8.1 *Voter preferences and aggregated measures of member of parliament (MP) interparty mobility.*

MP Moves	Voter preferences for candidate partisan loyalty	
	Widespread	Limited
Low	BR: MPs from districts with partisan voters CZ: 10.5% returning candidates between 1996 and 1998 elections CH: 0.5–1% / term 1999–2007 DK: 3% 1966–1968 FI: zero MPs 1990s HU: 6% 1998–2002, 1.6% 2006–2010 terms NO: 5 MPs total 1990s NZ: Pre-1996 reform ZA: 6% 1999–2004; 8% 2004–2009	JP: Pre-1990s, save for 1976 LDP breakaway
High	EP: 16% MPs 1989–1994 IL: 12–25% MPs / term 1992–2006 NZ: 13% MPs 1993–1996; 9% 1996–1999	BG: ~20–25% MPs / term 1991–2005 BR: 33–39% / term 1991–2001 CZ: 62% returning candidates between 1990 and 1992; 55% returning candidates between 1992 and 1996 EC: ~10% / year 1979–2002 EE: 75% returning candidates between 1992 and 1995; 43% returning candidates between 1995 and 1999 GT: 35% 2000–03; 52% 2004–07 HU: 24% 1990–1994; 12% 1994–1998 ID: Rare solo, many mass moves 1999–2004 IN: Eight major party splits over 1952–1985 terms IT: 22% 1948–1953 JP: 40.7% at least once 1990–1998 KR: 60.6% at least once 1988–2007 LS: At least 15% 2002–2007 LT: 29% returning candidates between 1992 and 1996; 33% returning candidates between 1996 and 2000 LV: 33% returning candidates between 1993 and 1995; 53% returning candidates between 1995 and 1998; 30% returning candidates between 1998 and 2002 ML: Mean 35% / term 1994–2007

TABLE 8.1 (cont.)

MP Moves	Voter preferences for candidate partisan loyalty	
	Widespread	Limited
		PG: "Frantic" hopping 1975–1990s
PH: "Rampant" 1990s; 48% 1992–1995
PO: *44% returning candidates between 1991 and 1993; 61% returning candidates between 1993 and 1997*
TH: Switching "abounded" 1979–1996
TR: 28% at least once 1987–2007
UA: 56% 1998–2002

Given diversity across available studies, we use four distinct measures here: mean percentage of MPs switched per year, mean percentage of MPs switched per term, percentage of MPs switched at least once over multiple terms, and percentage of legislative candidates who run on different labels in two successive elections, which taps some unknown component of MP behavior. Italics indicate electoral as opposed to parliamentary switching.

Sources on legislator behavior: Heller and Mershon (2009c, 11) and the two dozen sources therein. In addition: ACE (2011); Desposato (2009); Electoral Institute for the Sustainability of Democracy in Africa (2010); Fortín (2008); Hicken (2006b, 388; 2009, 152–156); Israel, Knesset (2011); Tan (2006, 108); Khelmko (2011, 203); Kopecký and Spirova (2008, 144); Kreuzer and Pettai (2003, 85); Kselman (2009, 175–176); McElroy (2003, 4); Mejía Acosta (2004, 163); Nemoto (2011, 113, 116); Nikolenyi and Shenhav (2009, 16, 19, 23); Owens (2003, 18, citing personal communication); Matti Wiberg (2002); Reilly (1999); Shabad and Slomczynski (2004, 153–154); South Africa, Parliament (2010); Switzerland, Parliament (2008); Thai (2006); Vowles (2000, 687); Vowles, Banducci, and Karp (2006, 280); Young (2012).

Sources on voter preferences: Dalton and Weldon (2007, citing CSES Modules I and II); Hicken (2009a, 154); Tan (2004; 2006); Kselman (2009, esp. 198–199); Norris (2004, 132, citing CSES Module I); Sayarı (2007); Vowles, Banducci, and Karp (2006, 278); Vowles, Karp, and Banducci (2000); Young (2012).

Key to country acronyms: BG, Bulgaria; BR, Brazil; CH, Switzerland; CZ, Czech Republic; DK, Denmark; EC, Ecuador; EE, Estonia; EP, European Parliament; FI, Finland; GT, Guatemala; HU, Hungary; ID, Indonesia; IL, Israel; IN, India; IT, Italy; JP, Japan; KR, South Korea; LS, Lesotho; LT, Lithuania; LV, Latvia; ML, Malawi; NO, Norway; NZ, New Zealand; PG, Papua New Guinea; PH, Philippines; PO, Poland; TH, Thailand; TR, Turkey; UA, Ukraine; ZA, South Africa

multiterm span (e.g., South Korea). The fourth measure taps some unknown component of MP behavior: the percentage of legislative candidates who run under different labels in two successive elections (e.g., Latvia). Given the diversity just described, we adopt crude rules of thumb to dichotomize switching frequency as relatively low or high. For characterizations of voter preferences, we rely on what amounts to expert judgments. That is, we synthesize how country experts describe voters' views of their representatives; survey data on party identification are available to inform such judgments for only some countries. The judgments we report on voter preferences are also dichotomized. The proposition just outlined means that observations should cluster in the

Comparative Statics

upper left and the lower right cells of the table. Few cases should populate the two other cells.[1]

The clearest feature of the table is that most cases fall into place as expected. This finding aligns with highly influential work on party system institutionalization (e.g., Mainwaring 1999). In what follows, we offer thumbnail sketches of several – not all – systems meeting expectations. We then discuss all systems that qualify as anomalous; that is, all that appear in the upper right and lower left cells of Table 8.1.

8.2.1 Illustrative Cases Meeting Expectations

We start with the upper left of the table. Those cases in which legislative switching is relatively low and voter preferences for candidate partisan loyalty are relatively widespread differ in numerous ways, including number of parties in the party system, relationship between the executive and legislature, and age of democracy. Notably, in the Czech Republic and Hungary, the emergence of a partisan electorate seems to have roughly coincided with a decline in incumbent interparty mobility.

Now turn to the lower right quadrant of the table. In post-Marcos Philippines, legislators, candidates, and voters attach little importance to the party label (Hicken 2009a, 151, 154; cf. Hicken 2009b, 11–12). Party platforms are virtually indistinguishable in policy terms; in fact, in one recent election, it was merely a different font that set apart the platforms of several parties because the same set of consultants had composed otherwise similar platforms for the parties (Hicken 2009a, 155). In a similar vein, "Thailand lacks politicized or particized ethnic or religious cleavages" (Hicken 2006b, 390). Moreover, Thailand ranked second to last in the percentage of respondents with party identification among the thirty-two countries included in the 1996–2002 Comparative Study of Electoral Systems (CSES, as reported in Norris 2004, 132). In both the Philippines and Thailand, incumbent interparty mobility is "rampant" (Hicken 2009a, 149).

In South Korea as well, voters tend to focus on personality rather than ideology (Nemoto 2011, esp. 3–4). Presidents, parties, and individual legislators alike leave aside policy concerns and are motivated by office and its perks – posts, pork, and patronage. Indeed, the ideological profiles of legislators show remarkable overlap (Nemoto 2009, 104–108; 2011, 16). Party organizations exist "on paper, but they are only cliques (*bungdang*) or factions (*padang*), ... depend[ing] on single notable politicians' personal ambitions."[2] As the president

---

[1] Our coding here accounts for whether percentages are computed annually or observed over a multiyear span; hence, we regard the mean of 10 percent MPs switching annually in Ecuador as higher than the 10.5 percent mobile nonincumbent and MP candidates observed over a multiyear span in the Czech Republic.

[2] Former speaker of the South Korean National Assembly, as quoted by Nemoto (2011, 8).

approaches the end of her constitutionally mandated single five-year term, her public approval tends to fall and, some evidence suggests, those contending for the presidency begin to promise some MPs office benefits as a lure to join their party (Nemoto 2011, 10–11). The aggregate upshot is that 60.6 percent of South Korean legislators have switched at least once over the 1998–2007 span (Nemoto 2009, 116).[3]

Voters in Papua New Guinea have long voted for candidates as individuals, not partisan representatives, focusing on clan identity and the incumbent's capacity "to deliver direct benefits to the community" (Reilly 2005, 51). Parties have been so weak that analysts deem them "largely irrelevant to the electoral process" (Okole 2008, 183). Legislators have switched party so often that country specialists deem it "impossible to keep track of the affiliations of many of them" (Okole 2008, 199).

Personalism dominates politics in Ecuador. As one former president put it, "in Ecuador, parties have a last name and a first name."[4] From 1979 to 2002, on average, 10 percent of Ecuadorian deputies switched per year (Mejía Acosta 2004, 163). Moreover, "since voters apparently place little weight on the party label, legislators ... switch parties without jeopardizing their electoral prospects" (Morgenstern 2002, 422).

Personalistic voting has also long prevailed in Brazil. One scholar takes stock of the evidence as follows: "most [Brazilian] voters have little interest in parties per se as collective entities" (Samuels 2006, 20; cf. Desposato 2006a; Desposato and Scheiner 2008). From 1991 to 2001, at least one-third of MPs switched at least once per term (Desposato 2009, 110; cf. Ames 2001; Desposato 2006a,b; Mainwaring 1999; Mainwaring and Pérez-Liñan 1997). Desposato (2006a, 70) reports that most mobile incumbents he interviewed "seemed to think that voters simply didn't care about party membership."

Brazil is where we find the within-nation variation that lends additional support to the proposition here. In Brazilian districts with relatively partisan electorates (as proxied by mean education levels), relatively few MPs defected (Desposato 2006a). Moreover, temporal variation in Brazil speaks to the importance of voters' preferences in deterring switching: overall, Brazilian MPs were more, not less, likely to switch in proximity to the next national legislative election (Desposato 2009). With a relatively nonpartisan electorate nationwide, this pattern comports with our *H2* in reverse. What we assume about voters is central to fulfillment of the second hypothesis in this study.

In much of sub-Saharan Africa, with the notable exception of South Africa, parties display "programmatic homogeneity" (van de Walle 2003, 304), and voters identify and vote along ethnic – often ethno-regional – lines (e.g., Ferree 2010; Ferree and Horowitz 2010). To one team of experts, evidence from

---

[3] Analyzing a dataset of monthly observations on South Korean MP behavior, Nemoto (2011) finds that the likelihood of switching rises as presidential elections near.
[4] Jamil Mahuad, former president of Ecuador, as quoted by O'Neill (2005, 168).

Malawi "confirms a generally established pattern for African party systems in which the combination of presidentialism and clientelism offers incentives for individuals to maintain small, personalized parties rather than consolidating strong opposition parties" (Rakner, Svåsand, and Khembo 2007, 1132). In Malawi, politicians pursue votes and office, not policy, and switch in efforts to achieve those aims; on average, 35 percent of MPs changed affiliation per term from 1994 to 2007 (Young 2007; cf. Young 2012).

The relatively partisan South African electorate deserves attention. One nuanced study finds that "party labels are heavily racialized in South Africa and play a powerful [role] in shaping voting behavior" (Ferree 2006, 804; cf. Ferree 2011). As Table 8.1 indicates, legislative party switching was relatively limited in South Africa after the lifting of a constitutional ban on this form of elite discretion.

8.2.2 Anomalies

Only four anomalies emerge in Table 8.1. Consider Japan, where "voters are mobilized at election time mainly by the lure of pork barrel, only marginally by policy issues, and even less by ideals and visions" (Fukui and Fukai 1996, 268–269, as cited by Desposato and Scheiner 2008, 512). Yet Japan witnessed limited switching before the early 1990s, save for a 1976 splinter from the ruling Liberal Democratic Party (LDP) – and the 1955 merger that created the LDP itself. The LDP's secure hold on national governing power long glued its MPs to their party label. Once the largest LDP faction broke away from the party in late 1992, other defections ensued and the party lost its grip on power (Cox and Rosenbluth 1995; Kato 1998; Reed and Scheiner 2003). By one estimate, 40.7 percent of Japanese legislators switched at least once between 1990 and 1998 (Nemoto 2009, 113). As long as the LDP stood as the invulnerable governing party, its power seems to have frozen legislators' party affiliations in place between elections.

Conversely, three systems exhibit greater switching than would be expected, given relatively partisan electorates. The European Parliament (EP) at first blush runs counter to our proposition. As McElroy (2003, 4) shows, 15 percent of members of the EP (MEPs) switched during the 1989–1994 term. This fits oddly with what we know about the relatively partisan national electorates of member states of the European Union (EU). Attention to the nature of EP elections resolves and removes the apparent discrepancy. National issues, not European-level ones, drive EP elections; voters often treat EP contests as an opportunity to punish national governments (e.g., Hix and Marsh 2007; Reif 1997; Reif and Schmitt 1980). National parties, not European-level party groups, compete in EP elections, so that "the value of the political group label in the context of European elections is minimal" (McElroy 2003, 5). What is more, for MEPs, electoral incentives are either "not obvious" or "absent" (McElroy 2003, 6, 5). Because the assumptions on which our logic is based do not operate, we should observe divergent outcomes – and we do. Largely freed of the electoral connection, MEPs switch for office benefits internal to the EP and for policy goals as well (McElroy 2003).

In New Zealand before the 1990s, legislative party switching was so rare as to go unremarked. As the transition to a new electoral system approached, however, "the first wave of 'party hopping'" unfurled between 1993 and 1996 (Vowles, Banducci, and Karp 2006, 280; cf. Vowles 2000; Vowles, Karp, and Banducci 2000). The backdrop to the electoral reform was a shift in voter opinion: in the 1970s and 1980s, minor parties drew rising voter support without commensurate legislative representation under the first-past-the-post (FPP) rules. Electoral volatility increased as well. In 1993, a binding popular referendum approved the introduction of a mixed-member proportional system (MMP). In one expert's judgment, "Most New Zealanders who voted for MMP did so because they believed the three most recent governments elected under FPP since 1975 had failed to keep faith with voters" (Vowles 2000, 684). In the first parliament elected under MMP (1996–1999), switching continued, although at a slightly lower level than in the last term under FPP (Vowles 2000, 687). Official changes of affiliation have subsided in the years since, as discussed later.

Israel presents the last anomaly in Table 8.1. Israel ranks second highest in the percentage of respondents with party identification among the thirty-two nations in the 1996–2002 CSES (Norris 2004, 132). Why, then, is MP interparty mobility as high as it is in and since the 1990s, as listed in Table 8.1? It is possible that legislators' actions have responded to and helped to influence a recent personalization of mass behavior and politics generally in Israel (Rahat and Sheafer 2007). The puzzle deepens in light of the 1991 constitutional amendment that penalized switching. We treat Israel further as we turn to institutional curbs on elite discretion.

8.3 ENFORCEMENT OF CONSTRAINTS ON SWITCHING AS A FUNCTION OF VOTER PREFERENCES

The reasoning just presented about voters and representatives in two states of the world points the way to another proposition. Where rules are adopted to prohibit changes of party during the legislative term or to limit switching in some way (e.g., by specifying a narrow window of time when moves may occur), they are likely to be upheld where legislators face a relatively partisan electorate. After all, where voters prefer steadfast partisanship on the part of their representatives, legislators who flout antiswitching laws risk electoral defeat. Strategic incumbents in such circumstances should obey the rules curbing elite discretion. Again consider the contrasting scenario: rules restricting switching are less likely to stick where voter preferences over the partisanship of their representatives are loosely defined. Therefore, relatively partisan electorates should make formal constraints on switching enforceable.

Comparative Statics

TABLE 8.2 *Voter preferences and the enforcement of curbs on member of parliament (MP) discretion in party affiliation.*

	Voter preferences for candidate partisan loyalty	
Enforcement	Widespread	Limited
Operative	Hungary New Zealand Spain South Africa	Brazil[b] Portugal[b]
Lax or limited	Israel[a]	Bulgaria Ecuador India[a] Lesotho Malawi Papua New Guinea Romania

We are forced to omit from the table those democracies with antiswitching legislation (as of ~2005–2007) for which data on switching are lacking.
[a] Evaluations are complex given confounds, as discussed in the text.
[b] For the boxed cases, as discussed in the text, questions of different kinds arise about voter preferences.

Table 8.2 builds on Table 8.1, borrowing the earlier portrayals of voter preferences and levels of switching. Table 8.2 focuses only on places and times where constraints on MP interparty mobility are in place, be they constitutional provisions, legislation, or parliamentary standing orders. We draw information on barriers to switching from Janda (2009, 4), who in turn relies on a survey of party officials conducted by the International Institute for Democracy and Assistance (IDEA 2006). We set up Table 8.2 so that, once more, cases aligning with expectations appear in the upper left and lower right cells.

Our proposition receives substantial support. Where electorates are relatively partisan, institutional constraints effectively deter legislators from changing party affiliation while in office. Where voter preferences for the partisan loyalty of their representatives are instead relatively weakly defined, enforcement of institutional curbs appears to be lax. Our narratives start with the most patent failures in enforcement.

8.3.1 Parchment Barriers

In Ecuador, the legislature in 1998 approved a Code of Ethics that would deprive a switcher of her seat as long as a plurality vote determined that she had violated the Code. The leaders of the governing Popular Democratic party had championed the law in an effort to ease the building of legislative coalitions (Mejía Acosta 2004, 201). As Mejía Acosta (2004, 201–202) demonstrates, however, "in practice [the Ethics Code] has never been applied to any particular case, since party leaders formed ad hoc coalitions to shield their new allies from being expelled." Mejía Acosta (2004) brands this repeated flouting of the formal rules "impunity by consent," a means by which Ecuadorian presidents have gained approval for their initiatives in a fragmented legislature. Presidents have reached agreements with legislative party leaders that typically are concealed from public view, dole out patronage, and span multiple parties. To supplement those deals, as needed, presidents have negotiated with small parties and single deputies, including mobile MPs. Because switchers have at times made pivotal contributions to legislative coalitions, the 1998 Code of Ethics has proven ineffective. Thus, on the whole, the Ethics Code stands as a "failed reform" (Mejía Acosta 2004, 259). Indeed, the actors who pushed for the reform have worked to render it inoperative: they found that the Code "tied their hands and feet" because leaders were left without bargaining chips available to entice political cooperation.[5]

The 1994 Malawian Constitution removes a switcher from legislative office, stipulating that the speaker of the national legislature is to pronounce a seat vacant if a legislator changes party and that a by-election is to ensue (Malawi 2010). Yet political actors have repeatedly maneuvered around these rules. The powerful president, who typically benefits from legislators flowing into his party, can truncate legislative sessions and prevent a vacancy from being declared. For his part, the speaker may not apply the rules if his party attracts new entrants (Young 2008, 16; cf. Bertelsmann-Stiftung 2009a, 4–5; Patel, Tambulasi, Molande, and Mpesi 2007, 34). At times, clusters of interparty moves have overwhelmed the electoral commission's capacity to organize by-elections. MPs have dodged penalties by, for instance, caucusing with a party without formally changing affiliation (Young 2008, 15–16). Any account of enforcement, however, must emphasize the power and the incentives of the Malawian president. Sitting presidents have, on occasion, called for a repeal of the constitutional punishment of switching (Art. 65) when it has threatened to deprive the presidential party of recent recruits to the party. Much stronger is their ongoing interest in preserving the possibility that MPs might cross the floor so that they can use their substantial resources to lure recruits in the future (Patel et al. 2007; cf. Kadima 2008, esp. 217; Young 2012). The constitutional prohibition on switching has amounted to the proverbial dead letter.

The standing orders of the Romanian Chamber of Deputies seem to protect the monopoly of current party leaders: MPs cannot enter a parliamentary party that has not already earned seats in elections (Chiva 2007, 203–204; Parlamentul României 2008b). Moves to join (or found) splinter parties or start-ups are impossible under these rules. Romania witnessed only one fusion from 1996 to 2004. In one sense, the rules had teeth, in that no splits or

---

[5] MP Ramiro Rivera, leader of Popular Democracy party, as quoted in Mejía Acosta (2004, 244).

Comparative Statics

brand-new parliamentary parties appeared. Overall and disregarding the single merger, interparty mobility has been relatively high. Switching has abounded in the presence of regulations that do not serve or strengthen the electoral connection. In this sense, the proposition just offered is upheld.

8.3.2 Loose Constraints

Political elites in Papua New Guinea introduced a package of reforms in 2002 with the status of constitutional laws. The Organic Law on the Integrity of Political Parties and Candidates was intended to foster greater stability in the executive and in the party system (Okole 2008; Reilly 2005; 2007). In particular, the Organic Law stipulates that partisan MPs have to toe the party line on such key divisions as votes of confidence "or face a possible by-election. As *every* government elected prior to 2002 fell prematurely due to party-hopping, these reforms constitute one of the most far-reaching attempts to engineer a party system anywhere in the Asia-Pacific region" (Reilly 2007, 67, emphasis in original). Moreover, the Organic Law imposes structure on parliamentary parties by, for example, requiring election of officers and naming of members (Okole 2008, 190–191, 193). Too, it requires defectors to face a commission charged with determining the validity of defection; the only valid grounds for exit are the party's insolvency or breach of its own constitution (Miskin 2003, 26). One report credits the Organic Law with stabilizing government, noting that the prime minister served a full term from 2002 to 2007; yet it observes as well that, during that span, eleven MPs hopped party without losing office (Bertelsmann-Stiftung 2009a, 9). This figure, 10.1 percent of all incumbents, even after the introduction of the Organic Law, suggests loose constraints.

8.3.3 Constraints with Confounds

Consider together two constitutional amendments whose effects and enforcement are difficult to pin down. In 1985, the Indian legislature approved a constitutional amendment that deprived switchers of their seats. In 1991, the Israeli parliament passed a similar constitutional amendment. In both systems, advocates of reform cited the aims of greater governmental stability and improved accountability (Nikolenyi and Shenhav 2009, 20, 24–28, 32). The Indian amendment immediately disqualified the mobile MP from legislative office. The Israeli one allowed a switcher to serve out her term but prohibited her from competing in the next election on the list of any party represented in the outgoing legislature. As a confound, both reforms stipulated that if the number of MPs moving to establish a splinter party overcame a threshold, the MPs involved would face no penalty for defection and the resulting new parliamentary group would gain recognition. The threshold in India was one-third the size of the original parliamentary group. In Israel, creating a new party through fusion or fission was the ticket to staying in parliamentary politics for the switchers; as few as two MPs, if moving from groups of fewer than six, and three from groups of six or more could claim entry into a new group.

On its face, the antidefection law in Israel proved ineffective. An average of 7.5 percent of MPs changed party per legislative term from 1949 to 1988, before the reform, and 7.5 percent hopped in the 1988–1992 Knesset, when the reform was enacted. A mean of 15.8 percent of MPs switched per term from 1992 to 2009 (drawn from Nikolenyi and Shenhev 2009, 23; Israel, Knesset 2011). By promoting the creation of new parliamentary parties, this amendment may have contributed to the personalization of Israeli politics, already under way (Rahat and Sheafer 2007).

For India, judgments diverge. Nikolenyi (2009, 23) contends that the Indian reform "discouraged party defections in the legislature ... [and] had the unintended consequence of encourag[ing] would-be deputies to form both smaller and ideologically more compact parties before the electoral race." Miskin (2003, 27) labels the antidefection amendment "problematic." India's Chief Election Commissioner in 2001 regarded it as "ineffective" and attributed the continuing "malaise of defection" to the partisan speaker of the legislature.[6] An official white paper in 2001 highlighted that defections increased rather than decreased after the reform; given the threshold provision, solo hops became rare but collective moves were quite common (Kashyap et al. 2001). Finally, since the late 1980s, ethnic parties have reappeared and flourished in India, after several decades of decline. In Chandra's (2005) analysis, this trend has resulted from institutional encouragement of politicized ethnic identities; these effects further confound appraisal of constraints on switching.

8.3.4 Clear Constraints with Questions on Voter Preferences

A different sort of question appears in Brazil. In March 2007, the Supreme Electoral Court (TSE) ruled that the electoral mandate for politicians elected under proportional representation (PR) pertained to parties, not individuals. In April 2007, the Supreme Court upheld that ruling, and, in October 2007, the TSE applied the ruling as well to politicians elected under plurality rules, such as federal Senators, mayors, and even the president (Desposato 2006a). Some observers interpret the Courts' rulings as "a response to a rash of party switching in 2002–2003 and 2006–2007 that facilitated President Lula's efforts to construct a coalition in Congress," and more broadly as part of a "judicialization of politics" in Brazil (Fleischer 2010, 3). Since October 2007, legislative party switching has disappeared, both in the national Chamber of Deputies and the State Assembly of São Paolo (Cunow 2010; Desposato 2009, 140–141).

The impact of the Courts' rulings seems clear. And yet complicating the assessment is not only the recent increase in the power of judicial actors but

---

[6] Manohar Singh Gill, Chief Election Commissioner, June 2001, as quoted in Miskin (2003, 28).

Comparative Statics

also, according to some scholars, a recent emergence of greater attention to party labels both in the electorate and among legislators. Hagopian, Gervasoni, and Moraes (2009) maintain that, since the early 1990s, some Brazilian legislators have become more party-oriented in response to a new programmatic cleavage created by market reforms. Hagopian and colleagues find in a 1999–2000 survey of parliamentary elites that those MPs who believe that voters care about party label are relatively unlikely to switch. They interpret the 2002 elimination of guaranteed renomination of candidates (the *candidato nato* rule), often seen as lowering the cost of switching, as possibly due to the rise of party-oriented deputies (2009, 382). Thus, the rallies around Lula aside, a change under way before the introduction of constraints might be inducing compliance now. The change in question is just the sort envisioned in our argument: if, over time, voters come to attach greater importance to partisan loyalty on the part of their representatives, then (some) deputies should come to switch less frequently. By our logic, any formal constraint should effectively rein in switching – and it does.

Readings of the Portuguese electorate differ. Significantly, party identification is relatively widespread (Norris 2004, 132), and some scholars stress that party sympathies structure the vote (e.g., Freire and Baum 2003; Magalhães 2008). Other scholars emphasize the relatively high aggregate shifts in vote shares registered in Portugal from one election to the next; even interbloc electoral volatility is high in Portugal (e.g., Gunther 2002; Gunther and Montero 2001). We do not attempt to take sides in this debate. The fact is that the Portuguese Constitution prohibits a legislative incumbent's entry into a new parliamentary party group but permits an incumbent's exit from her electoral party. That is, the constitution stipulates that deputies who enroll in a party different from the one in which they competed at election time will lose their seat. Another constitutional provision opens a door to mobile deputies, however, in that candidates can run on a party list without being formally enrolled in the party, and such candidates, if elected, may serve as independents without losing their mandate or may constitute a parliamentary group on their own. Any MP may move, moreover, to become and remain an independent (Portugal 2010b,c; Tomás Mallén 2002, 159–169). Thus, for instance, during the 1983–1985 term, two groups of independents, each elected on a distinct party list, coordinated to establish their own group, which represented 2.8 percent of MPs. During the 2005–2009 legislature, 0.8 percent of deputies changed affiliation (Portugal 2010a). Although we lack comprehensive data on Portugal, the available information suggests that switching is low. In this setting, rules stick.

8.3.5 Windows and Sunsets

The 1996 South African Constitution prohibited legislative party switching. In 2002, however, the governing African National Congress (ANC) introduced a constitutional amendment to permit representatives to change affiliation.

The bill gained approval in 2003 not only from the ANC but also from the largest opposition party, the Democratic Alliance, and several small opposition parties. Two kinds of limitations remained: switches were confined to two two-week windows per term, and defectors had to move simultaneously and make up at least 10 percent of their original party's legislative seats (Booysen 2006; Kadima 2008; Randall 2008; Reilly 2008). Logically, the 10 percent clause would favor large parties, in that the smaller the party, the fewer MPs needed to meet the threshold and the more easily they could coordinate to defect (cf. Kadima 2008). In practice, the rules enlarged the dominant ANC, expanding it beyond the two-thirds of the seats it typically won in national legislative elections (Booysen 2006, 635; Kadima 2008, 213–214; Randall 2008, 254; Reilly 2008, 16). In fact, the ANC lost not a single seat in the National Assembly or in provincial councils due to switching (De Jager 2009, 229). As for voter preferences on incumbent partisanship, a 2003 public opinion poll reported that 63 percent of South Africans, "across race and class divides," disapproved of floor crossing (De Jager 2009, 230). First, the dominant ANC in 2007 at its National Conference approved a resolution to abolish floor crossing entirely, and then the legislature in 2008 rescinded the law enabling switching (De Jager 2009, 115, 230).

The legislature in New Zealand passed an antidefection law in 2001 that would automatically expire after two elections. Writing before the sunset clause ended the law, Miskin deemed the law "unworkable" and a "dismal failure" (2003, 32, iii). We see a reason for this judgment, but read the outcomes differently. The law's particulars merit notice: switchers who informed the legislature's speaker in writing that they would resign from their electoral parties would be stripped of office, and a party leader could, with the support of two-thirds of the parliamentary group, force an errant MP out of office. Under these provisions, one of the main advocates of the antiswitching legislation split his parliamentary party with impunity. Internal party disagreements on interparty relations led MP Jim Anderton, leader of the Alliance party both in and out parliament, to announce in April 2002 his intention to found – later – a new party (Miskin 2003, 32; Van Beynen 2010). Anderton submitted nothing in writing to the speaker and mustered the backing of half of the Alliance MPs. He thus did not officially change party – although analysts concur that he helped bring on the early election of 2002 (Miskin 2003, 32–33; Vowles, Banducci, Karp 2006, 280). We emphasize that Anderton obeyed the letter of the law. In some settings, we have found, outright noncompliance is a frequently chosen option. This was not so in New Zealand, which corroborates the second proposition here. As the Minister of Health observed in 2005, "the number of [official] defections and resignations from parties has been very small over the past four years."[7] We also have additional evidence favoring the first

---

[7] MP Pete Hodgson, Minister of Health, speaking on behalf of the deputy prime minister, December 6, 2005, as recorded in New Zealand, Parliament (2005).

Comparative Statics 161

proposition: three MPs (2.5 percent) hopped party in the 2005–2008 term; one former MP and no sitting MPs jumped in the 2008–2011 term (New Zealand, Parliament 2011; 2012).

8.4 THE CASE OF SPAIN AS A REFERENCE GROUP AGAINST OUR MAIN FINDINGS

Voter preferences for candidate partisan loyalty in Spain may be viewed as reasonably widespread, as indicated by data on party identification (Norris 2004, 132) and relatively low interbloc electoral volatility (Gunther 2002; Gunther and Montero 2001). In this case, the assumption that is violated pertains to institutions: parliamentary rules open a very small window for interparty mobility in Spain. In February 1982, the Spanish legislature prohibited MPs from joining groups other than the Mixed Group later than five days after the start of the legislative session (personal communication from Bonnie Field, August 2011; Sánchez de Dios 1999, 151; Tomás Mallén 2002, 254). This constraint has largely served to dampen switching: only three of the thirty changes of affiliation in the 1979–1982 term occurred after February 1982; in four of the five legislatures over the 1982–2000 period, the percentage of MPs jumping party ranged from 0.3 to 2.3 per term. The 1986–1989 legislature stands apart: 12 percent of MPs switched, some more than once, as part of the evolution of the Spanish center-right (Tomás Mallén 2002, 197–209). About half of these MPs migrated to the Mixed Group and were thus abiding by the rules. Most of the rest belonged to either of two formations within the Mixed Group that flowed into the large center-right Popular Coalition (CP), in an apparent flexible interpretation of the rules. The CP would become what is today the Popular Party, one of Spain's two major parties. One centrist who crafted the parliamentary rules painted them as deliberately "not individualistic. ... We protected ... the authority of the head of the parliamentary groups over the parliamentarians."[8] The Spanish rules operate as intended, whether applied strictly, as is typical, or somewhat more flexibly. The second proposition is reinforced.

Spain aligns with other country cases in our main dataset, save for the presence of institutional constraints on MP interparty mobility. If not for the rules in effect, we would expect our theoretical argument to hold for the evolution of the Spanish interelectoral party system. It should thus be possible to attribute whatever differences might exist between Spanish patterns and our findings in Chapter 7 to this failure of the assumption on institutions.

Consider the cumulative raw number of MP interparty moves during the term, which Chapter 7 analyzed in explaining electoral volatility. Table 8.3 partitions the terms we study into subgroups according to whether a term

---

[8] MP from the former Union of the Democratic Center (UCD), as quoted in Field (2011, 15).

TABLE 8.3 *Parliamentary terms with cumulative raw counts of switches, by electoral system and change in number of parties during term.*

Cumulative N Switches	Terms without change in N parties			Terms with change in N parties		
	Terms in Main Dataset			Terms in Main Dataset		
	All	PR only	Spain (PR)	All	PR only	Spain (PR)
0	27.38%	0	0	0	0	0
1	25.00	0	16.67%	0	0	0
2–9	39.29	0	50.00	19.23	0	0
10–19	4.76	50.00%	0	11.54	0	0
≥20	3.57	50.00%	33.33	69.23	100%	0
	(84)	(2)	(6)	(26)	(11)	0

Cell entries are percentages, save for bottom row, where total terms in each column appear between parentheses.

witnessed a change in the number of parliamentary parties and what electoral rules are used to elect the parliament. The table also sets apart Spain, and the effects of the antiswitching rules are clear. The number of parliamentary parties has stayed the same across all Spanish terms here, in striking contrast to the other parliaments elected under PR in the main dataset.

To appreciate further the impact of the Spanish institutional constraints, consider analyses along the lines of those presented earlier. When we re-estimate models from Chapter 7 while including Spanish monthly observations, we find that the coefficient for the Spanish country effect is negative and statistically significant. What is more, the coefficient on the affiliation (A) stage dummy is boosted: this is when Spanish MPs are permitted to move. Given the restrictive rules in force, which define a short span for mobility, Spanish MPs stay put not only when the next election looms but also typically throughout the term. Examining Spain as a reference group against our main dataset highlights even more strongly the ability of our argument to identify the forces underpinning change and stability in interelectoral party systems.

8.5 CONCLUSION

The discussion in this chapter has entailed a journey around the world, allowing us to relax – to remove – the foundational assumption that voters prefer partisan loyalty on the part of the legislators they elect to represent them. This exercise in comparative statics has led us to observe variations that carry important lessons: traveling to places where the contrasting scenario on voter preferences holds *does* yield findings divergent from what we have shown where relatively partisan electorates are in place. The difference that assumptions make drives home the capacity of our argument to comprehend one scenario – and its mirror image.

In the theoretical framework set out in Chapters 2 and 3 and empirically supported in Chapters 4 through 7, particular institutions operate as incentives to MPs who bring about change in parliamentary parties and party systems, whereas voters' preferences, beliefs, and expectations impart caution to MPs and induce stability in parliamentary parties and party systems. This chapter has probed a reversal of that view: it removes the assumption that voters punish politicians who are turncoats, and it weighs institutional forces for stability.

We have demonstrated that where voter preferences over the partisanship of their representatives are weakly defined, switching can be frequent, and constraints on elite discretion are weakly enforced. Thus, the common and largely reasonable assumption that voters want representatives to stay where elections put them is an essential theoretical premise in explaining the stability of parliamentary party systems.

9

Conclusions

This book invites a rethinking of the sources of continuity and change in democratic parties and party systems. We seek not to replace the elections-dominant view of parties and party systems but rather to balance it by calling attention to and accounting for change in parties and party systems between elections.

Free, fair, and broadly inclusive elections are essential to the workings of democratic politics. Parties articulate and organize the choices that voters face at election time. The choices that voters make in elections convert a subset of candidates for legislative office into sitting legislators and shape the relative strength of parties as they arrive in the legislature. It is natural that influential schools of research in political science have investigated parties and party systems as creatures of elections. Naturally, too, the bulk of extant research has seen change in party systems as a product of the electoral arena.

This study moves outside the electoral arena. Political parties do not stand as fixed units from one national legislative election to the next. Parties and party systems can and, to variable degrees, do change between elections, without direct recourse to voter judgments, as a result of the decisions of individual members of parliament (MPs). When an individual legislator joins a new party, her switch is not a random characteristic or a behavioral quirk, but is instead an individually rational choice. Each such choice almost always realigns the parliamentary party system to some extent, as an individual incumbent, in choosing to change party, shifts the parliamentary balance of power and reorients possibilities in decision making.[1] We identify the individual-level rationale underlying any change in parliamentary parties: our theoretical argument identifies the forces that induce MPs to decide to change party and that inhibit them from

---

[1] MP interparty mobility would leave intact the overall distribution of party seat shares and party-member preferences only under very restrictive conditions, as noted.

Conclusions

doing so. The abundant, varied evidence we have examined substantiates the hypotheses we have proposed.

The first section of this chapter takes stock of what we have learned. The second addresses how our work can inform further research. The third section elaborates the broader implications of the theoretical argument for the discipline at large.

9.1 REAPPRAISAL: OF TIME AND PARTY SYSTEM STABILITY

Our theoretical and empirical results tell a tale of time and party system stability – and change – between elections. We deliberately invoke the title of Converse's (1969) landmark research, "Of Time and Partisan Stability," which analyzes an individual voter's party identification and also highlights the import of individual behavior for system-level characteristics. For us, voter preferences for party loyalty slow down individual incumbents' moves between parties; the moves of individual incumbents in turn alter the entire system of parliamentary parties. We analyze the MP's readiness to retain or change her party affiliation as a function of factors anchored in time, and we reveal the system-level consequences of individual-level behavior.

We look both at distinct temporal stages of legislative activity during a parliamentary term and at distances in time to the elections bracketing a term. We contend that when active stages of the parliamentary cycle hold out concrete office and policy benefits to representatives, they will be relatively likely to step out into another party to seize those benefits. Approaching the election closing the term, MPs will be averse to moving among parties, constrained by voter preferences for partisan loyalty on the part of representatives. The more the electoral system directs voter attention to individual candidates, the more likely MPs will also be wary of switching early in the term.

The formal model developed in Part One of the book assumes that incumbents care about policy, office, and reelection, whereas voters want legislators to evince loyalty to the party label. The formal model leads to several testable hypotheses, which distill to the notion that legislators should time any changes of party allegiance so as to secure policy and office gains and minimize electoral costs. Moreover, MPs should switch relatively rarely under relatively candidate-focused electoral rules because such rules magnify voters' attention to individual candidates' behavior.

In Chapters 4 through 7, we focus the empirical investigation mostly – although not exclusively – on systems with relatively partisan electorates. The case studies in Chapters 4 and 5 allow us to examine granular evidence bearing on our hypotheses. The most finely detailed data, from 1993–1995 Russia and 1996–2001 Italy, yield a range of findings at the individual level that shore up the hypotheses. Patterns in weekly aggregates of interparty mobility in both Russia and Italy comport with the theory. Even so, Russian MPs overall introduce a greater degree of interelectoral party system change than do their Italian counterparts. This we see as testament to the importance of weakly defined voter preferences in Russia relative to those in Italy. The secondary in-depth cases provide additional evidence that incumbents switch party so as to obtain benefits during active stages of the parliamentary cycle. MPs often also stand firm on party membership as an election nears. The secondary in-depth cases indicate as well that legislators elected under candidate-centered rules, relative to those elected on party lists, rarely jump party soon after the election initiating a term. Overall, interparty mobility is relatively infrequent in candidate-centered systems.

The comprehensive dataset allows us to gauge the applicability of our argument under a wide range of contexts. Chapter 6 sets up the extensive analysis and offers several simple comparisons across the broad swath of the data. Building on that basis, Chapter 7 submits the argument to numerous tests, using three measures of MP interparty mobility. The theory, stripped to its essentials, holds up in multiple estimations. We examine the impact of country specificities on the evolution of interelectoral party systems, incorporating country fixed effects into the models: the argument remains intact. The coefficients on the key indices tapping time-related inducements and deterrents to change continue to display the expected signs and statistical significance. We take into account the potential influence of institutional, socioeconomic, cultural, and international geopolitical conditions: in one step after another in the analysis, the hypotheses are sustained. Elected representatives respond to the pull of incentives held out during active stages of the parliamentary cycle, changing party at those times. Incumbents stay in their original party homes during the dormant stage of the parliamentary cycle and as the next election nears. Legislators elected under candidate-centered rules refrain from switching at the start of the term, in contrast to their counterparts elected on party lists. Overall, representatives in single-member district (SMD) systems move among parties relatively rarely. The theory and findings establish the significance of the timing of parliamentary inducements and electoral impediments to MPs' changing their affiliation and bringing on the interelectoral evolution of parliamentary party systems.

We observe patterns marching less closely with expectations in Romania, which, among the countries in the comprehensive dataset, least well approximates the key assumption that voters demand incumbent partisan loyalty. Romanian MPs tend to switch more often and less predictably than do legislators in systems with more partisan electorates. The results for Romania, like those for the Russian primary in-depth case, underscore the importance of looking at systems in which voter preferences are relatively loosely defined.

Chapter 8 then opens up to the general possibility that our premise on voter preferences might not apply. We journey to Africa, Asia, Eastern Europe, and Latin America to explore what happens where our model's assumptions do not hold. In systems where the electorate assigns little weight to candidate partisan

Conclusions

loyalty, MP interparty mobility is relatively frequent. In such settings, if formal institutions exist to constrain switching, they tend to be weakly enforced. Relaxing the model's assumptions should, and does, generate findings that diverge from those established in the case studies and the comprehensive dataset.

9.2 ILLUSTRATIVE APPLICATIONS IN FURTHER RESEARCH

This book has by no means exhausted the applications of our theoretical framework. To illustrate, we sketch but three examples of how our argument might guide additional research. First, consider what might happen if we relax the key assumption on voter preferences by traveling not around the world but back in time. Distinguished research in political science contends that voter attachments to parties and voter policy orientations solidified as the franchise was granted to and then exercised by a large electorate, and as, at the same time, parties mobilized the electorate and defended their niches in the electoral market (Lipset and Rokkan 1967; cf., e.g., Bartolini and Mair 1990; Caramani 2004; Mair 1997a). Thus, before and soon after the advent of mass suffrage, when voter preferences over the partisanship of their representatives were weakly defined, incumbent interparty mobility should have been relatively frequent. Observation of two contrasting systems supports this proposition. The available evidence on legislative parties in the United Kingdom reveals repeated episodes of upheaval in parliamentary party systems from 1835 to 1918. Even after 1884, when SMDs came to predominate under continued use of plurality rule, flux in the interelectoral party system was substantial in some parliaments (Mershon and Nokken 2008, esp. appendix B). This record obviously differs from the overall pattern in the United Kingdom since World War II. Moreover, the two legislatures elected in 1919–1922 Italy under proportional representation (PR) laws saw pronounced fragmentation of parliamentary groups during the term, with recurring interelectoral splinters and realignments between elections (Astraldi 1932; Farneti 1978, 24, 23–26; Giusti 1945, 75, 85–86; Grassi Orsini and Quagliarello 1996; Italy, Camera dei Deputati 1919a; 1919b; 1919c; 1920a; 1920b; 1920c; 1920d; 1920e).

Second, taking a completely different tack, our argument directly implies that shorter terms should lead to a lesser magnitude of interelectoral party system change. To see this idea, consider a simple transformation of the base model in Chapter 7: $Mobility_j = k + \beta_1 \text{ Time since start} + \beta_2 \text{ Time left}$ is equivalent to

$Mobility_j = k + \beta_1 \text{Time since start} + \beta_2 \text{ (Length}_w - \text{Time since start)}$, or
$Mobility_j = k + (\beta_1 - \beta_2) \text{ Time since start} + \beta_2 \text{ Length}_w$.

Because we expect for theoretical reasons, and because the evidence from estimations in Chapter 7 suggests that $\beta_2 > 0$, this implies that longer terms should evince more change. Our own initial empirical explorations of this notion indicate its plausibility. The shorter the term, the more limited the autonomy of MPs to reconstitute parties within the parliamentary arena.[2]

We invite other scholars to pursue yet a third question growing out of this study. If we relax our assumption that incumbents anticipate future election timing (Chapter 3, note 8), then where the duration of the parliamentary term is flexible, legislators elected in governing parties would have better information about a snap election than would the opposition. The argument would thus imply that government MPs, compared to opposition MPs, could better time their interparty moves. Hypothesis 2 should hold more strongly for incumbents originating in ruling parties. A robust test of the proposition would have to involve comparisons between systems with flexible and fixed election timing.[3]

These additional applications of the argument direct attention to the relationship between the elaboration of the theory and the empirical analysis. When we first studied 1993–1995 Russia and 1996–2001 Italy (Mershon and Shvetsova 2005a; 2008), we expected, and found, variations in MP interparty mobility according to stage of the parliamentary cycle. That initial examination also pointed to a midterm peak in interparty mobility, unanticipated by our hypotheses at the time. We were guided by the early findings and questions from those two legislatures when we developed a formal model of the inducements and deterrents to MPs' changes of party affiliation. That is why it was necessary for us here to present that model and assess hypotheses extracted from it against the new dataset that extends far beyond the evidence that fed into the elaboration of the model. Our analysis has led us to scrutinize new data on the primary in-depth case studies; for instance, in Chapter 5, we compare the number and timing of interparty moves across subsets of MPs. Our investigation in Chapters 4 through 7 expands first to thirty-three legislatures and then even further to 110 legislatures and more than 4,000 monthly observations of legislator behavior. Chapter 8 opens out the empirical inquiry yet again, relaxing assumptions basic to our theory and drawing on secondary evidence from more than two dozen countries outside our comprehensive dataset. Thus, although a portion of the empirical analysis here was intertwined with the development of the theory, throughout the study, we strive to scrub away any "tautological residue on the models" (Greif and Laitin 2004, 649).[4]

---

[2] Omitting the United States, given its fixed terms, a zero-inflated Poisson estimation discloses that:

Raw N switches (cap of 50) = 0.682 − 0.023 *Time since start* + 0.022 *Length*

The SMD inflation variable and the inflation model are statistically significant at the 0.001 level, as are the coefficients in this model.

[3] We thank George Krause for suggesting this line of research.

[4] To quote in full: "unless the observable implications of our models are statistically examined over a range of cases that were not from the set of cases from which we developed our theory, there will remain a tautological residue on those models. However, statistical tests of the observable implications of the model on aspects of the society that were not analyzed in the formation of the model can serve as a test of the model's validity" (Greif and Laitin 2004, 649).

9.3 BROADER THEORETICAL IMPLICATIONS FOR THE FIELD

This analysis sheds new light on change and stability in parties and party systems. The argument also has broader ramifications for what drives change in institutions, who governs in a democracy, and how parties and party systems operate as instruments of democracy. We turn first to the implication that is perhaps least obviously bound up with the theory.

9.3.1 Sources of Institutional Change

The study of institutions is central to political science. Different approaches, concepts, assumptions, and methods distinguish the three major schools of research: rational choice institutionalism, historical institutionalism, and constructivist institutionalism (e.g., Calvert 1995; Knight 1992; Hall and Taylor 1996; Hay 2006; Rhodes, Binder, and Rockman 2006; Riker 1990; Sanders 2006; Shepsle 2006; Thelen 1999; Thelen and Steinmo 1992). Yet, as analysts have increasingly recognized, work in all schools shares a common problem: difficulty in explaining institutional change. Even while some scholars have taken up the challenge and developed accounts of change, others have continued to emphasize that the "three varieties of institutionalism ... do not provide ... a general model of change, particularly one that can comprehend both exogenous and endogenous sources of change" (Mahoney and Thelen 2010, 6; cf., e.g., Greif and Kingston 2011; Greif and Laitin 2004; North 1990; Pierson 2000; Weyland 2008).

The main task of this book is not to advance a theory of institutional change. All the same, our argument implies that, when it is parliament that enacts institutional reform, an interelectoral shift in the party system ensuing from MP interparty mobility can make possible elite bargains on institutions that were not feasible at the outset of a legislative term. Legislators who care about office, policy, and reelection read and react to information about each of their goals. The role that information plays for strategic MPs is an engine of endogenous change in our story: once again, incentives to incumbents to reconsider party allegiance arise endogenously during the term, as different stages of legislative activity convey information about the varying salience of office and policy benefits; disincentives to MP interparty mobility evolve endogenously, as MPs observe the passage of time from one legislative election to the next. The reasoning also suggests that legislators are alert to new information about voters. Some events revealing such information are endogenous, such as subnational elections, investigated in Chapter 4. Other events are exogenous, such as polls showing public opinion on economic shocks. When legislators move among parties in response to new information about voters, they can transform the balance of power in parliament and create a new coalition capable of approving institutional change.

Episodes of institutional reform illustrate this process. Interelectoral change in the Polish parliamentary party system in the 1990s, partly fueled by MP updating of expectations on popular opinion via polling data, helped create the enacting coalitions for repeated redesigns of electoral laws (Benoit and Hayden 2004). In Japan, it was voter disaffection that spurred defections from the Liberal Democratic Party (LDP), and those defections in turn enabled the passage of a new electoral law in 1994 (Cox and Rosenbluth 1995; Giannetti and Grofman 2011; Kato 1998; Reed and Scheiner 2003).

9.3.2 Control of Government and the Legislative Agenda

Our study also enriches the understanding of who controls the executive in parliamentary and semi-presidential systems and who controls the legislative agenda in presidential systems. The bulk of the large, diverse literature on parliamentary government is grounded in the assumption that executives comprise parties whose weights are established at election time and do not vary between elections (e.g., Diermeier 2006; Lupia and Strøm 1995; Martin and Stevenson 2001; Schofield 1986; 1987; 1993; Schofield, Grofman, and Feld 1988; Schofield and Sened 2006; Strøm 1990b; Strøm, Budge, and Laver 1994; Strøm, Müller, and Bergman 2008). Nonetheless, some contributors to this school explore intraparty politics, such as Laver and Shepsle, who extend their portfolio allocation model by focusing on the impact of party splits and mergers (1999, 36–47; 2006, 257–258; cf. Giannetti and Benoit 2009; Laver 2008). Some work on legislative party switching considers its influence on control of government (e.g., Giannetti and Laver 2001; Laver and Benoit 2003; Laver and Kato 2001; cf. Laver 1989). We offer insights into the mechanism by which individual MPs bring differing degrees of change to parliamentary party systems. We show that the configuration of parties dominating the legislature hinges in part on realignments worked by MPs who choose to change affiliation during the course of a parliamentary term. By redefining party seat shares between elections, incumbents can disrupt the decisive structures put in place at election time; at times, they intentionally do so. MP strategic behavior has consequences for agenda control in presidential systems and for executives in parliamentary and semi-presidential systems.

In presidential systems, incumbents who change party can affect control of the legislative agenda. In the United States, in one move made in May 2001, Senator Jeffords handed control of the Senate to the Democrats and initiated a phase of divided government. Mobile MPs in Brazil and the Ukraine have enlarged the presidential majority (Ames 2001, 191–192, 273–276; Thames 2005, 9, 24). Ecuadorian presidents, as narrated, have secured passage of their initiatives by negotiating with switchers (Mejía Acosta 2004).

In semi-presidential and parliamentary systems, MP interparty mobility can enable minority governments to enact policy and survive. The French Socialist minority government launched after the 1988 election gained approval for its budget with the backing of the Center parliamentary group, founded shortly after the election (Huber 1996, 21, 151–170). After New Zealand's 1996 election, the Nationals and New Zealand First forged a majority coalition that was ended by the 1998 split of NZ First. The Nationals, as a minority, continued in office thanks to former NZ First incumbents who became independents or entered new parties (Vowles 2000, 688). After the 2000 Japanese election, the LDP governed with a lower house minority. Enough Diet members switched by 2001 to give the LDP a majority (Kato and Yamamoto 2009).

Incumbent choices to change party during a term can erode or destroy the legislative majority that had emerged at the preceding election. For instance, in Lesotho, the ruling Congress for Democracy (LCD) saw MP interparty mobility reduce its parliamentary majority from 65.8 percent of the seats, won in 2002, to 50.8 percent by late 2006. The LCD called an early election in an apparent attempt to prevent further attrition (ACE 2011; Thai 2006). In India, splits in the governing party in both 1969 and 1979 deprived the executive of a legislative majority and triggered early elections (Nikolenyi and Shenhav 2009, 16). As Chapter 8 recounted, switchers toppled all governments in Papua New Guinea before 2002 (Reilly 2007, 67). Less dramatically, in 1956, mobile German MPs left the Free Democratic Party, rupturing one majority coalition and ushering in another (Keesing's Contemporary Archives 1957, 15757–15759). British Labour won a narrow majority in October 1974, which dwindled to a minority by April 1976, given three defections and a by-election defeat; by early March 1979, Labour suffered another MP exit and multiple by-election losses. In late March 1979, Labour lost a vote of confidence by a margin of one (BBC 1979; 1997; Butler and Butler 1986 238, 244). That result forced the election that inaugurated eighteen years of Conservative rule.

The Irish case is telling. The November 1982 election reproduced the familiar line-up: Fianna Fáil (FF) as the largest party, Fine Gael (FG) as the second-largest, and Labour as a distant third. This balance broke in December 1985, when FF notable Desmond O'Malley bolted to found the Progressive Democrats (PD), joined by three FF MPs and one from FG. By February 1986, opinion polls revealed the PD as Ireland's second most popular party (*Irish Times*, February 10, 1986), and the PD trumpeted its "Claim to be Cause of Cabinet Reshuffle" (*Irish Times*, February 18, 1986). The PD fed tensions within the FG-Labour government (e.g., Lupia and Strøm 1995, 650–651) and "demoralized" FF deputies (*Irish Times*, January 24, 1986). In December 1986, given PD votes, the Speaker was needed to decide two ties in the lower house (*Irish Times*, December 18, 1986). After the 1989 election, FF abandoned its long-standing refusal to govern in coalition: when FF allied with the PD, "one of the basic parameters of Irish politics" fell away (Marsh and Mitchell 1999, 55). The party system saw fundamental change (Mair 1997c, 219–220; 2006, 67–68; cf. Mair 1989a). We emphasize that the FF's historic coalition was possible because the PD, established outside elections, offered a new alternative to Irish voters at the 1987 and 1989 elections.

Voter choices, as translated by electoral laws, create the configuration of parties capable of dominating decision making in the legislature. MP decisions during a term can modify that configuration and redefine the options for voter choice. Once voters respond to new options at subsequent elections, new alternatives for government composition can open up. The third implication follows and permits us to drive home the lessons and contributions of this study.

9.4 REBALANCING THE CONCEPT OF PARTY SYSTEMS

Distinguished work analyzes political parties as endogenous coalitions of incumbents (e.g., Aldrich 1995; 2011; Cox 1987; 2006; Cox and McCubbins 2005; 2007 [1993]; Laver and Shepsle 1999). A recurring theme is that the leadership of a legislative party cultivates a party brand name, which is perpetuated through the actions of its elected legislators and advertised at election time. This research tradition spotlights the value of party labels to legislative leaders, the legislative rank-and-file, and voters. Elected representatives, by virtue of their behavior, maintain enough fidelity to their districts to pass muster in elections, yet they play the parliamentary game to reap as many benefits as they can. These analyses treat the politician's relationship with a party, on the one hand, and voters, on the other, as an equation that requires careful balancing.

Our argument is similar, yet connects a politician with the entire party system, not just a single party. We understand an entire party system as an endogenous coalitional structure in a democracy, in which coalitions shift as opportunities shift, but a degree of stability is upheld: some stability is valuable because it supports the communication process with voters. An individual incumbent, as a potential recipient of parliamentary benefits, wrestles to identify the optimal strategy in her relationships with voters and her party or parties. Legislative partisanship is, in fact, one of the dimensions of her choice. The combination of optimization problems of multiple incumbents, in turn, reshapes the partisan array as it is perceived in the next round by both voters and politicians. The entire system of parties is altered, in subtle or at times sudden ways.

Hence, our concept of what constitutes a party system and how to characterize it needs amendment in order to incorporate these newly identified moving parts. A party system is less solid and unyielding than might be imagined. Although its component parties are certainly influenced by institutions and have their own multilayered organizations, a party system is not so much a fixture in politics as a result of the ongoing choices of many individual actors. Parliamentary parties and party systems change continuously through time. Any observed stability in a party system should not be viewed with finality, as a settled state prescribed by the rules of the game. Instead, it is a delicate equilibrium balance sustained through the rational actions of multiple sophisticated players within the political elite and through the oversight of rational voters who

Conclusions

are wary of unreliable representatives. Party systems, as malleable alliances of sitting politicians, serve as instruments of democracy, along with regularly occurring competitive elections (cf. Powell 2000). Strategic incumbents have the capacity to reconfigure the party system as established in elections. Representatives are motivated to bring about change by opportunities arising during the parliamentary term. They are deterred from doing so by the elemental democratic practice of elections.

Bibliography

Parliamentary Records

Arnold, Terence. 2005. "Electoral (Integrity) Amendment Bill: Legal Advice, Consistency with the New Zealand Bill of Rights Act 1990." Crown Law Office, Attorney-General, New Zealand Ministry of Justice, November 3. http://www.courts.govt.nz/policy-and-consultation/legislation/bill-of-rights/electoral-integrity-amendment-bill.

Australia, Australian Electoral Commission. 2011. "Australian Voting History in Action." http://www.aec.gov.au/About_AEC/25/theme1-voting-history.htm.

Australia, Parliament, House of Representatives. 2008. *House of Representatives Practice* (5th Edition). http://www.aph.gov.au/house/pubs/PRACTICE/index.htm

Australia, Parliament. 2011. "Parliamentary Handbook." http://www.aph.gov.au/library/handbook/index.htm.

Canada, House of Commons. 2009. "Members of the House of Commons Who Were Suspended from Their Caucus or Who Quit Their Caucus, 1867 to Date." http://www2.parl.gc.ca/Parlinfo/Compilations/HouseOfCommons/OutOfCaucus.aspx?Language=E&Section=Members.

Canada, Parliament. 1997. Hansard. February 4. http://www.parl.gc.ca/HouseChamberBusiness/ChamberIndex.aspx?File=b-38-1_2-e.htm&Language=E&Mode=1&Parl=38&Ses=1&View=H.

Canada, Parliament. 2011. "About the Federal Government." http://www.parl.gc.ca/Parlinfo/pages/federalgovernment.aspx?Menu=Federal.

France, Assemblée Nationale. 2009a. "Archives de la XIIe Législature (2002–2007)." http://www.assemblee-nationale.fr/12/documents/archives-12leg.asp.

France, Assemblée Nationale. 2009b. "Archives de la XIe Législature (1997–2002)." http://www.assemblee-nationale.fr/11/documents/archives-11leg.asp.

France, Assemblée Nationale. 2009c. "Régimes politiques, constitutions et législatures depuis 1789." http://www.assemblee-nationale.fr/histoire/legislatures.asp

France, Ministère de L'Intérieur. 2010. "Résultats électoraux en France." http://www.interieur.gouv.fr/sections/a_votre_service/elections/resultats.

Germany, Bundestag. 2010. "Fraktionsstärken und Fraktionswechsel." In *Datenhandbuch.* http://www.bundestag.de/dokumente/datenhandbuch/05/05_04/index.html Accessed January 2012.
Israel, Knesset. 2011. "Mergers and Splits Among Parliamentary Groups." http://www.knesset.gov.il/faction/eng/FactionHistoryAll_eng.asp.
Italy, Camera dei Deputati. 1919a. *Atti parlamentari Camera dei Deputati*, Sessione 1913–1919, vol. 270, 1 marzo-12 luglio 1919. Roma: Tipografia della Camera dei Deputati.
Italy, Camera dei Deputati. 1919b. *Atti parlamentari Camera dei Deputati*, Sessione 1913–1919, vol. 271, 13 luglio-3 agosto 1919. Roma: Tipografia della Camera dei Deputati.
Italy, Camera dei Deputati. 1919c. *Atti parlamentari Camera dei Deputati*, Sessione 1913–1919, vol. 272, 4 agosto-28 settembre 1919. Roma: Tipografia della Camera dei Deputati.
Italy, Camera dei Deputati. 1920a. *Atti parlamentari Camera dei Deputati*, Sessione 1919–1920, vol. 273, 10 dicembre 1919–7 febbraio 1920. Roma: Tipografia della Camera dei Deputati.
Italy, Camera dei Deputati. 1920b. *Atti parlamentari Camera dei Deputati*, Sessione 1919–1920, vol. 274, 22 marzo-8 maggio 1920. Roma: Tipografia della Camera dei Deputati.
Italy, Camera dei Deputati. 1920c. *Atti parlamentari Camera dei Deputati*, Sessione 1919–1920, vol. 275, 10 maggio-9 luglio 1920. Roma: Tipografia della Camera dei Deputati.
Italy, Camera dei Deputati. 1920d. *Atti parlamentari Camera dei Deputati*, Sessione 1919–1920, vol. 276, 10–28 luglio 1920. Roma: Tipografia della Camera dei Deputati.
Italy, Camera dei Deputati. 1920e. *Atti parlamentari Camera dei Deputati*, Sessione 1919–1920, vol. 277, 29 luglio-9 agosto 1920. Roma: Tipografia della Camera dei Deputati.
Italy, Camera dei Deputati. 2008a. Legislature precedenti. http://legislature.camera.it/.
Italy, Camera dei Deputati. 2008b. XIII [Tredicesima] legislatura. http://leg13.camera.it/.
Italy, Camera dei Deputati. 2009. Legislature precedenti. http://legislature.camera.it/.
Italy, Camera dei Deputati. 2010. Legislature precedenti. http://legislature.camera.it/.
Italy, Camera dei Deputati. 2011. *Commissione parlamentare per le riforme costituzionali. Commisione plenaria.* http://leg13.camera.it/_dati/leg13/lavori/rifcost/composiz/plenaria.htm.
Italy, Ministero dell'Interno. 2008. "Archivio storico delle elezioni." http://elezionistorico.interno.it/index.php.
Malawi, 2010. *Constitution of the Republic of Malawi.* http://www.sdnp.org.mw/constitut/dtlindx.html.
New Zealand, Parliament. 2005. "Electoral (Integrity) Amendment Bill—First Reading." *Hansard Debates*, 6 December. http://202.68.89.83/en-NZ/PB/Debates/Debates/4/f/5/48HansD_20051206_00001032-Electoral-Integrity-Amendment-Bill-First.htm Accessed August 2011.
New Zealand, Parliament. 2011. *Members of Parliament: Former MPs.* http://202.68.89.83/en-NZ/MPP/MPs/Former/default.htm?ps=0.
New Zealand, Parliament. 2012. *Members of Parliament: Former MPs.* http://www.parliament.nz/en-NZ/MPP/MPs/Former/.

Bibliography

Portugal, Assembleia da República. 2010a. "Deputados e grupos parlamentares." http://www.parlamento.pt/DeputadoGP/Paginas/GruposParlamentaresI.aspx.
Portugal, Assembleia da República. 2010b. "Deputados e grupos parlamentares: Resultados Eleitorais." http://www.parlamento.pt/DeputadoGP/Paginas/resultadoseleitorais.aspx.
Portugal, Assembleia da República. 2010c. "Estatuto dos Deputados." http://www.parlamento.pt/Legislacao/Paginas/EstatutoDeputados.aspxart8.
Portugal, Assembleia da República. 2010d. "Revisões Constitucionais." http://www.parlamento.pt/RevisoesConstitucionais/Paginas/default.aspx.
Romania, Agenţia Naţională de Presă, 2011. Guvernele româniei. http://documentare.rompres.ro/guverne.php.
Romania, Parlamentul României, Camera Deputaţilor. 2008a. "Activitate parlamentară." http://www.cdep.ro/pls/steno/steno.home?idl=2.
Romania, Parlamentul României, Camera Deputaţilor. 2008b. "Organizarea şi funcţionarea camerei deputaţilor: Grupurile parlamentare." http://www.cdep.ro/pls/dic/site.page?id=134&idl=1.
Romania, Parlamentul României, Camera Deputaţilor. 2008c. "Prima pagina." http://www.cdep.ro/.
South Africa, Parliament. 2010. "State of Parties in the NA." http://www.parliament.gov/za.live/content.php?Category_ID=148.
Switzerland, Parlement. 2008. *Les groupes parlementaires.* http://www.parlament.ch/f/organe-mitglieder/bundesversammlung/fraktionen/Pages/default.aspx
Switzerland, Parlement. 2012. *Effectifs des groupes parlementaires de la 48e législature 2007–2011.* http://www.parlament.ch/f/organe-mitglieder/bundesversammlung/fraktionen/fraktionen-48-legislatur/Pages/default.aspx.
United Kingdom, Parliament. 2008. "List of Previous Commons Recess Dates." http://www.parliament.uk/faq/recess.ccfm.
United Kingdom, Parliament. 2010. "Hansard 1803–2005." http://hansard.millbanksystems.com/
United States Congressional Biographical Directory. 2008. http://bioguide.congress.gov/biosearch/biosearch.asp.
United States, House of Representatives, Office of the Clerk. 2008. "Official House Information: House Floor Proceedings." http://clerk.ouse.gov/index.html.
United States, House of Representatives, Office of the Clerk. 2009. *House Floor Proceedings.* http://clerk.house.gov/legislative/.
United States, House of Representatives, Office of the Majority Leader. 2008. "U.S. House Vote Schedule." http://majorityleader.house.gov/docUploads/2008-CALENDAR.pdf.

Newspapers and Periodicals

Ballot Access News. 2001a. "Candidates Elected to the House, 1902–2000, Who Weren't Nominees of the Democratic or Republican Parties." 17, 3 (June 1). http://web.archive.org/web/20030417164754/http://www.ballot-access.org/2001/0601.html17.

Ballot Access News. 2001b. "Minor Party Candidates Elected to the House, 1902–2000, Who Were Nominated by Their Own Minor Party, Plus Major Party." 17, 3 (June 1). http://web.archive.org/web/20030417164754/http://www.ballot-access.org/2001/0601.html17.

BBC. 1979. "Early Election as Callaghan Defeated." http://news.bbc.co.uk/onthisday/hi/dates/stories/march/28/newsid_2531000/2531007.stm.

BBC. 1997. "Politics 97: Background, Past Elections, 1979." http://www.bbc.co.uk/news/special/politics97/background/pastelec/ge79.shtml.

BBC. 1998. "Romania's Coalition Democrats Urge Formation of New Government." March 13. http://news.bbc.co.uk/2/hi/world/monitoring/65158.stm.

BBC. 2005. "Canada PM Wins No–Confidence Vote." May 20. http://news.bbc.co.uk/2/hi/americas/4561799.stm.

Congressional Quarterly (CQ) Weekly. Various dates. http://library.cqpress.com/cqweekly.

Corriere della Sera, Archivio storico. Various dates. http://archiviostorico.corriere.it/.

De Vito, Francesco. 1982. "San Marco scaccia il Diavolo." *Radio radicale* 11/14. http://www.radioradicale.it/exagora/san-marco-scaccia-il-diavolo.

Economist. 2005a. "After the Vote." May 26.

Economist. 2005b. "Belinda's Leap." May 21, 40.

Hickey, Jennifer G. 2003. "Gillespie Focuses on Growth of GOP." *Insight on the News*, October 27, 2003. http://www.questia.com/read/1G1-109128676/gillespie-focuses-on-growth-of-gop-while-republican.

Irish Times. Various dates. http://www.irishtimes.com/archive/.

Keesing's Contemporary Archives. 1957. Bristol: Longman.

Keesing's Record of World Events. Various dates. www.keesings.com.

Larraz, Teresa. 2003. "Historia de otras traiciones." *El Siglo de Europa*, June 16.

Los Angeles Times. Various dates. http://articles.latimes.com/.

Melega, Gianluigi. 1982. "Per chi vota il radicale?" Archivio Partito radicale 10/23. http://old.radicali.it/search_view.php?id=48048&lang=IT+cms=H.

Santero, F. Javier. 1998. "Pacto de los partidos contra el transfuguismo en los ayuntamientos." *El Mundo*, July 8. http://www.elmundo.es/1998/07/08/espana/08N0026.html.

Thai, Bethuel. 2006. "Lesotho will go to the polls in February 2007." *IOL News*, December 1. http://www.iol.co.za/news/africa/lesotho-will-go-to-the-polls-in-february-2007-1.305718.

United Press International. 1984. "Campaign notes: County official wins Florida run off election." *New York Times*, October 3. http://query.nytimes.com/gst/fullpage.html?res=9C0CE0DB123BF930A35753C1A962948260&n=Top%2fReference%2fTimes%20Topics%2fOrganizations%2fR%2fRepublican%20Party.

Van Beynen, Martin. 2010. "The Final Push: Political Warhorse." *The Press*, July 27. http://www.stuff.co.nz/the-press/3954688/The-final-push.

Other Primary and Secondary Sources

ACE, The Electoral Knowledge Network. 2010. "Ecuador: The Search for Democratic Governance." http://aceproject.org/ace-en/topics/es/esy/esy_ec.

Bibliography

ACE, The Electoral Knowledge Network. 2011. "The MMP Electoral System Faces Political Challenges in Lesotho." http://aceproject.org/today/feature-articles/the-mmp-electoral-system-faces-political-challenges-in-lesotho.

Aldrich, John H. 1995. *Why Parties? The Origin and Transformation of Political Parties in America*. Chicago: University of Chicago Press.

Aldrich, John H. 2001. "Congress: The Electoral Connection: Reflections on Its First Quarter-Century." *PS: Political Science and Politics* 34 (2): 255–256.

Aldrich, John H. 2006. "Political Parties In and Out of Legislatures," in *Oxford Handbook of Political Institutions*, eds. R. A. W. Rhodes, Sarah A. Binder, and Bert A. Rockman. Oxford: Oxford University Press. 555–576.

Aldrich, John H. 2011. *Why Parties? The Origin and Transformation of Political Parties in America*. Chicago: University of Chicago Press.

Aldrich, John H., and William T. Bianco. 1992. "A Game-Theoretic Model of Party Affiliation of Candidates and Office Holders." *Mathematical and Computer Modelling* 16 (8–9): 103–116.

Aldrich, John H. Christopher Gelpi, Peter Feaver, Jason Reifler, and Kristin Thompson Sharp. 2006. "Foreign Policy and the Electoral Connection." *Annual Review of Political Science* 9: 477–502.

Aldrich, John H., John L. Sullivan, and Eugene Borgida. 1989. "Foreign Affairs and Issue Voting: Do Presidential Candidates 'Waltz Before a Blind Audience?'" *The American Political Science Review* 83 (1): 123–141.

Alesina, Alberto, Arnaud Devleeschauwer, William Easterly, Sergio Kurlat, and Romain Wacziarg. 2003. "Fractionalization." *Journal of Economic Growth* 8: 155–194.

Alesina, Alberto, Arnaud Devleeschauwer, William Easterly, Sergio Kurlat, and Romain Wacziarg. 2011. "Fractionalization Dataset." http://www.nsd.uib.no/macrodataguide/set.html?id=16&sub=1.

Ames, Barry. 2001. *The Deadlock of Democracy in Brazil*. Ann Arbor: University of Michigan Press.

Amorim Neto, Octavio, and Gary W. Cox. 1997. "Electoral Institutions, Cleavage Structures, and the Number of Parties." *American Journal of Political Science* 41 (1): 149–174.

Andersen, Robert, James Tilley, and Anthony F. Heath. 2005. "Political Knowledge and Enlightened Preferences: Party Choice through the Electoral Cycle." *British Journal of Political Science* 35 (2): 285–302.

Anderson, Christopher J. 1995. *Blaming the Government: Citizens and the Economy in Five European Democracies*. Armonk, NY: M.E. Sharpe.

Anderson, Christopher J. 2000. "Economic Voting and Political Context: A Comparative Perspective." *Electoral Studies* 19 (2–3): 151–170.

Anderson, Christopher J. 2007. "The End of Economic Voting? Contingency Dilemmas and the Limits of Democratic Accountability." *Annual Review of Political Science* 10: 271–296.

Arriola, Leonardo R. 2009. "Patronage and Political Stability in Africa." *Comparative Political Studies* 42 (10): 1339–1362.

Astraldi, Romolo. 1932. *Le norme regolamentari del parlamento italiano. Storia, esposizione sistematica e confronto con regolamenti stranieri*. Roma: Tipografia della Camera dei deputati.

Austen-Smith, David, and Jeffrey Banks. 1988. "Elections, Coalitions, and Legislative Outcomes." *American Political Science Review* 82 (2): 405–422.

Austen-Smith, David, and Jeffrey Banks. 1990. "Stable Governments and the Allocation of Policy Portfolios." *American Political Science Review* 84 (3): 891–906.

Baldassarri, Delia. 2005. *La semplice arte di votare. Le scorciatoie cognitive degli elettori italiani*. Bologna: Il Mulino.

Baldassarri, Delia, and Hans Schadee. 2004. "Il fascino della coalizione. Come e perché le alleanze elettorali influenzano il modo in cui gli elettori interpretano la politica." *Rivista italiana di scienza politica* 34 (2): 249–276.

Baldassarri, Delia, and Hans Schadee. 2005. "Voter Heuristics and Political Cognition in Italy: An Empirical Typology." *Electoral Studies* 25: 448–466.

Baron, David P. 1991. "A Spatial Theory of Government Formation in Parliamentary Systems." *American Political Science Review* 85 (1): 137–164.

Baron, David P., and John Ferejohn. 1989. "Bargaining in Legislatures." *American Political Science Review* 83 (4): 1181–1206.

Barro, Robert J., and Jong-Wha Lee. 2010. "A New Data Set of Educational Attainment in the World, 1950–2010." NBER Working Paper No. 15902. http://www.nber.org/papers/w15902.pdf?new_window=1

Barro, Robert J., and Jong-Wha Lee. 2011. "Barro-Lee Educational Attainment Dataset." http://www.barrolee.com/.

Bartolini, Stefano, and Peter Mair. 1990. *Identity, Competition, and Electoral Availability: The Stabilization of European Electorates 1885–1985*. Cambridge: Cambridge University Press.

Beck, Thorsten, George Clarke, Alberto Groff, Philip Keefer, and Patrick Walsh. 2001. "New Tools in Comparative Political Economy: The Database of Political Institutions." *World Bank Economic Review* 15 (1): 165–176. http://go.worldbank.org/2EAGGLRZ40.

Bélanger, Érik, and Jean-François Godbout. 2010. "Why Do Parties Merge? The Case of the Conservative Party of Canada." *Parliamentary Affairs* 63 (1): 41–65.

Benoit, Kenneth. 2001. "District Magnitude, Electoral Formula and the Number of Parties." *European Journal of Political Research* 39 (2): 203–224.

Benoit, Kenneth. 2007. "Electoral Laws as Political Consequences: Explaining the Origins and Change of Electoral Institutions." *Annual Review of Political Science* 10: 363–390.

Benoit, Kenneth, and Jacqueline Hayden. 2004. "Institutional Change and Persistence: The Evolution of Poland's Electoral System, 1989–2001." *Journal of Politics* 66 (2): 396–427.

Bertelsmann-Stiftung. 2009a. *BTI 2010: Malawi Country Report*. Gütersloh: Bertelsmann Stiftung. http://www.bertelsmann-transformation-index.de/fileadmin/pdf/Gutachten_BTI2010/ESA/Malawi.pdf.

Bertelsmann-Stiftung. 2009b. *BTI 2010: Papua New Country Report*. Gütersloh: Bertelsmann Stiftung. http://www.bertelsmann-transformation-index.de/fileadmin/pdf/Gutachten_BTI2010/ASO/Papua_New_Guinea.pdf.

Bhavnani, Ravi, and Dan Miodownik. 2009. "Ethnic Polarization, Ethnic Salience and Civil War." *Journal of Conflict Resolution* 53 (1): 30–49.

Birnir, Jóhanna Kristín. 2004. "Institutionalization of the Party System," in *Romania since 1989: Politics, Economics, Society*, ed. Henry F. Carey. Lanham, MD: Lexington Books. 139–158.

Bibliography

Birnir, Jóhanna Kristín. 2007. "Divergence in Diversity? The Dissimilar Effects of Cleavages on Electoral Politics in New Democracies." *American Journal of Political Science* 51 (3): 602–619.
Black, Duncan. 1948. "On the Rationale of Group Decision Making." *Journal of Political Economy* 56 (1): 23–34.
Black, Duncan. 1958. *The Theory of Committees and Elections.* Cambridge: Cambridge University Press.
Blimes, Randall J. 2006. "The Indirect Effect of Ethnic Heterogeneity on the Likelihood of Civil War Onset." *Journal of Conflict Resolution* 50 (4): 536–547.
Boix, Carles, and Susan C. Stokes, eds. 2007. *The Oxford Handbook of Comparative Politics.* Oxford: Oxford University Press.
Booysen, Susan. 2006. "The Will of the Parties Versus the Will of the People? Defections, Elections, and Alliances in South Africa." *Party Politics* 12 (6): 727–746.
Bowler, Shaun, David M. Farrell, and Richard S. Katz, eds. 1999. *Party Discipline and Parliamentary Government.* Columbus: Ohio State University Press.
Budge, Ian, Hans-Dieter Klingemann, Andrea Volkens, Judith Bara, and Eric Tannenbaum. 2001. *Mapping Policy Preferences. Estimates for Parties, Electors and Governments, 1945–1998.* Oxford: Oxford University Press.
Bull, Martin J. 1991. "The Italian Communist Party's Twentieth Congress and the Painful Birth of the Partito Democratico della Sinistra." *Journal of Communist Studies and Transition Politics* 7 (2): 257–264.
Butler, David E., and Gareth Butler. 1986. *British Political Facts, 1900–1985.* New York: St. Martin's Press.
Butler, David, and Gareth Butler. 2000. *Twentieth Century British Political Facts, 1900–2000.* New York: Palgrave Macmillan.
Butler, David, and Gareth Butler. 2006. *British Political Facts since 1979.* New York: Palgrave Macmillan.
Calvert, Randall L. 1995. "Rational Actors, Equilibrium, and Social Institutions," in *Explaining Social Institutions*, eds. Jack Knight and Itai Sened. Ann Arbor: University of Michigan Press. 57–94.
Canada. 2011. *Elections Canada.* http://www.elections.ca/home.aspx.
Canon, David T., and David J. Sousa. 1992. "Party System Change and Political Career Structures in the U.S. Congress." *Legislative Studies Quarterly* 17 (3): 347–363.
Capano, Gilberto, and Marco Giuliani. 2001a. "Governing Without Surviving? An Italian Paradox: Law-Making in Italy, 1987–2001." *The Journal of Legislative Studies* 7 (4): 13–36.
Capano, Giliberto, and Marco Giuliani. 2001b. "I laberinti del legislativo," in *Parlamento e processo legislativo in Italia. Continuità e mutamento*, eds. Giliberto Capano and Marco Giuliani. Bologna: Il Mulino.
Capano, Giliberto, and Marco Giuliani. 2003. "The Italian Parliament: In Search of a New Role?" *The Journal of Legislative Studies* 9 (2): 8–34.
Caramani, Daniele. 2004. *The Nationalization of Politics: The Formation of National Electorates and Party Systems in Western Europe.* Cambridge: Cambridge University Press.
Caramani, Daniele. 2006. "Is There a European Electorate and What Does It Look Like? Evidence from Electoral Volatility Measures, 1976–2004." *West European Politics* 29 (1): 1–27.

Carey, John M., and Simon Hix. 2008. "Maximizing Representation and Accountability in the Design of Electoral Systems." Data Codebook, Version 1.0. http://www.dartmouth.edu/~jcarey/Data_Archive.html.

Carey, John M., and Simon Hix. 2010. "Carey and Hix 'Electoral Sweet Spot' Data." (Stata data file). March. http://www.dartmouth.edu/~jcarey/Data_Archive.html.

Carey, John M., and Simon Hix. 2011. "The Electoral Sweet Spot: Low-Magnitude Proportional Electoral Systems." *American Journal of Political Science* 55 (2): 383–397.

Carey, John M., and Matthew Soberg Shugart. 1995. "Incentives to Cultivate a Personal Vote: A Rank Ordering of Electoral Formulas." *Electoral Studies* 14 (4): 417–439.

Chandra, Kanchan. 2005. "Ethnic Parties and Democratic Stability." *Perspectives on Politics* 3 (2): 235–252.

Chandra, Kanchan. 2008. "Making Causal Claims about Ethnic Politics," in *Comparative Politics: Rationality, Culture, and Structure*, eds. Mark Lichbach and Alan Zuckerman. Cambridge: Cambridge University Press.

Chandra, Kanchan, and Steven Wilkinson. 2008. "Measuring the Effect of 'Ethnicity.'" *Comparative Political Studies* 41 (4–5): 515–563.

Cheibub, José Antonio. 2006. "Electoral Identifiability and Budget Balances in Democratic Systems." *American Political Science Review* 100 (3): 335–350.

Cheibub, José Antonio. 2007. *Presidentialism, Parliamentarism, and Democracy*. Cambridge: Cambridge University Press.

Cheibub, José Antonio, and Fernando Limongi. 2002. "Democratic Institutions and Regime Survival: Parliamentary and Presidential Democracies Reconsidered." *Annual Review of Political Science* 5: 151–179.

Chhibber, Pradeep K., and Ken Kollman. 1998. "Party Aggregation and the Number of Parties in India and the United States." *American Political Science Review* 92: 329–342.

Chhibber, Pradeep K., and Ken Kollman. 2004. *The Formation of National Party Systems: Federalism and Party Competition in Canada, Great Britain, India, and the United States*. Princeton, NJ: Princeton University Press.

Chiva, Cristina. 2007. "The Institutionalization of Post-Communist Parliaments: Hungary and Romania in Comparative Perspective." *Parliamentary Affairs* 60 (2): 187–211.

Clarke, Harold D., and Allan Kornberg. 1996. "Partisan Dealignment, Electoral Choice and Party-System Change in Canada." *Party Politics* 2: 455–478.

Colton, Timothy J. 2000. *Transitional Citizens: Voters and What Influences Them in the New Russia*. Cambridge: Harvard University Press.

Constitutional Change and Parliamentary Democracies (CCPD). 2011. Comparative Parliamentary Democracy Data Archive, CCPD. http://www.erdda.se/index.php/projects/cpd/data-archive.

Converse, Philip E. 1964. "The Nature of Belief Systems in Mass Publics," in *Ideology and Discontent*, ed. David E. Apter. New York: Free Press. 206–261.

Converse, Philip E. 1969. "Of Time and Partisan Stability." *Comparative Political Studies*, 2 (2): 139–171.

Coppedge, Michael, Angel Alvarez, and Claudia Maldonado. 2008. "Two Persistent Dimensions of Democracy: Contestation and Inclusiveness." *Journal of Politics* 70 (3): 632–647.

Corbetta, Piergiogio, and Arturo M. L. Parisi, eds. 1997. *A domanda risponde. Il cambiamento del voto degli italiani nelle elezioni del 1994 e del 1996*. Bologna: Il Mulino.

Covington, Cary R. 2006. "Testing for the Effects of Party in the Senate: The Jeffords' Switch." Paper presented at the annual meeting of the Midwest Political Science Association, Chicago, Illinois.
Cox, Gary W. 1987. *The Efficient Secret: The Cabinet and the Development of Political Parties in Victorian England*. Cambridge: Cambridge University Press.
Cox, Gary W. 1997. *Making Votes Count: Strategic Coordination in the World's Electoral Systems*. New York: Cambridge University Press.
Cox, Gary W. 1999. "Electoral Rules and Electoral Coordination." *Annual Review of Political Science* 2: 145–161.
Cox, Gary W. 2006. "The Organization of Democratic Legislatures," in *The Oxford Handbook of Political Economy*, eds. Barry Weingast and Donald Wittman. Oxford: Oxford University Press. 141–161.
Cox, Gary W., and Mathew D. McCubbins. 1993. *Legislative Leviathan: Party Government in the House*. Berkeley: University of California Press.
Cox, Gary W., and Mathew D. McCubbins. 2007. *Legislative Leviathan: Party Government in the House*, 2nd edition. Cambridge: Cambridge University Press.
Cox, Gary W., and Mathew D. McCubbins. 2005. *Setting the Agenda: Responsible Party Government in the U.S. House of Representatives*. Cambridge: Cambridge University Press.
Cox, Gary W., and Frances M. Rosenbluth. 1995. "Anatomy of a Split: The Liberal Democrats of Japan." *Electoral Studies* 14 (4): 355–376.
Crawford, Sue E. S., and Elinor Ostrom. 1995. "A Grammar of Institutions." *The American Political Science Review* 89 (3): 582–600.
Crewe, Ivor, and Anthony King. 1995. *SDP: The Birth, Life, and Death of the Social Democratic Party*. Oxford: Oxford University Press.
Cunow, Saul. 2010. "Party Switching and Legislative Behavior: Evidence from Brazil's National and Sub-national Legislatures of the Impact of Party Switching on Legislative Behavior." Paper presented at the annual meeting of the Midwest Political Science Association, Chicago, Illinois.
D'Alimonte, Roberto. 2001. "Mixed Electoral Rules, Partisan Realignment, and Party System Change in Italy," in *Mixed-Member Electoral Rules: The Best of Both Worlds?*, eds. Matthew Sobert Shugart and Martin P. Wattenberg. Oxford: Oxford University Press. 323–350.
D'Alimonte, Roberto, and Stefano Bartolini. 2002. *Maggioritario finalmente? La transizione elettorale 1994–2001*. Bologna: Il Mulino.
Dahl, Robert A. 1966. *Political Oppositions in Western Democracies*. New Haven, CT: Yale University Press.
Dahl, Robert A. 1971. *Polyarchy: Participation and Opposition*. New Haven, CT: Yale University Press.
Dalton, Russell J. 2000. "The Decline of Party Identification," in *Parties without Partisans: Political Change in Advanced Industrial Democracies*, eds. Russell J. Dalton and Martin P. Wattenberg. Oxford: Oxford University Press. 19–36.
Dalton, Russell J., Paul Allen Beck, and Scott C. Flanagan. 1984. "Electoral Change in Advanced Industrial Democracies," in *Electoral Change in Advanced Industrial Democracies*, eds. Russell J. Dalton, Paul Allen Beck, and Scott C. Flanagan. Princeton, NJ: Princeton University Press.

Dalton, Russell J., Ian McAllister, and Martin P. Wattenberg. 2000. "The Consequences of Partisan Dealignment," in *Parties Without Partisans: Political Change in Advanced Industrial Democracies,* eds. Russell J. Dalton and Martin P. Wattenberg. Oxford: Oxford University Press. 37–63.

Dalton, Russell J., and Martin P. Wattenberg. 2000. *Parties without Partisans: Political Change in Advanced Industrial Societies.* Oxford: Oxford University Press.

Dalton, Russell J., and Steven Weldon. 2007. "Partisanship and Party System Institutionalization." *Party Politics* 13 (2): 179–196.

Daniels, Philip A. 2001. "Le elezioni del Parlamento europeo del 1999," in *Politica in Italia. I fatti dell'anno e le interpretazioni. Edizione 2001,* eds. Mark Gilbert and Gianfranco Pasquino. Bologna: Il Mulino. 46–67.

De Jager, Nicola Louise. 2009. "Voice and Accountability in One-Party Dominant Systems: A Comparative Case Study of Mexico and South Africa." Ph.D. diss., University of Pretoria, South Africa. http://upetd.up.ac.za/thesis/available/etd-05162010-005403/unrestricted/thesis.pdf.

Den Hartog, Christopher, and Nathan W. Monroe. 2008. "The Value of Majority Status: The Effect of Jeffords's Switch on Asset Prices of Republican and Democratic Firms." *Legislative Studies Quarterly* 33 (1): 63–84.

Desposato, Scott W. 2006a. "The Impact of Electoral Rules on Legislative Parties: Lessons from the Brazilian Senate and Chamber of Deputies." *Journal of Politics* 68 (4): 1015–1027.

Desposato, Scott. 2006b. "Parties for Rent? Careerism, Ideology, and Party Switching in Brazil's Chamber of Deputies." *American Journal of Political Science* 50 (1): 62–80.

Desposato, Scott. 2009. "Party Switching in Brazil: Causes, Effects, and Representation," in *Political Parties and Legislative Party Switching,* eds. William B. Heller and Carol Mershon. New York: Palgrave Macmillan. 109–144.

Desposato, Scott, and Ethan Scheiner. 2008. "Governmental Centralization and Party Affiliation: Legislator Strategies in Brazil and Japan." *American Political Science Review* 102 (4): 509–524.

Desserud, Donald. 2006. "The Confidence Convention under the Canadian Parliamentary System." Canadian Study of Parliament Group working paper. http://www.studyparliament.ca/English/pdf/ongoing/Parliamentary_Perspectives_7_206_Eng.pdf

Diermeier, Daniel. 2006. "Coalition Government." *Oxford Handbook of Political Economy,* eds. Barry R. Weingast and Donald A. Wittman. Oxford: Oxford University Press.

Di Mascio, Fabrizio. 2007. "DL-La Margherita. Organizazzione, strategia, cultura." Unpublished manuscript. Università di Firenze, Florence, Italy.

Di Palma, Giuseppe. 1977. *Surviving Without Governing: The Italian Parties in Parliament.* Berkeley: University of California Press.

Di Scala, Spencer M. 1988. *Renewing Italian Socialism: From Nenni to Craxi.* New York: Oxford University Press.

Di Virgilio, Aldo. 1997. "Le alleanze elettorali. Identità partitiche e logiche coalizionali," in *Maggioritario per caso. Le elezioni politiche del 1996,* eds. Roberto D'Alimonte and Stefano Bartolini. Bologna: Il Mulino. 71–136.

Di Virgilio, Aldo. 2002. "L'offerta elettorale. La politica delle alleanze si istituzionalizza," in *Maggioritario finalmente? La transizione elettorale 1994–2001,* eds. Roberto D'Alimonte and Stefano Bartolini. Bologna: Il Mulino. 79–129.

Diermeier, Daniel. 1995. "Commitment, Deference, and Legislative Institutions." *American Political Science Review* 89 (2): 344–355.
Donovan, Mark, and James L. Newell. 2008. "Centrism in Italian Politics." *Modern Italy* 13 (4): 381–397.
Döring, Herbert. 2001. "Parliamentary Agenda Control and Legislative Outcomes in Western Europe." *Legislative Studies Quarterly* 26 (1): 145–165.
Downs, Anthony. 1957. *An Economic Theory of Democracy*. New York: Harper and Row.
Drucker, Henry. 1977. *Breakaway: The Scottish Labour Party*. Edinburgh: EUSPB.
Duch, Raymond M., and Randolph T. Stevenson. 2008. *The Economic Vote: How Political and Economic Institutions Condition Election Results*. Cambridge: Cambridge University Press.
Duverger, Maurice. 1954. *Political Parties: Their Organization and Activity in the Modern State*. London: Methuen.
Electoral Institute for the Sustainability of Democracy in Africa. 2010. South Africa Election Archive. http://www.eisa.org.za/WEP/souelectarchive.htm.
Ellis, Faron, and Peter Woolstencroft. 2004. "New Conservatives, Old Realities: The 2004 Election Campaign," in *The Canadian General Election of 2004*, eds. Jon H. Pammett and Christopher Dornan. Toronto: Dundurn Press. 66–105.
Erdmann, Gero, Matthias Basedau, and Andreas Mehler. 2007. "The Research Agenda Ahead," in *Votes, Money and Violence: Political Parties and Elections in Sub-Saharan Africa*, eds. Matthias Basedau, Gero Erdmann, and Andreas Mehler. Scottsville, South Africa: University of KwaZulu-Natal Press. 276–292.
Evans, Geoffrey, and Stephen Whitefield. 1995. "The Politics and Economics of Democratic Commitment: Support for Democracy in Transition Societies." *British Journal of Political Science* 25 (4): 485–514.
Farneti, Paolo. 1978. "Social Conflict, Parliamentary Fragmentation, Institutional Shift, and the Rise of Fascism: Italy," in *The Breakdown of Democratic Regimes: Europe*, eds. Juan J. Linz and Alfred Stepan. Baltimore and London: Johns Hopkins University Press. 3–33.
Fearon, James D. 2003. "Ethnic Structure and Cultural Diversity by Country." *Journal of Economic Growth* 8 (2): 195–222.
Ferree, Karen E. 2006. "Explaining South Africa's Racial Census." *Journal of Politics* 68 (4): 803–815.
Ferree, Karen E. 2010. "The Social Origins of Electoral Volatility in Africa." *British Journal of Political Science* 40 (4): 759–779.
Ferree, Karen E. 2011. *Framing the Race in South Africa: The Political Origins of Racial-Census Elections*. Cambridge: Cambridge University Press.
Ferree, Karen E., and Jeremy Horowitz. 2010. "Ties that Bind? The Rise and Decline of Ethno-Regional Partisanship in Malawi, 1994–2009." *Democratization* 17 (3): 534–563.
Field, Bonnie N. 2006. "Transitions to Democracy and Internal Party Rules: Spain in Comparative Perspective." *Comparative Politics* 39 (1): 83–102.
Field, Bonnie N. 2011. "Bringing Party Leaders into Explanations of Party Unity: Lessons from Spain." Manuscript. Bentley University, Waltham, Massachusetts.
Filippov, Mikhail G., Peter C. Ordeshook, and Olga V. Shvetsova. 1999. "Party Fragmentation and Presidential Elections in Post-Communist Democracies." *Constitutional Political Economy* 10 (1): 3–26.

Filippov, Mikhail G., Peter C. Ordeshook, and Olga V. Shvetsova. 2004. *Designing Federalism: A Theory of Self-Sustainable Federal Institutions.* Cambridge: Cambridge University Press.
Fleischer, David. 2010. "Brazil." Freedom House, *Countries at the Crossroads.* http://www.freedomhouse.org/uploads/ccr/country-7788-9.pdf.
Fortín, Javier. 2008. "Transfuguismo parlamentario en Guatemala." Cuadernos de información política, No. 15. Guatemala: Editorial de Ciencias Sociales.
Fox, Graham. 2005. "The Conservatives and the Minority House: A Tale of Two Harpers." *Policy Options* 26 (8): 15–18.
Franchino, Fabio, and Bjørn Høyland. 2009. "Legislative Involvement in Parliamentary Systems: Opportunities, Conflict, and Institutional Constraints." *American Political Science Review* 103 (4): 607–621.
Franklin, Mark N., Thomas T. Mackie, and Henry Valen, eds. 1992. *Electoral Change: Responses to Evolving Social and Attitudinal Structures in Western Countries.* Cambridge: Cambridge University Press.
Freire, André, and Michael A. Baum. 2003. "Referenda Voting in Portugal, 1998: The Effects of Party Sympathies, Social Structure and Pressure Groups." *European Journal of Political Research* 42 (1): 135–161.
Fukui, Haruhiro, and Shigeko N. Fukai. 1996. "Pork Barrel Politics, Networks, and Local Economic Development in Contemporary Japan." *Asian Survey* 36 (3): 268–286.
Gallagher, Michael. 2011. *Election Indices.* http://www.tcd.ie/Political_Science/staff/michael_gallagher/ElSystems/Docts/ElectionIndices.pdf.
Gallagher, Michael, Michael Laver, and Peter Mair. 2006. *Representative Government in Modern Europe,* 4th edition. Boston, MA: McGraw-Hill.
Gallagher, Michael, and Paul Mitchell. 2008. *The Politics of Electoral Systems.* Oxford: Oxford University Press.
Giannetti, Daniela, and Kenneth Benoit, eds. 2009. *Intra-Party Politics and Coalition Governments.* New York: Routledge.
Giannetti, Daniela, and Bernard Grofman, eds. 2011. *A Natural Experiment on Electoral Law Reform: Evaluating the Long Run Consequences of 1990s Electoral Reform in Italy and Japan.* New York: Springer.
Giannetti, Daniela, and Michael Laver. 2001. "Party System Dynamics and the Making and Breaking of Italian Governments." *Electoral Studies* 20 (4): 529–553.
Giannetti, Daniela, and Itai Sened. 2004. "Party Competition and Coalition Formation, Italy 1994–96." *Journal of Theoretical Politics* 16 (4): 483–515.
Ginsborg, Paul. 1989. *Storia d'Italia dal dopoguerra a oggi. Società e politica 1943–1988.* Turin: Einaudi.
Giusti, Ugo. 1945. *Dai plebisciti alla costituente.* Rome: Editrice Faro.
Golder, Matt. 2005. "Democratic Electoral Systems around the World, 1946–2000." *Electoral Studies* 24 (1): 103–121.
Golosov, Grigorii V. 2003. "Electoral Systems and Party Formation in Russia: A Cross-Regional Analysis." *Comparative Political Studies* 36 (8): 912–935.
Grassi Orsini, Fabio, and Gaetano Quagliariello. 1996. *Il partito politico dalla grande guerra al fascismo. Crisi della rappresentanza e riforma dello Stato nell'età dei sistemi politici di massa (1918–1925).* Bologna: Il Mulino.

Greif, Avner, and Christopher Kingston. 2011. "Institutions: Rules or Equilibria?" in *Political Economy of Institutions, Democracy and Voting*, eds. Norman Schofield and Gonzalo Caballero. New York: Springer. 13–44.
Greif, Avner, and David D. Laitin. 2004. "A Theory of Endogenous Institutional Change." *American Political Science Review* 98 (4): 633–652.
Gunther, Richard. 2002. "Parties and Electoral Behavior in Southern Europe." Paper presented at the Portugal at the Polls – Legislative Elections 2002 conference. http://www.ics.ul.pt/ceapp/english/conferences/portugalatthepolls/index.htm
Gunther, Richard, and José R. Montero. 2001. "The Anchors of Partisanship: A Comparative Analysis of Voting Behavior in Four Southern European Democracies," in *Parties, Politics and Democracy in the New Southern Europe*, eds. Nikiforos P. Diamandouros and Richard Gunther. Baltimore, MD and London: Johns Hopkins University Press.
Gunther, Richard, Giacomo Sani, and Goldie Shabad. 1988. *Spain after Franco: The Making of a Competitive Party System*. Berkeley: University of California Press.
Gussow, David. 2006."Crossing the Floor, Conflict of Interest and the Parliament of Canada Act." *Canadian Parliamentary Review* 29 (2): 9–11.
Habyarimana, James, Macartan Humphreys, Daniel N. Posner, and Jeremy M. Weinstein. 2007. "Why Does Ethnic Diversity Undermine Public Goods Provision?" *The American Political Science Review* 101 (4): 709–725.
Haggard, Stephan, and Mathew D. McCubbins. 2001. *Presidents, Parliaments, and Policy*. Cambridge: Cambridge University Press.
Hagopian, Frances, Carlos Gervasoni, and Juan Andres Moraes. 2009. "From Patronage to Program: The Emergence of Party-Oriented Legislators in Brazil." *Comparative Political Studies* 42 (3): 360–391.
Hall, Peter, and Rosemary C. R. Taylor. 1996 "Political Science and the Three New Institutionalisms." *Political Studies* 44 (5): 936–957.
Hallerberg, Mark. 2004. *Domestic Budgets in a United Europe: Fiscal Governance from the End of Bretton Woods to EMU*. Ithaca, NY: Cornell University Press.
Hay, Colin. 2006. "Constructivist Institutionalism," in *Oxford Handbook of Political Institutions*, eds. R. A. W. Rhodes, Sarah A. Binder, and Bert A. Rockman. Oxford: Oxford University Press.
Heller, William B., and Carol Mershon. 2005. "Party Switching in the Italian Chamber of Deputies, 1996–2001." *Journal of Politics* 67 (2): 536–559.
Heller, William B., and Carol Mershon. 2008. "Dealing in Discipline: Party Switching and Legislative Voting in the Italian Chamber of Deputies, 1988–2000." *American Journal of Political Science* 52 (4): 910–925.
Heller, William B., and Carol Mershon. 2009a. "Conclusions." In William B. Heller and Carol Mershon, eds., *Political Parties and Legislative Party Switching*. New York: Palgrave Macmillan.
Heller, William B., and Carol Mershon. 2009b. "Integrating Theoretical and Empirical Models of Party Switching." In William B. Heller and Carol Mershon, eds., *Political Parties and Legislative Party Switching*. New York: Palgrave Macmillan.
Heller, William B., and Carol Mershon. 2009c. "Introduction: Legislative Party Switching, Parties, and Party Systems." In William B. Heller and Carol Mershon, eds., *Political Parties and Legislative Party Switching*. New York: Palgrave Macmillan.

Heller, William B., and Carol Mershon. 2009d. "Legislator Preferences, Party Desires: Party Switching and the Foundations of Policy Making in Legislatures." In William B. Heller and Carol Mershon, eds., *Political Parties and Legislative Party Switching*. New York: Palgrave Macmillan.

Heller, William B., and Carol Mershon, eds. 2009e. *Political Parties and Legislative Party Switching*. New York: Palgrave Macmillan.

Hellman, Stephen. 1977. "The Longest Campaign: Communist Party Strategy and the Elections of 1976," in *Italy at the Polls: The Parliamentary Elections of 1976*, ed. Howard R. Penniman. Washington, DC: American Enterprise Institute.

Hellwig, Timothy, and David Samuels. 2008. "Electoral Accountability and the Variety of Democratic Regimes." *British Journal of Political Science* 37 (1): 65–90.

Herron, Erik S., and Misa Nishikawa. 2001. "Contamination Effects and the Number of Parties in Mixed-Superposition Electoral Systems." *Electoral Studies* 20 (1): 63–86.

Hicken, Allen D. 2006a. "How Effective Are Institutional Reforms?" in *Political Parties in Conflict-Prone Societies: Regulation, Engineering and Democratic Development*, eds. Benjamin Reilly and Per Nordlund. New York and Tokyo: United Nations University Press.

Hicken, Allen D. 2006b. "Party Fabrication: Constitutional Reform and the Rise of Thai Rak Thai." *Journal of East Asian Studies* 6 (3): 381–407.

Hicken, Allen D. 2006c. "Stuck in the Mud: Parties and Party Systems in Democratic Southeast Asia." *Taiwan Journal of Democracy* 2 (2): 23–46.

Hicken, Allen D. 2008. "Political Engineering and Party Regulation in Southeast Asia," in *Political Parties in Conflict-Prone Societies: Regulation, Engineering and Democratic Development*, eds. Benjamin Reilly and Per Nordlund. New York: United Nations University Press.

Hicken, Allen D. 2009a. *Building Party Systems in Developing Democracies*. New York and Cambridge: Cambridge University Press.

Hicken, Allen D. 2009b. "Party and Party System Institutionalization in the Philippines." Paper presented at the Workshop on Party and Party System Institutionalization in Asia, Montréal, Québec, August. http://www.mcgill.ca/isid/research/party/papers/.

Hirschman, Albert O. 1970. *Exit, Voice and Loyalty*. Cambridge: Harvard University Press.

Hix, Simon, and Michael Marsh. 2007. "Punishment or Protest? Understanding European Parliament Elections." *The Journal of Politics* 69 (2): 495–510.

Hopkin, Jonathan, and Piero Ignazi. 2008. "Newly Governing Parties in Italy: Comparing the PDS/DS, Lega Nord and Forza Italia," in *New Parties in Government: In Power for the First Time*, ed. Kris Deschouwer. Oxford: Routledge. 45–64.

Horowitz, Donald L. 1985. *Ethnic Groups in Conflict*. Berkeley: University of California Press.

Huber, John D. 1996. *Rationalizing Parliament: Legislative Institutions and Party Politics in France*. Cambridge: Cambridge University Press.

Hug, Simon. 2001. *Altering Party Systems: Strategic Behavior and the Emergence of New Political Parties in Western Democracies*. Ann Arbor: University of Michigan Press.

Humphreys, Macartan. 2008. "Coalitions." *Annual Review of Political Science* 11: 351–386.

IDEA (International Institute for Democracy and Electoral Assistance). 2006. *Research and Dialogue with Political Parties*. http://political-parties.org/.

Ieraci, Giuseppe. 2008. *L'Ulivo e la Libertà. Governi e partiti in Italia nella democrazia dell'alternanza*. Trieste: EUT, Edizioni Università di Trieste.
Ignazi, Piero. 1989. *Il polo escluso. Profilo del movimento sociale italiano*. Bologna: Il Mulino.
Ignazi, Piero. 1992. *Dal PCI al PDS*. Bologna: Il Mulino.
INDEM Foundation. 2000. INDEM-Statistics 2000 Project. Bolshoi Zlatoustinskii Pereulok, Moscow, Russia.
Inglehart, Ronald F. 1971. "The Silent Revolution in Europe: Intergenerational Change in Post- Industrial Societies." *American Political Science Review* 65 (4): 991–1017.
Inglehart, Ronald F. 1977. *The Silent Revolution: Changing Values and Political Styles among Western Publics*. Princeton, NJ: Princeton University Press.
Inglehart, Ronald F. 1997. *Modernization and Postmodernization: Cultural, Economic, and Political Change in 43 Societies*. Princeton, NJ: Princeton University Press.
Inglehart, Ronald F. 2011. National-Level Value Scores by Country. http://www.world valuessurvey.org/wvs/articles/folder_published/article_base_111.
Istituto Cattaneo. 2010. "Archivi crono. Cronologia dei principali avvenimenti politici e sociali." http://www.cattaneo.org/index.asp?l1=archivi&l2=crono.
Istituto Luigi Sturzo. 2011. "Archivi della DC." http://www.sturzo.it/
ITANES. 1996. Italian National Election Studies. http://www.itanes.org.
ITANES. 2001. Italian National Election Studies. http://www.itanes.org.
Janda, Kenneth. 2009. "Laws against Party Switching, Defecting, or Floor-Crossing in National Parliaments." Paper presented at the 2009 World Congress of the International Political Science Association, Santiago, Chile, July 12–16. http://www.partylaw.bham.ac.uk/pdfs/wp0209.pdf.
Jayachandran, Seema. 2004. "The Jeffords Effect." University of California Los Angeles: California Center for Population Research. http://escholarship.org/uc/item/25p4z52g.
Kadima, Denis K. 2008. "Party Regulations, Nation-Building and Party Systems in Southern and East Africa," in *Political Parties in Conflict-Prone Societies: Regulation, Engineering and Democratic Development*, eds. Benjamin Reilly and Per Nordlund. New York and Tokyo: United Nations University Press.
Kam, Christopher J. 2009. *Party Discipline and Parliamentary Politics*. New York: Cambridge University Press.
Kam, Christopher, and Indriði Indriðason. 2005. "The Timing of Cabinet Reshuffles in Five Westminster Parliamentary Systems," *Legislative Studies Quarterly* 39 (3): 327–363.
Kaminski, Marek M. 2002. "Do Parties Benefit from Electoral Manipulation? Electoral Laws and Heresthetics in Poland, 1989–93." *Journal of Theoretical Politics* 14 (3): 325–358.
Kashyap, Subhash, et al. 2001. "Advisory Panel on Electoral Reforms: Standards in Political Life, Review of the Electoral Law, Processes and Reform Options." Consultation paper prepared for the National Commission to Review the Working of the Constitution, New Delhi, January.
Kato, Junko. 1998. "When the Party Breaks Up: Exit and Voice among Japanese Legislators." *American Political Science Review* 92 (4): 857–870.
Kato, Junko, and Kentaro Yamamoto. 2009. "Competition for Power: Party Switching and Party System Change in Japan," in *Political Parties and Legislative Party Switching*, eds. William B. Heller and Carol Mershon. New York: Palgrave Macmillan.

Katz, Richard S. 1995. "The 1993 Parliamentary Electoral Reform," in *Italian Politics: Ending the First Republic*, eds. Carol Mershon and Gianfranco Pasquino. Boulder, CO: Westview Press.

Katz, Richard S. 1996. "Electoral Reform and the Transformation of Party Politics in Italy." *Party Politics* 2 (1): 31–54.

Katz, Richard S. 1997. *Democracy and Elections*. Oxford: Oxford University Press.

Katz, Richard S. 1980. *A Theory of Parties and Electoral Systems*. Reprint, Baltimore: Johns Hopkins University Press, 2007.

Katz, Richard S., and Peter Mair, eds. 1994. *How Parties Organize: Change and Adaptation in Party Organizations in Western Democracies*. London: Sage Publications.

Katz, Richard S., and Peter Mair. 1995. "Changing Models of Party Organization and Party Democracy: The Emergence of the Cartel Party." *Party Politics* 1 (1): 5–28.

Katz, Richard S., Hans Rattinger, and Mogens N. Pedersen. 1997. "The Dynamics of European Party Systems." *European Journal of Political Research* 31 (1): 83–97.

Key, V. O. 1958. *Politics, Parties, and Pressure Groups*. New York: Crowell.

Key, V. O. 1964. *Politics, Parties, and Pressure Groups*. New York: Crowell.

Khelmko, Irina S. 2011. "Internal Organization of Post-Communist Parliaments over Two Decades: Leadership, Parties, Committees." *Journal of Legislative Studies* 17 (2): 193–214.

Knight, Jack. 1992. *Institutions and Social Conflict*. Cambridge: Cambridge University Press.

Kollman, Kenneth, Allen Hicken, Daniele Caramani, and David Backer. 2011. *Constituency-Level Elections Archive (CLEA), Appendix 1, Country Descriptions*. http://www.electiondataarchive.org/.

Kopecký, Petr, and Maria Spirova. 2008. "Parliamentary Opposition in Post-Communist Democracies: Power of the Powerless." *Journal of Legislative Studies* 14: 133–159.

Korguniuk, Yu G., and S. E. Zaslavskii. 1996. *Possiiskaia Mnogopartiinost: Stanovlenie, funktsionirovnie, razvitie*. Moscow: INDEM Foundation.

Kreuzer, Marcus, and Vello Pettai. 2003. "Patterns of Political Instability: Affiliation Patterns of Politicians and Voters in Post-Communist Estonia, Latvia, and Lithuania." *Studies in Comparative International Development* 38 (2): 76–98.

Kselman, Daniel M. 2009. Electoral Institutions, Party Organizations, and Political Instability. Ph.D. diss., Duke University.

Kunicová, Jana, and Thomas F. Remington. 2005. "The Effect of Electoral Rules on Distributive Voting: Some Evidence from the Russian State Duma, 1994–2003." Paper presented at the annual meeting of the Midwest Political Science Association, Chicago, Illinois.

Laakso, Markku, and Rein Taagepera. 1979. "'Effective' Number of Parties: A Measure with Application to West Europe." *Comparative Political Studies* 12 (1): 3–27.

Lassen, David Dreyer. 2007. "Ethnic Divisions, Trust, and the Size of the Informal Sector." *Journal of Economic Behavior & Organization* 63 (3): 423–438.

Laver, Michael. 1989. "Party Competition and Party System Change: The Interaction of Coalition Bargaining and Electoral Competition." *Journal of Theoretical Politics* 1 (3): 301–324.

Laver, Michael. 1998. "Models of Government Formation." *Annual Review of Political Science* 1: 1–25.

Bibliography

Laver, Michael. 2006. "Legislatures and Parliaments in Comparative Context," in *Oxford Handbook of Political Economy*, eds. Barry R. Weingast and Donald Wittman. Oxford: Oxford University Press. 121–140.
Laver, Michael. 2008. "Governmental Politics and the Dynamics of Multiparty Competition." *Political Research Quarterly* 61 (3): 532–536.
Laver, Michael, and Kenneth Benoit. 2003. "The Evolution of Party Systems between Elections." *American Journal of Political Science* 47 (2): 215–233.
Laver, Michael, and Junko Kato. 2001. "Dynamic Approaches to Government Formation and the Generic Instability of Decisive Structures in Japan." *Electoral Studies* 20 (4): 509–527.
Laver, Michael, and Norman Schofield. 1990. *Multiparty Government: The Politics of Coalition in Europe*. Oxford: Oxford University Press. Reprint, Ann Arbor: University of Michigan Press, 1998.
Laver, Michael, and Kenneth Shepsle. 1990a. "Coalitions and Cabinet Government." *American Political Science Review* 84 (3): 873–890.
Laver, Michael, and Kenneth Shepsle. 1990b. "Government Coalitions and Intraparty Politics." *British Journal of Political Science* 20 (4): 485–507.
Laver, Michael, and Kenneth Shepsle, eds. 1994. *Cabinet Ministers and Parliamentary Government*. Cambridge: Cambridge University Press.
Laver, Michael, and Kenneth Shepsle. 1996. *Making and Breaking Governments: Cabinets and Legislatures in Parliamentary Democracies*. Cambridge: Cambridge University Press.
Laver, Michael, and Kenneth Shepsle. 1999. "How Political Parties Emerged from the Primeval Slime: Party Cohesion, Party Discipline, and the Formation of Governments," in *Party Discipline and Parliamentary Government*, eds. Shaun Bowler, David M. Farrell, and Richard S. Katz. Columbus: Ohio State University Press. 23–48.
Leraci, Giuseppe. 2008. *Governments and Parties in Italy*. Leicester: Troubador Publishing Ltd.
Lewis-Beck, Michael S., and Mary Stegmaier. 2000. "Economic Determinants of Electoral Outcomes." *Annual Review of Political Science* 3: 183–219.
Lichbach, Mark I., and Alan S. Zuckerman. 1997. *Comparative Politics: Rationality, Culture and Structure*. Cambridge: Cambridge University Press.
Lijphart, Arend. 1984. *Democracies: Patterns of Majoritarian and Consensus Government in Twenty-One Countries*. New Haven, CT: Yale University Press.
Lindberg, Staffan I. 2007. "Institutionalization of Party Systems? Stability and Fluidity among Legislative Parties in Africa's Democracies." *Government and Opposition* 42 (2): 215–241.
Linz, Juan J. 1990. "The Perils of Presidentialism." *Journal of Democracy* 1 (1): 51–69.
Linz, Juan J. and Arturo Valenzuela, eds. 1994. *The Failure of Presidential Democracy*. Baltimore, MD: The Johns Hopkins University Press.
Lipset, Seymour Martin, and Stein Rokkan. 1967. "Cleavage Structures, Party Systems, and Voter Alignments: An Introduction," in *Party Systems and Voter Alignments: Cross-national Perspectives*, eds. Seymour Martin Lipset and Stein Rokkan. New York: Free Press.
Long, J. Scott. 1997. *Regression Models for Categorical and Limited Dependent Variables*, Number 7, in *Advanced Quantitative Techniques in the Social Sciences Series*. Thousand Oaks, CA: Sage Publications.

Long, J. S. and Freese, J. 2003. *Regression Models for Categorical and Limited Dependent Variables with Stata. Revised Edition*. College Station, TX: Stata Press.
Lovatt, Catherine, and David Lovatt. 2001. "PSD: A New Party of Government." *Central Europe Review* 3 (23). http://www.pecina.cz/files/www.ce-review.org/01/23/romania news23.html.
Löwenhardt, John. 1998. *Party Politics in Post-Communist Russia*. London: Frank Cass Publishers.
Luebbert, Gregory M. 1987. "Social Foundations of Political Order in Interwar Europe." *World Politics* 39 (4): 449–478.
Luebbert, Gregory M. 1991. *Liberalism, Fascism or Social Democracy: Social Classes and the Political Origins of Regimes in Interwar Europe*. Oxford: Oxford University Press.
Lupia, Arthur, and Mathew D. McCubbins. 1998. *The Democratic Dilemma: Can Citizens Learn What They Need to Know?* New York: Cambridge University Press.
Lupia, Arthur, and Kaare Strøm. 1995. "Coalition Termination and the Strategic Timing of Parliamentary Elections." *American Political Science Review* 90 (3): 648–665.
Lusztig, Michael, and J. Matthew Wilson. 2005. "A New Right: Anatomy of an Electoral Realignment in Canada." *Social Science Quarterly* 86 (1): 109–128.
Mackerras, Malcolm. 2004. "Australia." *European Journal of Political Research* 43 (7–8): 927–933.
Mackerras, Malcolm. 2005. "Australia." *European Journal of Political Research* 44 (7–8): 929–939.
Magalhães, Pedro C. 2008. "What are (Semi-) Presidential Elections About? The 2006 Presidential Elections in Portugal," in *The Multilevel Electoral System of the EU*, eds. Cees Van der Eijk and Hermann Schmitt. Mannheim, Germany: CONNEX-Network of Excellence, University of Mannheim.
Mahoney, James, and Kathleen Thelen. 2010. "A Theory of Gradual Institutional Change," in *Explaining Institutional Change: Ambiguity, Agency and Power*, eds. James Mahoney and Kathleen Thelen. New York: Cambridge University Press.
Mainwaring, Scott. 1992–1993. "Brazilian Party Underdevelopment in Comparative Perspective." *Political Science Quarterly* 107 (4): 677–707.
Mainwaring, Scott. 1998. "Party Systems in the Third Wave." *Journal of Democracy* 9 (3): 67–81.
Mainwaring, Scott. 1999. *Rethinking Party Systems in the Third Wave of Democratization: The Case of Brazil*. Stanford, CA: Stanford University Press.
Mainwaring, Scott, Carlos Gervasoni, and Annabella España-Nájera. 2010. "The Vote Share of New and Young Parties." The Helen Kellogg Institute for International Studies Working Paper 368.
Mainwaring, Scott, and Aníbal Pérez-Liñán. 1997. "Party Discipline in the Brazilian Constitutional Congress." *Legislative Studies Quarterly* 22 (4): 453–483.
Mainwaring, Scott, and Timothy R. Scully. 1995. *Building Democratic Institutions: Party Systems in Latin America*. Stanford, CA: Stanford University Press.
Mainwaring, Scott, and Timothy R. Scully. 2008. "Latin America: Eight Lessons for Governance." *Journal of Democracy* 19 (3): 113–127.

Mainwaring, Scott, and Mariano Torcal. 2006. "Party System Institutionalization and Party System Theory After the Third Wave of Democratization," in *Handbook of Party Politics*, eds. Richard S. Katz and William Crotty. London: Sage Publications.
Mainwaring, Scott, and Edurne Zoco. 2007. "Political Sequences and the Stabilization of Interparty Competition: Electoral Volatility in Old and New Democracies." *Party Politics* 13 (2): 155–178.
Mair, Peter. 1989a. "Continuity, Change and the Vulnerability of Party." *West European Politics* 12 (4): 169–187.
Mair, Peter. 1989b. "The Problem of Party System Change." *Journal of Theoretical Politics* 1 (3): 251–276.
Mair, Peter. 1997a. "On the Freezing of Party Systems," in *Party System Change: Approaches and Interpretations*. Oxford: Oxford University Press.
Mair, Peter. 1997b. *Party System Change: Approaches and Interpretations*. Oxford: Oxford University Press.
Mair, Peter. 1997c. "Party Systems and Structures of Competition," in *Party System Change: Approaches and Interpretations*. Oxford: Oxford University Press.
Mair, Peter. 2001. "The Freezing Hypothesis: An Evaluation," in *Party Systems and Voter Alignments Revisited*, eds. Lauri Karvonen and Stein Kuhnle. New York and London: Routledge.
Mair, Peter. 2006. "Party System Change," in *Handbook of Party Politics*, eds. Richard S. Katz and William J. Crotty. London: Sage Publications.
Mair, Peter, and Michael Marsh. 2004. "Political Parties in Electoral Markets in Postwar Ireland," in *Political Parties and Electoral Change: Party Responses to Electoral Markets*, eds. Peter Mair, Wolfgang C. Müller, and Fritz Plasser. Thousand Oaks, CA: Sage Publications.
Mair, Peter, Wolfgang C. Müller, and Fritz Plasser. 2004. *Political Parties and Electoral Change: Party Responses to Electoral Markets*. Thousand Oaks, CA: Sage.
Marsh, Michael, and Paul Mitchell. 1999. "Office, Votes, and Then Policy: Hard Choices for Political Parties in the Republic of Ireland 1981–1992." In Wolfgang C. and Strøm, Kaare, (eds.) *Policy, office or votes? How political parties in Western Europe Make hard decisions*. Cambridge University Press, New York, pp. 36–62.
Martin, Lanny W. 2004. "The Government Agenda in Parliamentary Democracies." *American Journal of Political Science* 48 (3): 445–461.
Martin, Lanny W., and Randolph T. Stevenson. 2001. "Government Formation in Parliamentary Democracies." *American Journal of Political Science* 45 (1): 33–50.
Martin, Lanny W., and Georg Vanberg. 2003. "Wasting Time? The Impact of Ideology and Size on Delay in Coalition Formation." *British Journal of Political Science* 33 (2): 323–332.
Martin, Lanny W., and Georg Vanberg. 2005. "Coalition Policymaking and Legislative Review." *American Political Science Review* 99 (1): 93–106.
Mayhew, David R. 1974. *Congress: The Electoral Connection*. New Haven, CT: Yale University Press.
Mayhew, David R. 2001. "Observations on Congress: The Electoral Connection a Quarter Century after Writing It." *PS: Political Science and Politics* 34 (2): 251–252.
McAllister, Ian. 2006. "Political Parties in Australia: Party Stability in a Utilitarian Society," in *Political Parties in Advanced Industrial Democracies*, eds. Paul Webb, David M. Farrell, and Ian Holliday. Oxford: Oxford University Press. 379–408.

McElroy, Gail. 2003. "Party Switching in the European Parliament: Why Bother?" Paper presented at the annual meeting of the Midwest Political Science Association, Chicago, Illinois.

McKelvey, Richard D. 1976. "Intransitivities in Multidimensional Voting Models and Some Implications for Agenda Control." *Journal of Economic Theory* 12 (3): 472–482.

McKelvey, Richard D. 1979. "General Conditions for Global Intransitivities in Formal Voting Models." *Econometrica* 47 (5): 1085–1112.

McKelvey, Richard D., and Norman Schofield. 1987. "Generalized Symmetry Conditions at a Core Point." *Econometrica* 55 (4): 923–933.

McLean, Iain. 2001. *Rational Choice and British Politics: An Analysis of Rhetoric and Manipulation from Peel to Blair.* Oxford: Oxford University Press.

Mejía Acosta, J. Andrés. 2003. "Partidos políticos. El eslabón político de la representación." http://www.fcs.edu.uy/enz/licenciaturas/cpolitica/sistemas%20latin oamericanos/antdemmejia.pdf.

Mejía Acosta, J. Andrés. 2004. "Ghost Coalitions: Economic Reforms, Fragmented Legislatures and Informal Institutions in Ecuador (1979–2002)." Ph.D. diss., University of Notre Dame.

Mershon, Carol. 1994. "Expectations and Informal Rules in Coalition Formation." *Comparative Political Studies* 27 (1): 40–79.

Mershon, Carol. 2001a. "Contending Models of Portfolio Allocation and Office Payoffs to Party Factions: Italy, 1963–79." *American Journal of Political Science* 45 (2): 277–293.

Mershon, Carol. 2002. *The Costs of Coalition.* Stanford, CA: Stanford University Press.

Mershon, Carol, and Timothy P. Nokken. 2008. "Party Formation and Changes of Party Affiliation among Legislators: The United States and Great Britain in the Nineteenth and Early Twentieth Centuries." Paper presented at the 2008 Annual Meetings of the Midwest Political Science Association, Chicago.

Mershon, Carol, and Olga Shvetsova. 2008a. "Parliamentary Cycles and Party Switching in Legislatures." *Comparative Political Studies* 41 (1): 99–127.

Mershon, Carol, and Olga Shvetsova. 2008b. "Party Switching in Sitting Parliaments and the Midterm Effect." Paper presented at the Annual Joint Sessions of the European Consortium for Political Research, Rennes, France.

Mershon, Carol, and Olga Shvetsova. 2009a. "Change and Stability in Parties and Party Systems between Elections." Paper presented at the 2009 Workshop on the Political Economy of Democratic Institutions, Hoover Institution, Stanford.

Mershon, Carol, and Olga Shvetsova. 2009b. "The Midterm Effect: Forces for Stability in Legislative Party Systems." Paper presented at the 2009 Annual Meetings of the Midwest Political Science Association, Chicago.

Mershon, Carol, and Olga Shvetsova. 2009c. "Timing Matters: Incentives for Party Switching and Stages of Parliamentary Cycles," in *Political Parties and Legislative Party Switching*, eds. William B. Heller and Carol Mershon. New York: Palgrave Macmillan.

Mershon, Carol, and Olga Shvetsova. 2011. "Moving in Time: Legislative Party Switching as Time-Contingent Choice," in *Political Economy of Institutions, Democracy and Voting*, eds. Norman Schofield and Gonzalo Caballero. New York: Springer.

Mershon, Carol, and Olga Shvetsova. 2013. "The Micro-Foundations of Party System Stability in Legislatures." *Journal of Politics.* 75 (4).

Mershon, Carol, and Olga Shvetsova. Forthcoming. "Change in Parliamentary Party Systems and Policy Outcomes: Hunting the Core." *Journal of Theoretical Politics*.
Miller, Arthur H., William M. Reisinger, and Vicki L. Hesli. 1998. "The Russian 1996 Presidential Election: Referendum on Democracy or Personality Contest?" *Electoral Studies* 17 (2): 175–196.
Miller, Gary, and Norman Schofield. 2003. "Activists and Partisan Realignment in the U. S." *American Political Science Review* 97 (2): 245–260.
Miller, William L., Stephen White, and Paul Heywood. 1996. "Twenty-Five Days To Go: Measuring and Interpreting the Trends in Public Opinion During the 1993 Russian Election Campaign." *Public Opinion Quarterly* 60 (1): 106–127.
Miskin, Sarah. 2003. "Politician Overboard: Jumping the Party Ship." Department of the Parliamentary Library, Australia, Research Paper No. 4, 2002–2003.
Monroe, Nathan W. 2010. "The Policy Impact of Unified Government: Evidence from 2000 to 2002." *Public Choice* 142 (1): 111–124.
Morgenstern, Scott. 2002. "Explaining Legislative Politics in Latin America," in *Legislative Politics in Latin America*, eds. Scott Morgenstern and Benito Nacif. New York and Cambridge: Cambridge University Press.
Morlino, Leonardo. 1996. "Crisis of Parties and Change of Party System in Italy." *Party Politics* 2 (1): 5–30.
Morton, Desmond. 2006. "A Note on Party-Switchers." *Canadian Parliamentary Review*. Summer: 4–8.
Moser, Robert G. 2001. *Unexpected Outcomes: Electoral Systems, Political Parties, and Representation in Russia*. Pittsburgh, PA: University of Pittsburgh Press.
Moser, Robert G., and Ethan Scheiner. 2004. "Mixed Electoral Systems and Electoral System Effects: Controlled Comparison and Cross-National Analysis." *Electoral Studies* 23 (4): 575–599.
Mullahy, John. 1986. "Specification and Testing of Some Modified Count Data Models." *Journal of Econometrics* 33 (3): 341–365.
Müller, Wolfgang C., and Kaare Strøm, eds. 1999. *Policy, Office, or Votes: How Political Parties in Western Europe Make Hard Decisions*. Cambridge: Cambridge University Press.
Munger, Michael C. 2010. "Endless Forms Most Beautiful and Most Wonderful: Elinor Ostrom and the Diversity of Institutions." *Public Choice* 143 (3): 263–268.
Murer, Jeffrey. 2002. "Mainstreaming Extremism: The Romanian PDSR in Comparative Perspective," in *Communist Successor Parties: Ten Years of Transformation*, eds. András Bozóki and John T. Ishiyama. Armonk, NY: M. E. Sharpe. 367–396.
Nemoto, Kuniaki. 2009. "Committing to the Party: The Costs of Governance in East Asian Democracies." Ph.D. diss., University of California, San Diego.
Nemoto, Kuniaki. 2011. "Presidential Term Limit and Party Switching in South Korea." Paper presented at the annual meetings of the Midwest Political Science Association, Chicago, Illinois.
Newell, James L., and Martin Bull. 1995. "Italy Changes Course? The 1994 Elections and the Victory of the Right." *Parliamentary Affairs* 48 (1): 72–99.
Newell, James L., and Martin Bull. 1997. "Party Organisations and Alliances in Italy in the 1990s: A Revolution of Sorts." *West European Politics* 20 (1) 81–109.
Nicholson, Stephen P. 2005. "The Jeffords Switch and Public Support for Divided Government." *British Journal of Political Science* 35 (2): 343–356.

Nikolenyi, Csaba. 2009. "An Asian Outlier? The Causes of Party System Institutionalization in India." Paper presented at the Workshop on Party System Institutionalization in Asia, McGill University, Montréal, Québec, Canada, August.

Nikolenyi, Csaba, and Shaul Shenhav. 2009. "In Search of Party Cohesion: The Emergence of Anti-Defection Legislation in Israel and India." Paper presented at the annual Meeting of the American Political Science Association, Toronto, Canada.

Nokken, Timothy P. 2009. "Party Switching and the Procedural Party Agenda in the US House of Representatives," in *Political Parties and Legislative Party Switching*, eds. William B. Heller and Carol Mershon. New York: Palgrave Macmillan.

Nokken, Timothy P., and Keith T. Poole. 2004. "Congressional Party Defection in American History." *Legislative Studies Quarterly* 29 (4): 545–568.

Norris, Pippa. 2004. *Electoral Engineering: Voting Rules and Political Behavior*. Cambridge: Cambridge University Press.

North, Douglass C. 1990. *Institutions, Institutional Change and Economic Performance*. New York: Cambridge University Press.

O'Neill, Kathleen. 2005. *Decentralizing the State: Elections, Parties, and Local Power in the Andes*. New York and Cambridge: Cambridge University Press.

Okole, Henry. 2008. "Party Regulation and Political Engineering in Papua New Guinea and the Pacific Islands," in *Political Parties in Conflict-Prone Societies: Regulation, Engineering and Democratic Development*, eds. Benjamin Reilly and Per Nordlund. New York and Tokyo: United Nations University Press. 182–200.

Ordeshook, Peter C., and Olga V. Shvetsova. 1994. "Ethnic Heterogeneity, District Magnitude, and the Number of Parties." *American Journal of Political Science* 38 (1): 100–123.

Ostrogorski, Moiseï. 1902. *Democracy and the Organization of Political Parties*. London: Macmillan.

Ostrom, Elinor. 1990. *Governing the Commons: The Evolution of Institutions for Collective Action*. Cambridge: Cambridge University Press.

Owens, John E. 2003. "Explaining Party Cohesion and Discipline in Democratic Legislatures: Purposiveness and Contexts." *Journal of Legislative Studies* 9 (4): 12–40.

Pasquino, Gianfranco. 1998. "New Government, Old Party Politics." *South European Society and Politics* 3 (2): 124–133.

Pasquino, Gianfranco. 1999. "Autopsia della Bicamerale," in *Politica in Italia. Edizione 99*, eds. David Hine and Salvatore Vassallo. Bologna: Il Mulino.

Patel, Nandini, Richard Tambulasi, Bright Molande, and Andrew Mpesi. 2007. *Consolidating Democratic Governance in Southern Africa: Malawi*. EISA Research Report No. 33. Johannesburg: EISA.

Pedersen, Mogens N. 1978. "La misurazione del mutamento nei sistemi partitici. Una critica." *Rivista italiana di scienza politica* 2: 243–261.

Pedersen, Mogens N. 1979. "The Dynamics of European Party Systems: Changing Patterns of Electoral Volatility." *European Journal of Political Research* 7 (1): 1–26.

Pedersen, Mogens N. 1983. "Changing Patterns of Electoral Volatility in European Party Systems, 1948–1977: Explorations in Explanation," in *Western European Party Systems: Continuity and Change*, eds. Hans Daalder and Peter Mair. London: Sage Publications.

Pierson, Paul. 2000. "Increasing Returns, Path Dependence and the Study of Politics." *American Political Science Review* 94 (2): 251–267.

Pizzorno, Alessandro. 1981. "Interests and Parties in Pluralism," in *Organizing Interests in Western Europe*, ed. Suzanne Berger. Cambridge: Cambridge University Press.
Pop-Eleches, Grigore. 2008. "A Party for All Seasons: Electoral Adaptation of Romanian Communist Successor Parties." *Communist and Post-Communist Studies* 41 (4): 465–479.
Posner, Daniel N. 2004. "Measuring Ethnic Fractionalization in Africa." *American Journal of Political Science* 48 (4): 849–863.
Powell, G. Bingham, Jr. 2000. *Elections as Instruments of Democracy: Majoritarian and Proportional Visions*. New Haven, CT: Yale University.
Powell, G. Bingham, Jr. 2004. "Political Representation in Comparative Politics." *Annual Review of Political Science* 7: 273–296.
Powell, G. Bingham, Jr., and Guy D. Whitten. 1993. "A Cross-National Analysis of Economic Voting: Taking Account of the Political Context." *American Journal of Political Science* 37 (2): 391–414.
Prodi, Romano, and Gioconda Marinelli. 2006. *Il pensiero politico di Romano Prodi*. Rome: Gremese Editore.
Project on Political Transformation and the Electoral Process in Post-Communist Europe, University of Essex. 2008. "Romania: Legislation." http://www2.essex.ac.uk/elect/database/indexCountry.asp?country=ROMANIA&opt=leg.
Przeworski, Adam, Michael E. Alvarez, Jose Antonio Cheibub, and Fernando Limongi. 2000. *Democracy and Development: Political Institutions and Well-Being in the World, 1950–1990*. Cambridge: Cambridge University Press.
Przeworski, Adam, and John Sprague. 1986. *Paper Stones: A History of Electoral Socialism*. Chicago: University of Chicago Press.
Rae, Douglas. 1971. *The Political Consequences of Electoral Laws*. 2nd edition. New Haven, CT: Yale University Press.
Rahat, Gideon, and Tamir Sheafer. 2007. "The Personalization(s) of Politics: Israel, 1949–2003." *Political Communication* 24 (1): 65–80.
Rakner, Lise, Lars Svåsand, and Nixon S. Khembo. 2007. "Fissions and Fusions, Foes and Friends: Party System Restructuring in Malawi in the 2004 General Elections." *Comparative Political Studies* 40 (9): 1112–1137.
Randall, Vicky. 2008. "Party Regulation in Conflict-Prone Societies: More Dangers than Opportunities?" in *Political Parties in Conflict-Prone Societies: Regulation, Engineering and Democratic Development*, eds. Benjamin Reilly and Per Nordlund. New York: United Nations University Press. 142–260.
Rasch, Bjørn Erik. 1999. "Electoral Systems, Parliamentary Committees, and Party Discipline: The Norwegian Storting in a Comparative Perspective," in *Party Discipline and Parliamentary Government*, eds. Shaun Bowler, David M. Farrell, and Richard S. Katz. Columbus: The Ohio State University Press. 121–140.
Reed, Stephen R., and Ethan Scheiner. 2003. "Electoral Incentives and Policy Preferences: Mixed Motives behind Party Defections in Japan." *British Journal of Political Science* 33 (3): 469–490.
Reif, Karlheinz. 1997. "Reflections: European Elections as Member State Second-Order Elections Revisited." *European Journal of Political Science* 31 (1): 115–124.
Reif, Karlheinz, and Hermann Schmitt. 1980. "Nine Second-Order National Elections: A Conceptual Framework for the Analysis of European Election Results." *European Journal of Political Research* 8 (1): 3–44.

Reilly, Benjamin. 1999. "Party Politics in Papua New Guinea: A Deviant Case?" *Pacific Affairs* 72 (2): 225–246.
Reilly, Benjamin. 2005. "Papua New Guinea: Electoral Incentives for Inter-Ethnic Accommodation," in *Electoral System Design: The New International IDEA Handbook*, eds. Andrew Reynolds, Benjamin Reilly, and Andrew Ellis. Stockholm: International Institute for Democracy and Electoral Assistance. 50–53.
Reilly, Benjamin. 2007. "Political Engineering in the Asia-Pacific." *Journal of Democracy* 18 (1): 58–72.
Reilly, Benjamin. 2008. "Introduction," in *Political Parties in Conflict-Prone Societies: Regulation, Engineering and Democratic Development*, eds. Benjamin Reilly and Per Nordlund. New York: United Nations University Press. 3–24.
Remington, Thomas F. 2001. *The Russian Parliament: Institutional Evolution in a Transitional Regime 1989–1999*. New Haven, CT: Yale University Press
Rhodes, R. A. W., Sarah A. Binder, and Bert A. Rockman, eds. 2006. *The Oxford Handbook of Political Institutions*. New York: Oxford University Press.
Riker, William H. 1962. *The Theory of Political Coalitions*. New Haven, CT: Yale University Press.
Riker, William H. 1982a. *Liberalism against Populism: A Confrontation between the Theory of Democracy and the Theory of Social Choice*. San Francisco: W. H. Freeman.
Riker, William H. 1982b. "The Two-Party System and Duverger's Law: An Essay on the History of Political Science." *American Political Science Review* 76 (4): 753–766.
Riker, William H. 1990. "Political Science and Rational Choice," in *Perspectives on Positive Political Economy*, eds. James E. Alt and Kenneth A. Shepsle. Cambridge: Cambridge University Press. 163–181.
Rodrik, Dani, and Romain Wacziarg. 2005. "Do Democratic Transitions Produce Bad Economic Outcomes?" *The American Economic Review* 95 (2): 50–55.
Rokkan, Stein. 1970. "Nation-building, Cleavage Formation and the Structuring of Mass Politics," in *Citizens, Elections, Parties: Approaches to the Comparative Study of the Processes of Development*, eds. Stein Rokkan, Angus Campbell, Per Torsvik, and Henry Valen. Oslo: Universitetforlag. 72–143.
Russian Warrior. 2008. "The First Chechnya Campaign (1993–1996)." At http://www.russianwarrior.com/STMMain.htm?1991_ChechHistoryFirst.htm&1.
Sakwa, Richard. 1995. "The Russian Elections of December 1993." *Europe-Asia Studies* 47 (2): 195–227.
Samuels, David. 2006. "Sources of Mass Partisanship in Brazil." *Latin American Politics and Society* 48 (2): 1–27.
Sánchez de Dios, Manuel. 1999. "Parliamentary Party Discipline in Spain," in *Party Discipline and Parliamentary Government*, eds. Shaun Bowler, David M. Farrell, and Richard S. Katz. Columbus: Ohio State University Press. 141–162.
Sanders, Elizabeth. 2006. "Historical Institutionalism," in *Oxford Handbook of Political Institutions*, eds. R. A. W. Rhodes, Sarah A. Binder, and Bert A. Rockman. Oxford: Oxford University Press. 39–55.
Sartori, Giovanni. 1976. *Parties and Party Systems: A Framework for Analysis*. New York: Cambridge University Press.
Sayarı, Sabri. 2007. "Towards a New Turkish Party System?" *Turkish Studies* 8 (2): 197–210.

Bibliography

Sayarı, Sabri. 2008. "Non-Electoral Sources of Party System Change in Turkey," in *Prof. Dr. Ergun Özbudun'a Armağan: Essays in Honor of Ergun Özbudun*, eds. Serap Yazıcı, Kemal Gözler, and Fuat Keyman. Ankara, Turkey: Yetkin Yayınları. 399–418.
Schattschneider, E. E. 1942. *Party Government*. New York: Rinehart & Company.
Schindler, Peter. 1984. *Datenhandbuch zur Geschichte des Deutschen Bundestages 1949 bis 1982*. Baden-Baden: Nomos.
Schindler, Peter. 1994. *Datenhandbuch zur Geschichte des Deutschen Bundestages 1983 bis 1991: Mit Anhang, Volkskammer der Deutschen Demokratischen Republik*. Baden-Baden: Nomos.
Schofield, Norman. 1986. "Existence of a 'Structurally Stable' Equilibrium for a Non-Collegial Voting Rule." *Public Choice* 51 (3): 267–284.
Schofield, Norman. 1987. "Coalitions in West European Democracies: 1945–1987." *The European Journal of Political Economy* 3: 555–591.
Schofield, Norman. 1993. "Political Competition and Multiparty Coalition Governments." *European Journal of Political Research* 23 (1): 1–33.
Schofield, Norman. 2008. *The Political Economy of Democracy and Tyranny*. Munich, Germany: Oldenbourg.
Schofield, Norman. 2009. "Switching Equilibria," in *Political Parties and Legislative Party Switching*, eds. William B. Heller and Carol Mershon. New York: Palgrave Macmillan.
Schofield, Norman, Bernard Grofman, and Scott L. Feld. 1988. "The Core and the Stability of Group Choice in Spatial Voting Games." *American Political Science Review* 8 (1): 195–211.
Schofield, Norman, and Itai Sened. 2006. *Multiparty Democracy: Elections and Legislative Politics*. Cambridge : Cambridge University Press.
Schüttemeyer, Suzanne S. 1994. "Hierarchy and Efficiency in the Bundestag: The German Answer for Institutionalizing Parliament," in *Parliaments in the Modern World: Changing Institutions*, eds. Gary W. Copeland and Samuel C. Patterson. Ann Arbor: University of Michigan Press. 29–58.
Setta, Sandro. 2005. *L'uomo qualunque. 1944–1948*. Rome: Editori Laterza.
Shabad, Goldie, and Kazimierz M. Slomczynski. 2004. "Inter-Party Mobility among Parliamentary Candidates in Post-Communist East Central Europe." *Party Politics* 10 (2): 151–176.
Shamir, Michael, Raphael Ventura, Asher Arian, and Orit Kedar. 2008. "Kadima: Forward in a Dealigned Party System," in *The Elections in Israel, 2006*, eds. Asher Arian and Michal Shamir. Edison, NJ: Transaction Publishers.
Shepsle, Kenneth A. 1979. "Institutional Arrangements and Equilibrium in Multidimensional Voting Models." *American Journal of Political Science* 23 (1): 27–59.
Shepsle, Kenneth A. 1986. "Institutional Equilibrium and Equilibrium Institutions." In Herbert F. Weisberg, ed., *Political Science: The Science of Politics*. New York: Agathon.
Shepsle, Kenneth A. 1989. "Studying Institutions: Some Lessons from the Rational Choice Approach." *Journal of Theoretical Politics* 1 (2): 131–147.
Shepsle, Kenneth A. 2006. "Rational Choice Institutionalism," in *Oxford Handbook of Political Institutions*, eds. R. A. W. Rhodes, Sarah A. Binder, and Bert A. Rockman. Oxford: Oxford University Press. 23–38.

Shepsle, Kenneth A., and Barry R. Weingast. 1987. "The Institutional Foundations of Committee Powers." *American Political Science Review* 81 (1): 85–104.

Shugart, Matthew Soberg. 1995. "The Electoral Cycle and Institutional Sources of Divided Presidential Government." *American Political Science Review* 89 (2): 327–343.

Shugart, Matthew Soberg, and Martin P. Wattenberg. 2001. *Mixed-Member Electoral Systems: The Best of Both Worlds?* Oxford: Oxford University Press.

Shvetsova, Olga. 2002. "Gaining Legislative Control Through Strategic District Nomination: The Case of the Russian Left in 1995." *Legislative Studies Quarterly* 27: 635–657.

Shvetsova, Olga. 2003. "Resolving the Problem of Pre-Election Coordination: The 1999 Parliamentary Election as Elite Presidential 'Primary,'" in *Elections, Parties, and the Future of Russia*, eds. Vicki Hesli and William S. Reisinger. Cambridge: Cambridge University Press.

Shvetsova, Olga. 2005. "Compromising a Long Lasting Transitional Formula," in *Handbook of Electoral System Design*, ed. Josep M. Colomer. New York: St. Martin's Press. 382–397.

Sinnott, Richard. 1995. *Irish Voters Decide: Voting Behaviour in Elections and Referendums Since 1918*. Manchester: Manchester University Press.

Smyth, Regina. 2006. *Candidate Strategies and Electoral Competition in the Russian Federation: Democracy without Foundation*. New York and Cambridge: Cambridge University Press.

Snyder, James M., Jr., and Michael M. Ting. 2002. "An Informational Rationale for Political Parties." *American Journal of Political Science* 46 (1): 90–110.

Somer-Topcu, Zeynep, and Laron K. Williams. 2008. "Survival of the Fittest? Cabinet Duration in Postcommunist Europe." *Comparative Politics* 40 (3): 313–329.

Stepan, Alfred, and Cindy Skach. 1993. "Constitutional Frameworks and Democratic Consolidation: Parliamentarianism Versus Presidentialism." *World Politics* 46 (1): 1–22.

Stokes, Susan C. 1999. "Political Parties and Democracy." *Annual Review of Political Science* 2: 243–267.

Strøm, Kaare. 1985. "Party Goals and Government Performance in Parliamentary Democracies." *American Political Science Review* 79 (3): 738–754.

Strøm, Kaare. 1990a. "A Behavioral Theory of Competitive Political Parties." *American Journal of Political Science* 34 (2): 565–598.

Strøm, Kaare. 1990b. *Minority Government and Majority Rule*. Cambridge: Cambridge University Press.

Strøm, Kaare, Ian Budge, and Michael J. Laver. 1994. "Constraints on Cabinet Formation in Parliamentary Democracies." *American Journal of Political Science* 38 (2): 303–335.

Strøm, Kaare, Wolfgang C. Müller, and Torbjorn Bergman, eds. 2008. *Cabinets and Coalition Bargaining*. Oxford: Oxford University Press.

Szarka, Joseph. 1997. "Snatching Defeat from the Jaws of Victory: The French Parliamentary Elections of 25 May and 1 June 1997." *West European Politics* 20 (4): 192–199.

Taagepera, Rein. 1997. "Effective Number of Parties for Incomplete Data." *Electoral Studies* 16 (2): 145–151.

Taagepera, Rein. 1999. "Supplementing the Effective Number of Parties." *Electoral Studies* 18 (4): 497–504.
Taagepera, Rein, and Matthew Soberg Shugart. 1989. *Seats and Votes: The Effects and Determinants of Electoral Systems.* New Haven, CT: Yale University Press.
Tan, Paige Johnson. 2004. "Party Rooting, Political Operators, and Instability in Indonesia: A Consideration of Party System Institutionalization in a Communally Charged Society." Paper presented at the Annual Meetings of the Southern Political Science Association, New Orleans, January.
Tan, Paige Johnson. 2006. "Indonesia's Seven Years after Suharto: Party System Institutionalization in a New Democracy." *Contemporary Southeast Asia* 28 (1): 88–114.
Tavits, Margit. 2008. "Party Systems in the Making: The Emergence and Success of New Parties in New Democracies." *British Journal of Political Science* 38 (1): 113–133.
Thames, Frank C. 2005. "Parliamentary Party Switching in the Ukrainian Rada, 1998–2002." Paper presented at the annual meeting of the Midwest Political Science Association, Chicago, Illinois.
Thames, Frank C. 2007. "Searching for the Electoral Connection: Parliamentary Party Switching in the Ukrainian Rada, 1998–2002." *Legislative Studies Quarterly* 32 (2): 223–246.
Thelen, Kathleen. 1999. "Historical Institutionalism in Comparative Politics." *Annual Review of Political Science* 2: 369–404.
Thelen, Kathleen, and Sven Steinmo. 1992. "Historical Institutionalism in Comparative Politics." In *Structuring Politics: Historical Institutionalism in Comparative Analysis*, eds. Sven Steinmo, Kathleen Thelen, and Frank Longstreth. New York: Cambridge University Press.
Tomás Mallén, Beatriz. 2002. *Transfuguismo parlamentario y democracia de partidos.* Madrid: Centro de Estudios Politicos y Constitucionales.
Valenzuela, Arturo. 2004. "Latin American Presidencies Interrupted." *Journal of Democracy* 15 (4): 5–19.
van de Walle, Nicolas. 2003. "Presidentialism and Clientelism in Africa's Emerging Party Systems." *Journal of Modern African Studies* 41 (2): 297–321.
Verzichelli, Luca. 1996. "I gruppi parlamentari dopo il 1994. Fluidità e riaggregazioni." *Rivista italiana di scienza politica* 26 (2): 391–413.
Verzichelli, Luca. 2003. "Much Ado about Something? Parliamentary Politics in Italy Amid the Rhetoric of Majority Rule and an Uncertain Party System." *Journal of Legislative Studies* 9 (2): 35–55.
Vowles, Jack. 2000. "Introducing Proportional Representation: The New Zealand Experience." *Parliamentary Affairs* 53: 680–696.
Vowles, Jack, Susan A. Banducci, and Jeffrey A. Karp. 2006. "Forecasting and Evaluating the Consequences of Electoral Change in New Zealand." *Acta Politica* 41: 267–284.
Vowles, Jack, Jeffrey A. Karp, and Susan A. Banducci. 2000. "Proportional Representation on Trial: Elites vs. Mass Opinion on Electoral System Change in New Zealand." Paper presented at the annual meetings of the American Political Science Association, Washington, DC.
Warner, Steven, and Diego Gambetta. 1994. *La retorica della riforma. Fine del sistema proporzionale in Italia.* Turin: Einaudi.

Weinberg, Leonard B. 1995. *The Transformation of Italian Communism*. Piscataway, NJ: Transaction Publishers.
Weingast, Barry R. 1995. "The Economic Role of Political Institutions: Market-Preserving Federalism and Economic Development." *Journal of Law, Economics, and Organization* 11 (1): 1–31.
Wertman, Douglas A. 1977. "The Italian Electoral Process," in *Italy at the Polls: The Parliamentary Elections of 1976*, ed. Howard R. Penniman. Washington, DC: American Enterprise Institute. 41–79.
Wertman, Douglas A. 1995. "The Last Year of the Christian Democratic Party," in *Italian Politics: Ending the First Republic*, eds. Carol Mershon and Gianfranco Pasquino. Boulder, CO: Westview Press.
Weyland, Kurt. 2008. "Toward a New Theory of Institutional Change." *World Politics* 60 (2): 281–314.
White, Stephen, Richard Rose, and Ian McAllister. 1997. *How Russia Votes*. Chatham, NJ: Chatham House.
Wolinetz, Steven. 2006. "Party Systems and Party System Types," in *Handbook of Party Politics*, eds. Richard S. Katz and William J. Crotty. Thousand Oaks, CA: Sage Publications.
Young, Daniel J. 2007. "Politics without Positions: Party Loyalty and Voting Behavior in Malawi." Paper presented at the meeting of the Working Group in African Political Economy, Stanford, California, December.
Young, Daniel J. 2008. "Where Ideology Does Not Divide: Political Behavior in Malawi's Multiparty Era." Ph.D. diss., University of California, Los Angeles.
Young, Daniel J. 2012. "An Initial Look into Party Switching in Africa: Evidence from Malawi." *Party Politics*. doi:10.1177/1354068811436041.
Zucchini, Francesco. 1997. "La decisione di voto. I tempi, l'oggetto, i modi," in *A domanda risponde. Il cambiamento del voto degli italiani nelle elezioni del 1994 e del 1996*, eds. Piergiorgio Corbetta and Arturo M. L. Parisi. Bologna: Il Mulino. 91–137.
Zucchini, Francesco. 2001. "La commissione affari costituzionali. Gli effetti paralizzanti del mutamento," in *Parlamento e processo legislativo in Italia. Continuità e mutamento*, eds. Giliberto Capano and Marco Giuliani. Bologna: Il Mulino. 153–186.

Appendixes

Appendix A: Chapter Appendixes

Chapter 3

3A.1 Proof of Proposition 1

Proposition 1: Strategic incumbents will change parties only during active parliamentary stages.

Proof: An incumbent legislator, i, will move to a new party, π, from her original party, o, during month j, when the utility differential for incumbent i is positive; that is, if
$u_i^j(\cdot, \pi) > u_i^j(\cdot, o)$, or equivalently

$$\lambda a_\pi^j + \theta b_\pi^j + \tau \sum_{k=1}^{n} p_k^{i\pi} > \lambda a_o^j + \theta b_o^j + \tau \sum_{k=1}^{n} p_k^{io.} \qquad (3.A1)$$

Because $\tau \sum_{k=1}^{n} p_k^{i\pi} < \tau \sum_{k=1}^{n} p_k^{io}$ by assumption, and $\lambda a_\pi^j + \theta b_\pi^j = 0$ whenever $a_\pi^j = 0$ and $b_\pi^j = 0$, which happens $\forall j \notin C \cup B$ (where C is the set of months in which legislators vie for control of an active policy agenda, and B is the set of months in which legislators seek a share of the benefits of legislative [and executive] office that are up for distribution), it follows that expression [3.A1] can hold only during active months in the parliamentary cycle.

3A.2 Proof of Proposition 2

Proposition 2: Conditional on the availability of partisan gains, strategic incumbents will time changes of party near the middle of a legislative term.

Proof: First incorporate the probability of receiving voter k's vote into the utility function of incumbent legislator i. That utility function, as stated in expression (3.1) from section 3.1.1, thus becomes:

$$u_i(\lambda, \theta, \tau) = f(\lambda, \theta) + \tau \sum_{k=1}^{n} p_k^i(x_i, I_i, H^i). \qquad (3.A2)$$

Assuming that all voters assign equal value to partisanship and loyalty, and that those factors additively contribute to the probability of voter k voting for incumbent i, we can rewrite (3.A2) as:

$$u_i(\cdot, \tau, H^i) = f(\lambda, \theta) + \tau \sum_{k=1}^{n} g_k^i(x_i, x_k) + \tau \nu(\sigma^2(I_i, H^i, \alpha)) \quad (3.\text{A}3)$$

The incumbent politician's utility in expression (3.A3) is a function of the parliamentary (policy and office) benefits she receives, $f(\lambda, \theta)$, and of her expected vote in the next election, $\tau \sum_{k=1}^{n} g_k^i(x_i, x_k) + \tau \nu(\sigma^2(I_i, H^i, \alpha))$. Her expected vote, in turn, reflects voters' reaction to her history of party loyalty – that is, steadfast (vs. inconstant) party affiliation – in addition to her policy proximity to her voters. We use $g_k^i(x_i, x_k)$ to designate the policy-related element of the probability that voter k would vote for candidate i. For each individual voter, this is a function of the distance between the policy locations of the voter and the candidate, $|x_i, x_k|$, where the policy location of the voter is her ideal point, and the policy location of the candidate is his perceived policy platform. Expression $\nu(\sigma^2(I_i, H^i, \alpha))$ is the component in a voter's probability of voting for candidate i that depends on the candidate's policy variance.[1] For convenience, we assume that all voters, regardless of their policy ideals, respond to candidates' variance in a similar way, which allows us to take $\nu(\sigma^2(I_i, H^i, \alpha))$ from under the summation sign and treat it as an additive component of the utility function of an incumbent politician. This is useful because this component is the only part of the politician's utility (negatively) affected by her history of switching during the term.

Note that $\nu(\sigma^2(I_i, H^i, \alpha))$ and thus also $u_i(\cdot, \tau, H^i, \alpha)$ are declining in $\sum_{j=0}^{m} h_j^i(\delta^{m-j}\Delta l + \phi^j \Delta L)$. The more recently and frequently an incumbent has changed parties near the initiating and the upcoming elections, the greater the utility loss she will suffer, other things equal. For incumbent legislator i in party o, who has remained loyal to the original electoral label:

$$u_i(\lambda, \theta, \tau) = f(\lambda, \theta) + \tau \sum_{k=1}^{n} p_k^i(x_i, I_i, L_o, \alpha) \quad (3.\text{A}4)$$

For the mobile incumbent now in party π, who switched just once during the given legislative term, in month j, this expression becomes

$$u_i(\lambda, \theta, \tau) = f(\lambda, \theta) + \tau \sum_{k=1}^{n} p_k^i(x_i, I_i, (L_o + \delta^{m-j}\Delta l + \phi^j \Delta L)) \quad (3.\text{A}5)$$

---

[1] Our model does not incorporate variation across party systems in relationships between candidates' policy stances and party platforms.

Appendixes

Observe that expression (3.A5) depicts the single move made by the recruit to party π as occurring before m, the month of the election for the subsequent legislature, yet after o, the month of the term coinciding with the election initiating the legislature. The logic here indicates that the minimum in electoral damage conditional on executing the switch would correspond to the maximum of $L_i(j) = L_o + \delta^{m-j}\Delta l + \phi^j \Delta L$ or, when $\Delta l, \Delta L < 0$, to the minimum of $\delta^{m-j}\Delta l + \phi^j \Delta L$. Differentiating by j, we obtain

$$\partial[\delta^{m-j}\Delta l + \phi^j \Delta L]/\partial j = \phi^j \log\phi\Delta L - \delta^{m-j}\log\delta\Delta l. \quad (3.A6)$$

This function attains the value of zero somewhere in the middle of the parliamentary term; that is, in the interval $[1; m]$. To illustrate, setting $\delta = \phi, \Delta l = \Delta L$, it becomes zero at

$$\phi^j \log\phi\Delta L = \phi^{m-j} \log\phi\Delta L, \text{ or at } j = m/2.$$

The conclusion is thus that legislative incumbents' utility loss from switching parties is minimized and their benefits are maximized, all else equal, if moves are timed near the middle of a legislative term.[2]

3A.3 Case Selection

This appendix supplements the discussion of case selection in Chapter 3. First, we aim to maximize institutional variation across country-terms in the effort to establish the generalizability of our argument. We strive in the comprehensive dataset for coverage starting with each country's first democratic election after World War II, but confront problems with the availability of monthly observations on legislator behavior for Australia and above all France. The timing of the advent of democracy shortens the data series for Spain and even more for Romania.

Second, the primary in-depth terms do not enter into the large-N analysis. The reason for this exclusion is indicated in Chapter 9: the 1996–2001 Italian and the 1993–1995 Russian legislatures were those whose analysis guided the development of the formal model we have presented here.

Third, we omit the Italian 1994–1996 legislature from the large-N dataset, given severe difficulties both in theorizing about voter and MP behavior and in operationalizing incumbent switching when the hybrid electoral rules came into effect in 1994. First, it strains credulity to assume voter preferences for MP partisan loyalty in 1994, because many of the party actors were new and because the phenomenon of SMD candidates identified with electoral cartels was new as well. In 1996, in contrast, voters could associate candidates (even SMD candidates) with party labels, given very rapid voter learning and given cartel leaders' explicit negotiation of SMD candidacies in proportion to expected party

---

[2] We invite the reader to note again that the loss parameters are a function of institutional variation (a). The maximization in (3.A6) occurs regardless of the value of a, of course.

strength (e.g., Corbetta and Parisi 1997; Di Virgilio 1997, esp. 91–135; 2002). For their part, the party leaders who headed electoral cartels in 1996 could estimate party strength and could bargain to "proportionalize" SMD candidacies because they had learned from experience in the 1994 legislative and 1995 regional elections (Di Virgilio 1997, esp. 106). Thus in 1996, all of the center-right cartel's SMD candidates and 93 per cent of the center-left cartel's SMD candidates were linked to just one PR party list, whereas in 1994, over 80 per cent of the two center-right cartels' candidates and roughly 40 per cent of the center-left cartel's candidates were linked to multiple PR lists (Di Virgilio 1994, 125; no information available on the nature of links for the 1994 centrist cartel, which did not compete in 1996). Second, all of this means that it is well nigh impossible to establish a firm baseline for MP switching in the 1994–1996 Italian term. Consider the deputy who, when the 1994–1996 legislature opens, declares affiliation with one of the four parliamentary groups that are the

TABLE 3A.4 *Descriptive statistics on dependent and independent variables, large-N analysis (N = 4,072).*

Variable	Mean	Min	Max	SD
Raw N moves	0.547	0	207	5.756
Fact of switching	0.127	0	1	0.334
Moves per 100 members of parliament (MPs)	0.116	0	49.541	1.208
Month	20.708	0	61	14.396
Month squared	636.002	0	3721	740.485
Length of term	42.416	7	62	13.117
Single-member district (SMD)	0.675	0	1	0.468
Proportional	0.159	0	1	0.366
Presidential	0.212	0	1	0.400
Federal	0.706	0	1	0.409
Weak party system institutionalization	0.024	0	1	0.153

TABLE 3A.5 *Descriptive statistics on dependent and independent variables, secondary in-depth legislative terms (N = 1,200).*

Variable	Mean	Min	Max	SD
Raw N moves	1.015	0	207	9.908
Fact of switching	0.148	0	1	0.355
Moves per 100 members of parliament (MPs)	0.194	0	49.541	1.996
Month	20.661	0	60	14.635
Month squared	640.876	0	3600	759.495
Length of term	42.322	7	61	13.952
Single-member district (SMD)	0.610	0	1	0.488
Proportional	0.390	0	1	0.488
Presidential	0.381	0	1	0.486
Federal	0.478	0	1	0.500
Weak party system institutionalization	0.081	0	1	0.273

Appendixes

legislative incarnations of the four party lists with which she was linked as an SMD candidate. Has she switched or not? The answer is unclear, and the question recurs for the many SMD candidates with links to multiple PR lists. Hence operationalizing switching in the 1994–1996 Italian term poses challenges not found in any other term we study.

Chapter 4

TABLE 4A.1 *Key to active stages and substages of the parliamentary cycle, Italian 1996–2001 Chamber*

Stage A is defined as the period when newly elected members of parliament (MPs) affiliate with parliamentary groups. This stage runs from election day (21-IV-96) to the last day that MPs must announce membership in parliamentary groups (14-V-96, two weekdays after first session of legislature on 9/10-V-96).

Stage B is the period of allocation of legislative and executive office benefits. In a legislative term featuring one executive, the executive B runs from the day groups are announced to the day all legislative and executive payoffs are completed; because multiple executives govern during the 1996–2001 Italian term, stage B is not continuous and is defined as the sum of substages B.1 through B.6.

B.1 = Day groups announced *(14-V-96)* to day payoffs in first cabinet are announced (*18-V-96*)

B.2 = Day executive payoffs allocated to day allocations of all legislative payoffs are completed (Chamber leadership is elected 9-V-96, 15-V-96; committee assignments are completed and committee chairs elected *5-VI-96*)

B.3 = Day *la Bicamerale* gains two-thirds approval in lower house (22-I-97) to day committee elects chair (includes days that committee appointments are made) (*5-II-97*)

B.4. = Day government falls (9-X-98) to day new cabinet offices are announced (21-X-98)

B.5. = Day government resigns (*18-XII-99*) to day new cabinet payoffs are named (21-XII-99)

B.6. = Day government resigns (*17-IV-00*) in light of preceding day's losses in regional elections, to day new executive payoffs are announced (*25-IV-00*)

Stage C is defined for decision making on the national budget and on constitutional reform. Substages are listed chronologically by start date, although some substages overlap.

C.1 = Day Senate transmits to lower house constitutional bill for establishment of Bicameral Committee on Constitutional Reform (30-VII-96), to the day lower house grants first approval of committee, known as *la Bicamerale* (2-VIII-96)

C.2 = Day executive presents 1997 budget bill (*legge finanziaria*) for first reading in Chamber (*30-IX-96*) to day 1997 budget gains final approval in both houses (22-XII-96)

C.3 = Day Senate grants second (two-thirds) approval of *la Bicamerale* and transmits revised bill to Chamber (*16-I-97*) to day *la Bicamerale* gains required two-thirds approval in Chamber (22-I-97)

C.4 = Day *la Bicamerale* chair begins to direct work of committee (*5-II-97*) to day Chamber President removes unified text of constitutional reforms from agenda due to interparty discord (*9-VI-98*); *la Bicamerale* dissolved same day. Some individual articles of the Constitution are amended after 9-VI-98, but effort to frame integrated package of reforms is abandoned.

C.5 = Day Senate transmits 1998 budget bill for first reading in lower house (*22-XI-97*) to day 1998 budget gains final approval from both houses (*18-XII-97*) (wholly subsumed within C.4)

TABLE 4A.1 (*cont.*)

C.6 = Day executive presents 1999 budget bill for first reading in lower house (*30-IX-98*) to day conflicts over budget (and to some degree foreign policy) lead to fall of government on confidence vote (*9-X-98*)

C.7 = Day committee work relevant to 1999 budget bill resumes in lower house (*28-X-98*) to day 1999 budget gains final approval from both houses (*20-XII-98*)

C.8 = Day Senate transmits 2000 budget bill for first reading in lower house (*15-XI-99*) to day 2000 budget gains final approval from both houses (*16-XII-99*)

C.9 = Day government presents 2001 budget bill for first reading in lower house (*30-IX-00*) to day 2001 budget gains final approval from both houses (*22-XII-00*)

Stage E is defined for major subnational elections and for European Parliament elections. "Major" subnational elections are identified as those involving numerous, populous, and prominent areas of the national territory.

E.1. Ninetieth day before first round of elections (*27-I-97*) to thirtieth day after second round (*10-VI-97*)

E.2. Ninetieth day before first round (*18-VIII-97*) to thirtieth day after second (*30-XII-97*)

E.3. Ninetieth day before first round (*23-II-98*) to thirtieth day after second round (*7-VII-98*)

E.4. Ninetieth day before first round (*15-III-99*) to thirtieth day after second (*27-VII-99*)

E.5. Ninetieth day before elections (*17-I-00*) to thirtieth day after (*16-V-00*)

Sources: Camera dei Deputati (2008b); Istituto Cattaneo (2010); Ministero dell'Interno (2008); Pasquino (1999).

TABLE 4A.2 *Key to active stages and substages of the parliamentary cycle, Russian 1993–1995 Duma.*

Stage A is the period for member of parliament (MP) affiliation with parliamentary groups (factions in the Duma).

A.1 = Election day to the day of factional selection by single-member district (SMD) MPs (*12-XII-93*).

A.2 = Day of the Duma's adoption of the procedure for factional announcement (*1-IV-94*) to day before start of decision making on budget (*11-V-94*). This was the first time proportional representation (PR) MPs could shop for a new faction and thus we code a recurrence of A.

Stage B = Allocation of committee posts as reflected in the content of considered legislation, from *10-I-94* to *1-IV-94*.

Stage C is defined for decision making on the national budget and internal security, with the latter entailing a constitutional crisis. We order substages chronologically.

C.1 = Day of the start of the intense budget legislative activity (*11-V-94*), to day of the legislative agenda shifting away from the budget (*6-VII-94*)

C.2 = Day marking start of First Chechen War (*29-XI-94*) to end of campaign (*19-I-95*); overlaps entirely with the legislative attempt to deal with the 1995 budget in January 1995.

C.3 = Day marking start of second major campaign of Chechen war (*6-III-95*) to end of campaign (*20-III-95*).

C.4 = Day marking start of hostage crisis, when insurgents capture civilians inside Budennovsk hospital (*14-VI-95*), to ceasefire (*30-VI-95*).

Sources: On the legislative agenda and content of passed and debated legislation: INDEM (2000). On the phases of the Chechen warfare, also: Russian Warrior (2008).

Appendixes

Chapter 6

TABLE 6A.1 *Multiple measures of incumbents' changes of party during month j and two views of frequency of interparty moves in comprehensive dataset.*

Variable name	Operationalization	Min	Max	SD	Mean
Move	Raw count interparty moves	0	207	5.756	0.547
Fact	Absence vs. occurrence of moves	0	1	0.334	0.127
Category	Absence, individual, collective moves	0	2	0.350	0.132
% units in data with counts of *Move*	0	1	2–5	6–9	10–19	≥20
% monthly observations (n = 4,072)	87.254	8.251	3.168	0.442	0.467	0.418
% parliamentary terms (n = 110)	20.909	19.091	26.364	8.182	6.364	19.091

TABLE 6A.2 *Three sets of independent variables for large-N analysis: measures and expectations.*

SET/SUBSET/Name of variable	Operationalization	Coefficient Sign
INDUCEMENTS (P1; C1; H1)		
Stage A, Affiliation	First two months of term, starting election day	+
Stage B, Benefits	For committees: First month that legislature in session; in parliamentary systems, any month in which cabinet(s) negotiated	+
Stage C, Control of policy	Any month that legislature is in session	+
Stage D, Dormant	As indicated by other stages (residual)	–
DETERRENTS (P2; H2–4)		
Time left in term (H2)	N months to next election; linear and squared	+
Time since start of term (H3)	N months since last election; linear and squared	+
Electoral rules (H4)	Proportional rules 1, 0 otherwise	+
RIVAL HYPOTHESES AND CONTROLS		(sign if alternative holds)
PARTY SYSTEM PROPERTIES		
Number of legislative parties	Raw N of legislative parties at election t	+
	Effective N of legislative parties at t	+

TABLE 6A.2 (cont.)

SET/SUBSET /Name of variable	Operationalization	Coefficient Sign
Electoral volatility	Electoral volatility election $t - 1$ to t	+
Party system institutionalization	Weak (Romania) 1, 0 otherwise	d.n.s.
DEMOCRATIC INSTITUTIONS		
Federalism	Federal and highly regionalized 1, 0 otherwise	+
District magnitude	Mean and median district magnitude	+
Run-up to election $t + 1$	Last six months of term before election $t + 1$	+
Presidentialism	(Semi-) presidential 1, 0 parliamentary	+
Age of democratic regime	N uninterrupted months since first democratic national election (+6 or above on Polity IV index)	–
SOCIOLOGICAL AND STRUCTURAL FACTORS		
Ethnic fractionalization	Fearon ethnic fractionalization index	d.n.s.
	Alesina indices (ethnicity; language; religion)	d.n.s.
Economic growth	Mean three-year growth in gross domestic product (GDP)	d.n.s.
Economic development	GDP per capita	d.n.s.
Economic inequality	Gini coefficient of income inequality	d.n.s.
CULTURAL FACTORS AND SALIENT ISSUES		
Education	National-level mean level of schooling for age 15+	+ / –
Cold War	Months 02/1947–12/1991 coded 1, 0 otherwise	+ / –

Key to abbreviations: P, Proposition; C, Corollary; H, Hypothesis; d.n.s., deterrents not significant: with this variable added, deterrents should lack significance
Multiple entries in right column indicate competing claims (see text).

Appendix B

TABLE B.1 *Operationalizing incumbents' changes of parliamentary party group and incumbents' formation of new parliamentary parties.*

Label	Definition	Rules for Coding
Individual-level behavior		
Move (or switch)	Change in party affiliation	Includes adoption or abandonment of independent status; for members of parliament (MPs) elected as independents, includes initial abandonment of that status.
		Includes rule-driven move to, e.g., Mixed Group for MPs elected from tiny parties. Such a move entails a departure from the MP's electoral label.
		Excludes reacquisition of electoral label when new interpretation of same parliamentary rules permits an MP once forced to sit in the Mixed Group to declare affiliation with her electoral label.
		Includes adoption of parliamentary party label different from electoral label, with one exception as noted below.
		If entire parliamentary party adopts name only slightly different from electoral label (so that voters see substantial continuity in label), do not code moves. This rule informs coding of, for example, Australian Country party (renamed National Country in 1975, National Party of Australia 1982, and then National Party 2003).
New parliamentary parties, as result of individual-level behavior		
Fission (or split)	Moves split extant party, creating one or more new parties	When split occurs, code as switchers only those MPs who break away from parent party, with two exceptions as noted below.
		When split reconstitutes two formerly separate parties, briefly merged, code as switchers MPs moving to both parties.

TABLE B.1 (*cont.*)

Label	Definition	Rules for Coding
		When split coincides with reorganization of parent party and breakaway is substantial in size, code as switchers all MPs involved. Voters do not see continuity in label. This rule informs coding of, for example, Italian Christian Democrats in 1994 (all MPs involved counted as switching) and Communists in 1991. Given some ambiguity in the latter case, we ran estimations with the alternative coding (only breakaway MPs counted as switchers) and no substantive impact on results emerged.
Fusion (or merger)	Moves merge two or more extant parties, creating one new party	When fusion occurs, count moves from all parties, with one exception as noted below.
		When splinter party rejoins parent party, reconstituting prior (old) party, count moves only from splinter; when breakaway is substantial in size, however, count all moves.
Start-up	Moves found new party with MPs from multiple parties	Exclude as a start-up any name change that triggers zero or very few moves. With no or very few moves, voters see substantial continuity in label; do count any of the few exits as moves.

Author Index

Aldrich, John H., 6, 9, 15, 20, 33, 37, 109, 116, 172
Alesina, Alberto 114, 133, 179, 210
Alvarez, Michael, 109
Ames, Barry, 152, 170
Amorim Neto, Octavio, 111, 114, 129, 133
Anderson, Christopher J., 114
Arriola, Leonardo R., 114
Astraldi, Romolo, 167
Austen-Smith, David, 20

Baldassarri, Delia, 61
Banducci, Susan A., 11, 150, 154, 160
Banks, Jeffrey, 20
Baron, David P., 20
Barro, Robert J., 115
Bartolini, Stefano, 6, 8, 12, 14, 78, 110, 167
Baum, Michael A., 159
Beck, Paul A., 6, 15
Benoit, Kenneth, 6, 9, 31, 109, 111, 170
Bergman, Torbjörn, 57, 70, 106, 170
Bertelsmann-Stiftung, 157
Bianco, William T., 9, 15, 20
Binder, Sarah A., 169
Birnir, Jóhanna K., 10, 70, 75
Black, Duncan, 20
Blimes, Randall J., 114
Boix, Carles, 109
Booysen, Susan, 160
Borgida, Eugene, 116
Bowler, Shaun, 21
Budge, Ian, 14, 21, 26, 170

Bull, Martin, 75
Butler, David, 49, 70, 77, 78, 103, 171
Butler, Gareth, 49, 70, 77, 78, 103, 171

Calvert, Randall L., 3, 169
Canon, David T., 9
Capano, Giliberto, 71, 88
Caramani, Daniele, 5, 49, 105, 108, 113, 114, 133, 167
Carey, John M., 38, 110, 111, 114, 115
Chandra, Kanchan, 114, 158
Cheibub, José A., 21, 109, 110, 112
Chhibber, Pradeep K., 6, 109, 111
Chiva, Cristina, 72, 75, 156
Colton, Timothy J., 61, 85, 86
Converse, Philip E., 38, 113, 165
Corbetta, Piergiorgio, 57, 63, 206
Covington, Cary R., 24
Cox, Gary W., 6, 21, 24, 35, 37, 111, 114, 129, 133, 153, 170, 172
Crawford, Sue E. S., 3
Crewe, Ivor, 73, 75, 77, 78, 93
Cunow, Saul, 158

Dahl, Robert A., 1, 7
Dalton, Russell J., 6, 115, 150
De Jager, Nicola, 160
De Vito, Francesco, 92
Den Hartog, Chris, 22, 24
Desposato, Scott W., 9, 11, 33, 115, 150, 152, 153, 158
Desserud, Donald A., 25
Di Mascio, Fabrizio, 29
Di Palma, Giuseppe, 88
Di Scala, Spencer M., 71, 75, 77

Di Virgilio, Francesco, 63, 78, 84, 206
Diermeier, Daniel, 6, 20, 37, 38, 170
Donovan, Mark, 28, 67
Döring, Herbert, 35
Downs, Anthony, 4, 6, 19, 33
Drucker, H. M., 75, 77
Duch, Raymond M., 109, 114
Duverger, Maurice, 6, 8

España-Nájera, Annabella, 110
Evans, Geoffrey, 61

Farneti, Paolo, 167
Farrell, David M., 21
Feaver, Peter D., 116
Feld, Scott, 20, 26, 170
Ferejohn, John A., 20
Ferree, Karen E., 5, 109, 114, 152, 153
Filippov, Mikhail, 6, 111, 112
Flanagan, Scott C., 6
Fleischer, David, 158
Fortín, Javier, 11, 150
Franchino, Fabio, 20
Franklin, Mark N., 4, 6, 114
Freire, André, 159
Fukai, Shigeko N., 153
Fukui, Haruhiro, 153

Gallagher, Michael, 12, 110
Gambetta, Diego, 77
Gelpi, Christopher F., 116
Gervasoni, Carlos, 110, 159
Giannetti, Daniela, 6, 26, 27, 28, 29, 30, 31, 170
Ginsborg, Paul, 13, 77
Giuliani, Marco, 71, 88
Giusti, Ugo, 167
Golder, Matt, 110
Golosov, Grigoriy, 58
Grassi Orsini, Fabio, 167
Greif, Avner, 3, 168, 169
Grofman, Bernard, 20, 26, 170
Gunther, Richard, 159, 161
Gussow, David, 25

Habyarimana, James, 114
Haggard, Stephen, 21, 57

Hagopian, Frances, 159
Hall, Peter A., 3, 169
Hallerberg, Mark, 57
Hayden, Jacqueline, 6, 170
Heath, Anthony F., 15
Heller, William B., 9, 11, 14, 27, 29, 31, 33, 37, 59, 68, 102, 150
Hellman, Stephen, 71
Hellwig, Timothy T., 15
Herron, Erik S., 109
Hesli, Vicki L., 61
Heywood, Paul, 61
Hicken, Allen, 105, 108, 113, 150, 151
Hickey, Jennifer G., 95
Hirschman, Albert O., 19
Hix, Simon, 110, 111, 114, 115, 153
Hopkin, Jonathan, 75
Horowitz, Donald L., 133, 152
Høyland, Bjørn, 20
Huber, John D., 171
Hug, Simon, 6
Humphreys, Macartan, 20, 114

Ieraci, Giuseppe, 31
Ignazi, Piero, 75
Indriðason, Indriði, 106
Inglehart, Ronald F., 6
Instituto Cattaneo, 67

Janda, Kenneth, 155
Jayachandran, Seema, 24

Kadima, Denis, 160
Kam, Christopher, 106
Kaminski, Marek M., 60
Kashyap, Subhash, 158
Karp, Jeffrey A., 11, 150, 154, 160
Kato, Junko, 9, 31, 153, 170, 171
Katz, Richard S., 5, 6, 8, 21, 60, 110
Key, V. O., 1, 4, 8, 46, 62, 70, 76, 107, 150, 207, 208, 210
Khelmko, Irina, 150
Khembo, Nixon S., 153
King, Anthony, 73, 75, 77, 78, 93
Kingston, Christopher, 169
Kopecký, Petr, 150
Klingemann, Hans-Dieter, 14, 21

Author Index

Knight, Jack, 3, 169
Kollman, Ken, 6, 105, 108, 109, 111, 113
Korguniuk, Yuri G., 66, 75
Kornberg, Allan, 6
Kreuzer, Marcus, 150
Kselman, Daniel M., 150
Kunicová, Jana, 60

Laakso, Markku, 5, 109
Laitin, David D., 3, 168, 169
Lassen, David D., 114
Laver, Michael J., 4, 6, 9, 12, 20, 31, 57, 58, 109, 170, 172
Lee, Jong-Wha, 115
Lewis-Beck, Michael S., 114
Lichbach, Mark I., 109
Lijphart, Arend, 57
Limongi, Fernando, 109, 112
Lindberg, Björn, 5
Linz, Juan J., 112
Lipset, Seymour M., 4, 5, 49, 114, 133, 167
Long, J. Scott, 119
Lovatt, Catherine (&) David, 72, 73, 75
Löwenhardt, John, 86
Luebbert, Gregory M., 49
Lupia, Arthur, 38, 170, 171

Mackie, Thomas, 4, 6, 114
Magalhães, Pedro C., 159
Mahoney, James, 169
Mainwaring, Scott P., 4, 7, 12, 14, 47, 110, 111, 113, 129, 151, 152
Mair, Peter, 4, 6, 7, 8, 12, 13, 14, 15, 49, 109, 110, 167, 171
Marinelli, Gioconda, 29
Marsh, Michael, 13, 153, 171
Martin, Lenny W., 20, 35, 170
Mayhew, David R., 33, 36, 148
McAllister, Ian, 6, 61
McCubbins, Mathew D., 6, 21, 24, 35, 37, 38, 57, 172
McElroy, Gail, 150, 153
McKelvey, Richard, 20, 22, 58
McLean, Iain, 6
Mejía Acosta, Andrés, 150, 152, 155, 156, 170

Melega, 92
Mershon, Carol, 9, 11, 14, 20, 23, 27, 29, 31, 33, 37, 46, 48, 59, 63, 68, 71, 83, 102, 112, 150, 167, 168
Miller, Gary, 6
Miller, William L., 6, 61
Miodownik, Dan, 114
Miskin, Sarah, 157, 158, 160
Mitchell, 171
Molande, Bright, 156
Monroe, Nathan W., 22, 24
Moraes, Juan A., 159
Morgenstern, Scott, 152
Morlino, Leonardo, 75
Morton, Desmond, 25
Moser, Robert G., 60, 85, 86
Mpesi, Andrew, 156
Mullahy, John, 119
Müller, Wolfgang C., 6, 8, 33, 57, 70, 106, 109, 170
Munger, Michael C., 3

Nemoto, Kuniaki, 150, 151, 152, 153
Newell, James L., 28, 67, 75
Nicholson, Stephen P., 24
Nikolenyi, Csaba, 11, 150, 157, 158, 171
Nishikawa, Misa, 109
Nokken, Timothy P., 23, 24, 49, 69, 70, 93, 167
Norris, Pippa, 150, 151, 154, 159, 161
North, Douglass C., 3, 169

Okole, Henry T., 152, 157
Ordeshook, Peter, 5, 6, 111, 112, 114, 129, 133
Ostrogorski, Moisei Y., 1, 8
Ostrom, Elinor, 3
Owens, John, 150

Parisi, Arturo M. L., 57, 63, 206
Pasquino, Gianfranco, 28, 62, 67, 75, 208
Patel, Nandini, 156
Pedersen, Mogens N., 5, 110
Pérez-Liñán, Aníbal, 152
Pettai, Vello, 150

Pierson, Paul, 169
Pizzorno, Alessandro, 20
Plasser, Fritz, 6, 8
Poole, Keith T., 23, 49, 69, 93
Pop-Eleches, Grigore, 72, 73
Posner, Daniel, 114, 187
Powell, G. Bingham, 4, 109, 114, 173
Prodi, Romano, 29
Przeworski, Adam, 4, 109

Quagliariello, Gaetano, 167

Rahat, Gideon, 154, 158
Rakner, Lise, 153
Randall, Vicky, 160
Rasch, Bjørn E., 21
Reed, Steven R., 9, 33, 153, 170
Reif, Karlheinz, 153, 197
Reifler, Jason, 116
Reilly, Benjamin, 150, 152, 157, 160, 171
Reisinger, William M., 61
Remington, Thomas F., 60, 88
Rhodes, R. A. W., 169
Riker, William H., 3, 20, 67, 169
Rockman, Bert A., 169
Rodrik, Dani, 114
Rokkan, Stein, 4, 5, 49, 114, 133, 167
Rose, Richard, 61
Rosenbluth, Frances M., 153, 170

Sakwa, Richard, 85
Samuels, David J., 15, 152
Sánchez de Dios, Manuel, 161
Sanders, Elizabeth, 169
Sartori, Giovanni, 4, 5, 6, 19, 21, 109
Sayari, Sabri, 150
Schadee, Hans, 61
Schattschneider, E. E., 1
Scheiner, Ethan, 9, 33, 152, 153, 170
Schindler, Peter, 49
Schmitt, Hermann, 153, 192
Schofield, Norman J., 4, 6, 9, 14, 16, 20, 22, 25, 26, 29, 31, 58, 109, 170
Scully, Timothy R., 7, 111
Sened, Itai, 4, 6, 14, 16, 20, 26, 27, 28, 29, 30, 109, 170

Shabad, Goldie, 9, 113, 150
Sheafer, Tamir, 154, 158
Shepsle, Kenneth A., 3, 6, 20, 24, 31, 57, 58, 169, 170, 172
Shugart, Matthew S., 5, 6, 15, 38, 60, 109, 111
Shenhav, Shaul, 11, 150, 157, 158, 171
Shvetsova, Olga V., 5, 6, 9, 20, 23, 27, 46, 59, 63, 66, 78, 83, 84, 108, 111, 112, 114, 120, 129, 133, 168
Skach, Cindy, 112
Slomczynski, Kazimierz M., 9, 113, 150
Smyth, Regina, 63, 85
Somer-Topcu, Zeynep, 20
Sousa, David J., 9
Spirova, Maria, 11, 150
Sprague, John, 4
Stegmaier, Mary A., 114
Stepan, Alfred, 112
Stevenson, Randolph T., 20, 109, 114, 170
Strøm, Kaare, 5, 15, 21, 33, 57, 70, 106, 109, 170, 171
Sullivan, John L., 116
Svåsand, Lars, 153
Szarka, Joseph, 49

Taagepera, Rein, 5, 109
Tambulasi, Richard, 156
Tan, Paige J., 150
Tavits, Margit, 142
Taylor, Rosemary C. R., 3, 169
Thames, Frank C., 9, 170
Thai, Bethuel, 150
Thelen, Kathleen, 3, 169
Tilley, James, 15
Tomás Mallén, Beatriz, 159, 161
Torcal Loriente, Mariano, 7, 12, 47, 111, 113

Valen, Henry, 4, 6, 114
Valenzuela, Arturo, 112
Van Beinen, 160
van de Walle, Nicolas, 152
Vanberg, Georg S., 20
Verzichelli, Luca, 60
Vowles, Jack, 11, 50, 150, 154, 160, 171

Author Index

Wacziarg, Romain, 114
Warner, Steven, 77
Wattenberg, Martin P., 6, 60, 115
Weingast, Barry R., 3, 24
Weinstein, Jeremy, 114
Wertman, Douglas A., 70, 75, 77
White, Stephen, 61
Whitefield, Stephen, 61
Whitten, Guy D., 114
Wiberg, Matti, 150

Wilkinson, Steven, 114
Williams, Laron K., 20
Wolinetz, Steven B., 4

Yamamoto, Kentaro, 9, 171
Young, Daniel J., 150, 153, 156

Zoco, Edurne, 110, 113, 129
Zucchini, Francesco, 60, 61, 88
Zuckerman, Alan S., 109

Subject Index

Agenda setting, 19–20, 65, 104, 170–172
Approaches to analyzing party systems, 1–9, 15–16, 164–165, 172–173
 institutional, 6, 15–16, 111–113
 sociological, 5–6, 114–116
 strategic, 6, 15–16
Assumptions
 on incumbents, 19, 32–34, 42, 165, 168, 203
 on institutions, relaxing, 17, 154–163
 on voter preferences, 37–38, 48–49, 60–61, 84, 163, 165–167
 on voter preferences, relaxing, 147–163, 165–167
Australia, 11, 48, 49, 106, 124, 133, 205, 211

Balance of power, partisan, 2, 9, 10, 24, 50, 104, 115, 141, 164, 169
Brazil, 11, 100, 150, 152, 155, 158–159, 170
 Silva, Luiz Inácio Lula da, 158, 159
 State Assembly of São Paolo, 158
 Supreme Electoral Court, 158
Bulgaria, 149, 155

Canada, 11, 25, 26
 House of Commons, 25
 Liberals, 25
 Stronach, Belinda, 25
Candidate selection, 70–71
Coalitions
 executive, 8, 18, 20–21, 25, 31, 55, 71, 170–172

legislative, 18, 20–21, 22, 29, 155, 158, 169–172
Cold War era, 115, 130, 210
Collective decision making, 19, 22, 169–171
Cooperative theory, 21
Core (Also see Median), 18, 19, 21–30
Cycle
 electoral, 15 (See also Volatility, electoral)
 parliamentary, 4, 15–17, 35–36, 42–48, 50–52, 53–79, 88–93, 101, 104–107, 118, 120–140, 143–146, 165–166, 168, 203, 207–209
Czech Republic, 149–151

Decisive coalitions, 19, 21, 22, 29, 31
Decisive structures, 18–19, 23, 141, 170–172
Denmark, 5–7, 11, 149–150
 Folketing, 5

Economic environment, 48, 114–115, 119, 126–132, 166, 210
Ecuador, 17, 148–152, 155–156, 170
Education level, 115, 126–132, 152, 210
Electoral
 reforms, 6, 72, 170
 dealignment, 5
 deterrents to change (Also see Party system, stability), 16–17, 32, 36–45, 50, 51, 80–97, 99, 101, 104–105, 107–108, 111–116, 117–140, 146, 165–166, 168, 209–210

218

Subject Index

laws (Also see Electoral laws), 6, 38, 47, 70–71, 77–78, 87, 95, 104–105, 108, 118–140, 170, 172
realignment, 5, 14
Electoral laws, 6, 38–39, 47–48, 57, 61, 70–72, 76–78, 84, 95, 104–105, 106–107, 108, 111, 118–123, 129, 145–146, 154, 162, 165–166, 170, 172
  candidate-centered, 38, 44, 46–47, 50, 81, 108, 118–123, 145–146, 165–166
  district magnitude, 111, 112, 114, 210
  Mixed, 60, 63, 78, 84–87, 145
  Proportional representation, 40, 49, 70–72, 76–77, 104–105, 108, 120–140, 145, 146, 158, 167, 208, 209
  Single-member district, 49, 69–72, 76, 104–108, 118–140, 145, 146, 166, 208
Electoral volatility, 5, 12–14, 110, 114, 141–144, 146, 159, 161
Enfranchisement, 5, 49
Estimations, general form, 117–118
Estimations, specification
  ordered probit, 118, 138
  Poisson, 118, 119
  probit, 118, 135
  zero-inflated Poisson, 118
European Parliament, 11, 29, 57, 68, 78, 149–150, 153–154, 208

Federalism, 6, 108, 111, 126, 129, 130, 135, 138
Fixed effects
  country, 48, 113, 118, 123–126, 162, 166
Formation of new parliamentary parties, 14, 65, 70, 73–79, 103–104, 135, 138, 142–145, 157–159, 211–212
France, 11, 170–171
Freezing thesis, 5, 167

Geopolitical context, 115–116, 129–132
Germany, 11, 49, 103, 104, 108, 120, 124, 145, 171
Guatemala, 11, 149

Heart (Also see spatial theory), 26, 29
Heterogeneity
  ethnic, 114, 126, 133–134, 151–152, 158, 210
  linguistic, 5, 133–134, 210
  religious, 5, 114, 133–134, 151, 210
Hungary, 11, 149–151, 155
Hypotheses
  H0 – Null, 47, 59, 64, 69, 73, 78, 111
  H1 – Time Moves to Seize Gains, 35, 43–44, 45, 48, 51, 53, 55, 58–60, 64–69, 73–79, 104–105, 123, 126, 130, 135, 165–166, 209
  H2 – Stay Put When Elections Loom, 44, 45, 51, 69, 81, 83–84, 86, 88, 94–96, 104, 111, 118, 120, 123, 143, 152, 165–166, 168, 209
  H3 – Wait to Jump Ship, 44–46, 51, 69, 81, 83–84, 88, 95, 118, 120, 126, 165–166, 209
  H4 – Move to the Law, 46–47, 52, 73, 81, 95, 104, 111, 118, 123, 126, 165–166, 209
  H5 – Limit Moves, 47, 81, 84, 89–90, 155

India, 17, 150, 155, 157, 158, 171
  Anti-Defection Amendment, 158
Indonesia, 149–150
Institutional change, sources of, 169–170
Institutional effects, 126–129, 136, 139, 166
  federalism, 6, 108, 111, 126–130, 135–138, 140
  presidentialism, 55, 108, 112–113, 126–130, 135–138, 140, 152–153
Ireland, 8, 171
  Fianna Fáil, 8, 171
  Fine Gael, 171
Israel, 11, 26, 29, 149–150, 154–155, 157–158
  Anti-Defection Law, 158
Italy
  Chamber of Deputies, 10–13, 25–31, 53, 54, 61–64, 66–68, 69–78, 82–90, 92, 167
  Christian Democratic Center, 27, 67, 76, 77

Italy (cont.)
  Christian Democratic Union, 27, 67, 76, 77
  Christian Democrats, 13, 71, 75, 76, 77, 94, 212
  Communist Party, 71, 75, 77, 94
  Communist Party of Italy, 30
  Communist Refounding, 26–27, 30–31, 67
  Constituent Right-National Democracy, 75, 76
  Cossiga, Francesco, 27, 29, 31, 67, 68
  Democrats-Olive Tree, 29, 31, 68, 77
  Greens, 63
  Italian Renewal, 25, 27
  Italian Social Democratic Party, 12, 71, 76–78, 102
  Italian Social Movement, 75
  Italian Socialist Party, 25, 71, 76, 77
  Mixed group, 12, 26, 63
  Party of the Democratic Left, 25, 27, 75–77
  Popular Party, 25, 27, 75, 76, 77
  Prodi, Romano, 29, 30, 67, 68, 77
  Proletarian Democracy-Communist group, 76, 77
  Radicals, 92
  Union of Democrats for Europe, 31, 68, 76
  Union of Democrats for the Republic, 27, 30, 67, 68, 76

Japan, 6, 11, 149–150, 153, 170
  Liberal Democratic Party, 149, 153, 170, 171

Latvia, 149–150
Legislative agenda, control of, 170–171
Lesotho, 149–150, 155, 171
Lithuania, 159–150

Malawi, 100, 148, 150, 153, 155, 156
Manipulating the core, 22–23
Measurement
  multiple measures of incumbents' changes of party, 102–104

Measurement influences and controls
  ascriptive cleavages and economic factors, 114–115
  cultural factors and salient issues, 115–116
  democratic institutions, 111–113
  deterrents to incumbent inter-party mobility, 107–109
  inducements to inter-party mobility (Also see Parliamentary cycle), 104–107
  party system properties at the most recent election, 109–110
Median (Unidimensional core), 26, 28, 29, 31, 112, 210
Mexico, 6
Midterm effect, 45, 51, 77, 79, 81, 83–84, 89, 95, 104, 120, 123, 135, 138, 145, 168
Model of inducements and deterrents to change, 2, 16, 15–16, 32–35, 37, 42, 43, 45, 47, 50, 80, 108–109, 118–119, 123, 126, 135, 144, 147, 165–170, 203–205
  candidate reputation, 36, 40
  incumbent's utility, 35
  loyalty parameter, 40
  MP's history of switching, 39–40, 204
  parliamentary benefits, 43, 88, 89, 92, 96, 172
  voters' calculus, 38–40

National executive
  coalition, 19
  competition for, 4–8, 14–15, 27, 33–34
  control of, 16, 19–21, 25, 31, 71, 77, 170–171
  formation, 16, 43, 45, 55–57
  impact of party system on, 15, 19–21, 25, 67
  veto override, 20
New Zealand, 6, 11, 150, 154, 155, 160, 171
  Alliance Party, 160
  Anderton, Jim, 160
  Anti-Defection Law, 160

Subject Index

Papua New Guinea, 150, 152, 155, 157, 171
  Organic Law on the Integrity of Political Parties and Candidates, 157
Parliamentary cycle, 4, 15–16, 35–36, 42, 43, 44, 45, 48, 50–46, 51, 53–56, 57, 58–61, 64, 69, 71, 73, 78–74, 79, 88, 92, 101, 104–106, 107, 118, 120, 123, 130, 135–138, 145, 165, 166, 168, 203, 207, 208
  operationalizing stages of (Also see Measurement, influences and controls)
    inducements to incumbent inter-party mobility, 54–58
Parliamentary rules
  committees, 37, 46, 72
  parliamentary groups, 63, 64–68, 71–72, 156, 161–162
Parliamentary terms
  and electoral volatility, 13
  and within-term seat volatility, 12, 13
  length and degree of party system change, 141–144, 167–168
  relationship between within-term seat volatility and electoral volatility, 141–144, 146
Party
  legislative as coalition of incumbents, 8, 15–16, 19–20, 32–33, 37, 172
  mergers, 22, 71, 72, 77, 78, 156, 157, 212
  splits, 22, 30, 67, 76, 77, 143, 149, 157, 170, 211–212
  start-ups, 66, 72, 78, 156, 212
Party system
  change, 1–17, 23, 31, 47, 50, 51, 54, 60, 66, 69, 74, 79, 80–81, 83–84, 97, 102–103, 109–110, 117, 119, 120–123, 129, 130–133, 141–145, 147, 165–167
  stability (Also see Electoral deterrents to change), 80, 89–90, 145–146, 165–167, 172–173
Philippines, 150, 151
Poland, 6, 150, 170
Portugal, 155, 159

Research design, 32, 47–50, 99–100, 102, 118, 168, 205–207
  choice of primary in-depth terms (Also see internal validity), 60–61
  choice of time frame, 48–49
Romania, 11, 49, 52, 53, 69–78, 90–91, 94–95, 123, 126, 130, 132–133, 135–136, 155–157, 166, 205, 210
Russia
  Agrarian Party, 66, 78
  Budennovsk Crisis, 65
  Chechen War, 65, 208
  Communist Party, 66
  Duma, 53–54, 58, 60–66, 76–78, 82–90, 208
  Liberal-Democratic Union, 66
Societal Division
  ethnic, 114, 126, 133–134, 151–152, 158, 210
  linguistic, 5, 133–134
  religious, 5, 114, 133–134, 151
South Africa, 11, 17, 149–150, 152–153, 155, 159–160
South Korea, 150, 151, 152
Spain, 11, 49, 101, 108, 155, 161, 162, 205
Spatial theory, 21, 25
Strategic choice
  disincentives to change, 16–17, 32, 51, 69, 80–81, 88, 90, 94–95, 99, 101, 104–105, 107, 111, 115–116, 117–118, 120, 123–126, 129–130, 133–135, 146, 166, 168–169
  Inducements to change, 4, 9, 15, 17, 32, 36–37, 42–43, 45, 51, 58, 60, 69, 72, 78, 86, 97, 101, 103–104, 106, 118, 120, 133–134, 138, 153, 156, 163, 166, 169
  office-driven, 33, 36, 45, 58, 63, 72, 95, 152, 154
  policy-driven, 20, 33, 42, 90, 165, 169
Switzerland, 11, 149

Temporal proximity to elections, 41, 120
Temporal variation
  in benefits (Also see temporal stages of parliamentary cycle), 6, 9, 16, 33, 34, 35, 37, 41, 42, 43, 44, 45, 53, 58, 64, 65, 67, 68, 71, 72, 78, 86, 92, 96, 101, 106, 117, 120, 123, 126, 138, 143, 152, 156, 165, 166, 172, 203, 204, 205
  in electoral costs (Also see temporal proximity to elections), 6, 35, 36, 43, 45, 96, 101
Thailand, 100, 150, 151
Turkey, 11, 150

Ukraine, 11, 150, 170
United Kingdom, 11, 49, 52, 53, 69, 70, 72, 73, 76, 78, 90, 91, 92, 94, 95, 125, 167
  Conservative Party, 26, 73, 93
  House of Commons, 70
  Labour Party, 73, 76, 77, 78, 92, 93, 102, 171
  Liberal Democrats, 75, 78
  Liberals, 75
  Scottish Labour Party, 77
  Social Democratic Party, 73, 75–76, 78, 92–93
  Thatcher, Margaret, 92
United States, 11, 22–25, 49, 52–53, 56, 69–74, 76, 78, 90–91, 93–95, 103–106, 113, 115–116, 123, 126, 133, 141–143, 168, 170
  House of Representatives, 23–24
  Jeffords, Jim, 22, 24, 25, 104, 170
  Republican Revolution, 24, 93
  Senate, 24–25, 170

Validity
  external, 17, 48, 99, 148, 205
  internal, 17, 48, 50, 51, 52, 56, 90, 99
Volatility
  electoral, 5, 12–14, 110, 114, 141–144, 146, 159, 161
  seat, within-term, 10–14

For EU product safety concerns, contact us at Calle de José Abascal, 56–1°,
28003 Madrid, Spain or eugpsr@cambridge.org.

www.ingramcontent.com/pod-product-compliance
Ingram Content Group UK Ltd.
Pitfield, Milton Keynes, MK11 3LW, UK
UKHW011316060825
461487UK00005B/119